What's New, Harry?

The Best of Buffalo Courier-Express
Columnist Phil Ranallo

by Paul Ranallo

NFB
Buffalo, New York

Printed in the United States of America

Ranallo, Paul

What's New, Harry? The Best of Buffalo Courier-Express Columnist Phil Ranallo/Ranallo - 1st Edition

ISBN: 978-0692553589

1. What's New, Harry? 2.Phil Ranallo 3. Courier-Express, Buffalo NY
4. Sports 5. Editorial 6. Historical/Sports 7. No Frills.

All articles were originally published in the Courier-Express newspaper and are reprinted with permission of the author's representative.

All interior photographs courtesy of Paul Ranallo.

Back cover photos courtesy of Buffalo Courier-Express Buffalo State College Archives and Collections.

Editorial support provided by Joe Kirchmyer,
Kirchmyer Media LLC,
West Seneca, NY.

NFB
<<<>>>
No Frills Buffalo/Amelia Press
119 Dorchester Road, Buffalo, New York 14213

For more information visit nofrillsbuffalo.com

This book is dedicated to the memory of my father and mother. Their union resulted in this extraordinary piece of literary history created in Buffalo, New York.

Your son, Paul

What's New, Harry?
The Best of Buffalo Courier-Express
Columnist Phil Ranallo

Table of Contents

Preface

Consider this a sports history book, but you will realize that the real story is about the lives that were touched by the writing of my father, Phil Ranallo. He was a sports columnist with the Buffalo Courier-Express. My father loved his work and the people who he wrote about. Many of those people are no longer here, but I wish they could see their stories brought to life again. This book is for those people, from Western New York and around the world. The Western New York families include the O'Sullivans, Masiellos, Ralstons, Kemps and Horrigans, just to name a few.

Phil called himself "Honest Harry" in the column, and he called my mother "Ruby." He also had a cast of characters based on real people, including "Sam the Immigrant," "Julie Potatoes" and "Loose Lip Louie." As I read his articles from the 1960s, I realized that his early work was based on his love and affection for my mother.

Phil started working as a copy boy at the Courier-Express in the 1940s. He continued to work there while attending Canisius College, and married my mother, Dorothy Eleey, on June 27, 1942. He joined the Marines during World War II as a tail gunner on an SBD Dauntless dive-bomber. The commanders recognized his writing skills and assigned him to the Intelligence Department as a report specialist. They asked him to stay for a period of six months after the war was over to assist in completion of the war reports. They even offered him a position in Washington, D.C., that he turned down to resume his career in the city that he loved, Buffalo, New York.

Phil went right back to the Courier-Express and covered high school sports for about ten more years. He traveled all over Western New York and met many great young athletes and their families. This "people connection" laid the foundation for his increasing popularity.

He became quite a wordsmith, and he was eventually promoted to Sports Columnist. The Courier-Express was home to some of the greatest sportswriters in the country at that time. The sports editor that I was most fond of was an Irishman named Mike Kanaley. Our families were very close. Mike and his wife, Marcella, lived in Kenmore, New York. Mike was totally devoted to his family and his work. I once complained to my father for never taking me to Crystal Beach in Ontario, Canada. When Mr. Kanaley heard about my complaint, he picked me up from my house and treated me to a full day at Crystal Beach with his family. He always drove a big station wagon. I still see his son, Mike, and I bought a car from his other son, Chris, who works at a local car dealership.

My father wrote his columns from our house in North Buffalo. I would tag along when he delivered his completed column to the Courier-Express. I remember taking the shiny, brass-trimmed elevator to the fourth floor where the Sports Department was located. The newspaper business was much different in those days. Game results were shown on the Western Union ticker machine, and writers pounded on manual typewriters. I would sit there and talk with the "sports guys" — copy editor Bill Coughlin, baseball and boxing write Joe Alli, and hockey writer Charlie Barton. I would also spend time with Willie, the security guard. He took me on tours of the building, and I even got to see the running presses. It was quite an experience for a young kid.

My father's telephone number was in the phone book, so my mother would screen his calls as he typed on his Olivetti-Underwood manual typewriter. I remember phone calls to our house from some very well known figures. The call that I remember most came from Muhammad Ali, and my brother Mark had the pleasure of answering. My father went to see Ali speak at Buffalo State College in the 1960s. He came home and told us that Ali was a great man who loved this country.

People would stop by all day long just to say hello. There was a local retired boxer named Tony Sciolino who would come over at least once a week. I remember light heavyweight Jimmy Ralston the most. His boxing career was gaining momentum back then. The boxing promoter at that time was Don Elbaum, and Jimmy's trainer was Spats Simpson. Spats ran a gym in the Riverside area where Jimmy grew up, and was a friend of my father. Spats loved Jimmy, and taught him the "sweet science."

Phil walked into the Courier-Express building when he was 16 years old and he walked out of that same building in 1982 when the newspaper went out of business. I will never forget that dark day — September 19, 1982 — for as long as I live. It was the day the last newspaper rolled off the presses. I went to see my father at his house in North Buffalo on that Sunday morning. He was sitting in his favorite chair in front of the television, staring at the last edition of that great newspaper. The front page read "Goodbye" in large red letters. My father had devoted his entire life to that company and he couldn't believe that it failed to survive the hard economic times of the 1980s. He never wrote another word after the newspaper closed.

Phil talked about getting a collection of his columns together and assembling them in a book, but the days went by too fast and the project remained a dream. He passed away in 1986 and the book was never brought to life. I could not let the project go undone in my lifetime. My father's columns were not syndicated. With a little luck, some of the people outside of Western New York may now have the chance to read his wonderful work.

I've read thousands of his columns while deciding which ones would be worthy of reprinting. When you read this book, you will notice names that you recognize, and others that you don't. The names that you don't recognize belong right up there with the names that have world recognition. They are all enjoyable stories about extraordinary people.

I hope you enjoy this collection and pass it along to others who will appreciate my father's timeless work. Many of the columns could serve as a teaching tool in homes and schools today. Most of the people he wrote about were great role models for others. My father was more impressed by a person's character than their skill. He was a humanitarian who cared about others, no matter what race or religion. He championed the underdog, and did anything he could to help those who are less fortunate.

I won't go on and on here. I just wanted to give some background on my father. He always said he was just a "Fan with a Typewriter."

— Paul Ranallo

Baseball — HENRY AARON

Aaron is not distracted by bigots as he is about to tie or break Babe Ruth's home run record.

Thursday, April 4, 1974

Phil Ranallo: What's New, Harry?

ONCE MORE A NEW BASEBALL season is upon us ... and a strange thing is about to happen — because this is not an ordinary season. The cry, "Play ball!" will not be greeted as it usually is — with little more than a large yawn.

For the first time since Abner Doubleday got his brainstorm and invented the diamond game, there will be as much drama crammed into the opening of a baseball season as there is in a World Series — maybe more.

Despite the distractions created by the dunking of basketballs and the icing of pucks and the super-raiding that's going on in pro football, baseball, as it leaves the starting gate, will command center-stage attention.

There is a reason.

The reason is named Henry Aaron.

Henry Aaron, the extraordinary man from Atlanta, resumes his pursuit of Babe Ruth's home run record today in Cincinnati's Riverfront Stadium.

BAD HENRY AARON, who somehow managed to survive the tremendous pressure of last year's long, hot summer, today comes out of a long winter of semi-hibernation with 713 home runs — one short of the Babe's record and two short of immortality.

So the "Great Debate" will be resumed — between those who resent Aaron's inevitable intrusion on hallowed ground and those who don't.

Aaron has not had an easy time of it since the beginning of the "Great Debate," about a year ago, because some of the defenders of Ruth base their argument on race and believe that Aaron, a black man, has no right to break the record of so noble a caucasian as the Babe.

These bigots, for a year now, have been taking dead aim at the absolutely splendid baseball player, Aaron, by illusions to his race and by sending him threatening letters.

AT FIRST, LAST SEASON, Aaron let it be known that the badgering was only vocal and that he heard the threats while patrolling his sector of the Atlanta ballpark.

Then he disclosed that his mail was loaded with diatribes that challenged his right to exist in the land of his birth.

Aaron fixed the bigots with his bat — by hitting more home runs.

He never mentioned that Ruth never had to face a Bob Gibson or a Don Newcombe ... or a Willie Mays or a Roberto Clemente wasn't around to streak to the outer rim of a park, leap and turn a homer into an out.

AARON NEVER MENTIONED that Ruth had the big advantage of playing in an era when the game of baseball was restricted to only four-fifths of the population — only whites.

He never mentioned that, since the coming of Jackie Robinson, it has been made clear that one-fifth of the population — the blacks — are athletically superior to the other four-fifths.

Not every defender of Ruth's place in history is a racist, of course.

These defenders repeatedly make the point that Aaron can't really break Ruth's record because by the time he connects for his 715th home run he will have been to the plate about 3,000 times oftener than the Babe.

THIS IS TRUE, BUT IT has noth-

ing to do with the record. The Book of
Baseball Records could not have put
it more simply — "Most Home Runs,
Lifetime."

There's no mention of the number
of seasons, games, times at bat, caliber
of pitching, liveliness of ball, size of
parks, day games or night.

So why the Great Debate over
whether Henry Aaron will really have
broken a record if, in different times,
under different conditions, he hits
home run No. 715?

When Bad Henry hits No. 715, he
will have "Most Home Runs, Lifetime."

Period.

I'll be delighted if Bad Henry cracks
two today.

Baseball — LOU BROCK

Brock breaks baseball's base-stealing record.
Wednesday, August 31, 1977
Phil Ranallo: What's New, Harry?

WELL, LOU BROCK HAS won his foot-race with history.

The marvelous St. Louis Cardinal did it Monday night, in San Diego. Louis Clark Brock gave Ty Cobb a nudge, made the legendary Cobb move over, and became No. 1 — baseball's all-time champion base-stealer.

I don't believe Lou Brock!

Brock's accomplishments as a baseball "thief" the last four seasons — since be-coming an "old man" — boggle the imagination. Compared to Brock, Willie Sutton, in his heyday, was an honest man.

In 1974, at age 35, Brock stole 118 bases to rub out Maury Wills' record of 104. And Monday night, at age 38, he swiped the 893rd base of his career to break Cobb's record of 892.

Amazing!

It's like Methuselah winning the Olympic 100 meters.

Brock's achievements since he blew out 35 candles on his birthday cake — since he became one of baseball's "senior citizens" — are testament perhaps less to his speed than to his durability.

Imagine, the last four seasons Brock has stolen a total of 258 bases — 118 in 1974, 56 in 1975, 56 again in 1976, and 28 so far this season!

Now, let me tell you just how extraordinary it is for a guy to steal 258 bases after reaching age 35.

WITH THE EXCEPTION of Lou Brock, there has never been a baseball player who, after his 35th birthday, was not all washed up as a base-stealer. Ty Cobb, at 35, for example, stole only 22.

Brock, in his career, has set himself apart from the other great base-steal-ers with his durability, his will to succeed — and his love of pressure.

"You can't be afraid to fail," he said in Buffalo a couple of years ago, at the Dunlop Pro-Am awards dinner. "And you have to want to be on the spot. Pressure, I respond to it. I welcome it. It's the part of the game I like most."

Brock has been a star baseball player for 15 years. Right now he's in the twilight of his career, but he's still an exciting player.

He still runs. He still hits.

But nothing like "yesterday" — when he was a bit younger.

"YESTERDAY," sparks flew whether Brock was at bat or on base. When he was on base, he made a Nervous Nellie out of every catcher in the National League. The catchers knew he was going, but they couldn't stop him.

Brock, when he was younger, set up an anxiety complex in the opposition. The perspiring catchers felt like lawmen with cap-pistols when they tried to shoot down the stealing Brock.

And the younger Brock, the compulsive thief whose burglar tools were a pair of shoes with spikes on them, made a tremendous contribution to the game of baseball.

The game, primarily because of Brock, has changed. Everybody in both leagues is running, going wild on the base paths — and the running is making baseball more exciting.

BROCK OPENED THEIR EYES.

"Speed — running on the base paths — starts rallies," Brock says. "When a team runs, it forces the other team into mistakes. When a runner takes off from first, the shortstop and second baseman both move to cover him

— and that opens a hole in the infield that shouldn't be there.

"Another thing — when the pitcher fears you'll run he starts throwing fastballs in order to give the catcher a better chance to handle the ball and make the throw on a steal.

"And that gives the batter a break, because most batters like nothing better than fastballs, especially when they're anticipating fastballs."

What makes Brock's achievement — as the all-time champ base stealer — most astonishing is that he never worked at piling up thefts until he was in the majors for "six or seven years."

"IT WAS THE MESSAGE boards in the new stadiums that made me aware that I had a significant number of steals," he says. "We'd sit in the dugouts and read all that stuff. Statistics on everything, every record imaginable.

"One night, they put up the 10 base stealers in history. Cobb was up there with his 892. Then they put up the top 10 active stealers. Maury Wills was No. 1 and I was No. 10.

"I hadn't been aware I was that high and it was like making the honor roll. I started to figure how I might do if I could steal 50 a year. I was startled at how I could move up. So, I figured I'd give it a try."

Brock tried — and never failed. He has stolen 50 bases, or more, the last 12 years.

He may not hit 50 this season. But it's not necessary. For Brock, it was mission accomplished Monday night, in San Diego — when he swiped No. 893.

STEALING NO. 893, by the way, did provide Brock with his greatest thrill — or give him his deepest satisfaction. Breaking the single-season record is No. 1 with Brock.

"To me, 1974 was my greatest test and accomplishment," Brock said. "And it meant even more — it was all that more of a challenge — because I was 35 years old.

"There were so many people, including Maury Wills, who didn't believe anyone could do it at that age. When I broke Maury's record, it was special — because of my age.

"If I had done it at 25, I don't think I would have thought that much about it."

Baseball — JOE BROWN

A crafty guy who knew how to "fix" a playing field to the home team's advantage.

Friday, July 30, 1971

Phil Ranallo: What's New, Harry

ONE OF THE MORE NOTICE- ABLE things about life, as the years go fleeting by, is the final roll call. The obituary columns of a newspaper become familiar reading. Wednesday's list included the name of an old friend — Joe Brown, baseball diamond care-taker, high school athletic coach and official, fun lover.

In 1925, Joe Brown was hired by the Buffalo baseball club on a temporary basis — "for three or four weeks" — and was part of the Offermann Stadium scenery for 28 years.

There had been a flooding problem at the stadium the previous year, the first full season of operation at Offer-mann after the construction of new stands.

It was discovered, much to the em-barrassment of the construction engi-neers, that the playing field was lower than the water level of the stands. On rainy nights, this made things very risky for outfielders who were not strong swimmers.

THEN CRAFTY JOE BROWN WAS called to the rescue, from his na-tive Rochester. Joe rolled up his sleeves and went to work. He installed a sys-tem of natural drainage — by raising the field five or six feet in some places.

Brown's rescue job so delighted the Buffalo baseball brass that they refused to let him go. He stayed in Buffalo until 1953, when he moved to the major league — to Baltimore — in the company of Paul Richards.

Brown's artistry with a baseball diamond extended beyond its prepa-ration and maintenance — and it was this extra talent, plus his loyalty to Boss Richards, that endeared him to Richards and induced Paul to lure Joe to Baltimore.

Joe Brown you see was master "fix-er" of diamonds. He was an artist at doctoring diamonds for the visiting teams — to rob them of some of their strong points.

IF THE VISITING CLUB had a superb bunter, for example, Brown would roll the baselines in a manner that would "encourage" bunted balls to roll foul. Or he'd raise or lower the pitching mound to fit the Baltimore pitcher and "unfit" the visiting pitch-er.

Brown would also "fix" the batter's box — to work to the disadvantage of the visiting team's big hitter.

Joe especially liked to do this when Ted Williams came to town. Familiar with the positions of Williams' feet in the batter's box, Brown would replace the dirt in those spots with sawdust — so Ted couldn't take a hold.

On more than one occasion, Wil-liams, after taking his first swing in the batter's box, turned to Brown and, laughed and said, "You've done it again you bum you."

JOE BROWN WAS A HIGHLY successful coach at St. Joseph's Colle-giate Institute, where he directed the football, basketball and baseball teams for 13 years.

His biggest thrills at St. Joe's came from two football games. One was against Canisius.

"They had won seven straight and we had lost five or six," Brown often recalled, with a relish. "So were sup-posed to get buried, but late in the game we were leading by, 12-7.

"Then Canisius put on a drive to our one yard line. Their backs got into an argument about who should carry the ball in for the winning touchdown — but the clock ran out before they could get the play off."

The other "big thrill" was a 14-0 victory over South Park, a strong team which won the Harvard Cup. The memory of that one stayed with Brown — because "we did it all on the ground; we never threw a pass."

JOE BROWN DIDN'T CONFINE his teachings to football, basketball and baseball. He had a habit of also giving his athletes — and their friends — valuable lessons in the value of money.

The story of one of those money lessons has been told a thousand times by Bob Smith, who went on to make millions with Howdy Doody.

One night after a boxing match at Offermann Stadium, Brown got Smith and Neil O'Donnell, the policeman of PAL fame, and two other kids to clean the stadium — for $3 apiece.

Smith and O'Donnell and the other two kids were very happy with their pay, even though it took them a dozen hours to do the job.

"There's a lesson to be learned here," Brown said as he handed each of the exhausted boys, but happy kids, their three dollars. "You boys busted your boilers to clean the place for a total of $12. They gave me $100 to get the job done. So you've been had. Remember that."

Joe Brown was a good man. It is saddening to learn he had answered the final roll call.

Baseball — JOE DiMAGGIO

Phil recalls DiMaggio's 56-game hitting streak and Pete Rose's run at the record.

Wednesday, July 19, 1978

Phil Ranallo: What's New, Harry?

ALTHOUGH MORE THAN 25 years have passed since he took his last classic swing of the bat for the New York Yankees, Joseph Paul DiMaggio is still the "people's choice" — still No. 1 — among millions of baseball fans on the wrong side of 40.

The older generations remember Joe DiMaggio and his diamond exploits vividly — as if he'd performed them only yesterday.

They recall the rhythm and effortless grace that made DiMag perhaps the greatest center fielder of all time.

They recall Joe D.'s big bat, with which he directed the Yankees' charge to 10 American League pennants and nine World Series championships between 1936 and 1951.

But, alas, the young set, the members of the current generation, generally speaking — they don't know Joe DiMag. They don't know what they missed.

The young folks know Joe DiMaggio only as a tall, silver-haired salesman — an aging gentleman in a conservative business suit who pops up on their television screens, rather regularly, and makes a pitch for an electric coffee-maker.

They associate DiMag only with the teevee commercial and with the line, "Where have you gone, Joe DiMaggio?" — the line that's part of the lyrics of that hit tune of a few years back, "Mrs. Robinson."

BUT THE YOUNG GUYS and gals, if they're reading the sports pages these days, should be getting to know a little more about DiMag — thanks to Pete Rose, that remarkable hustler for the Cincinnati Reds.

Rose, of course, currently is chasing Joe DiMaggio's record, Yankee Clipper's feat of hitting in 56 consecutive games in 1941 — the record that for 37 years has been labeled "the baseball record that may never be broken."

If Pete Rose continues to keep alive his consecutive-game hitting streak — which stood at 30 games going into Tuesday night's contest with Montreal — the young folks are going to learn all about Joe DiMaggio.

They're going to find out who DiMaggio was, and where he was — before he was gone.

They're going to learn that DiMaggio was one of the last of America's classic sports folk heroes.

ALSO, THAT HE WAS THE opposite of most of the athletes now populating the world of sports, a dignified contrast to the anti-heroes of today, with their agents, seven-figure salaries and controversies.

That he was one of the all-time giants of the game, succeeding Babe Ruth as the greatest performer and box office attraction in all of professional sports.

That he was the first $100,000-a-year athlete.

That he in no way would fit in with the guys who inhabit Yankee clubhouse today, since he was timid and retiring, avoiding controversy and fanfare, guarded his private life, and wasn't a party guy.

That he struck out less than any slugger who ever breathed, 13 times in one year, which is less than Reggie Jackson sometimes does in a week.

That he was a majestic figure in center field or at the plate, and that in his final year, when he felt himself slipping a trifle, that was it. He took off the pinstripes and was gone.

AND THE YOUNG FOLKS, if Pete Rose manages to keep rolling along for a while, will learn all about DiMaggio's 56-game hitting streak — the astonishing feat that enables DiMag to stand alone in the record book.

The streak ended in Cleveland, in Game No. 57 — a game in which DiMaggio was robbed of the hits by the marvelous fielding of Indian third baseman Ken Keltner.

DiMaggio twice hammered hot shots down the third base line — and twice Keltner backhanded the ball, whirled around, and threw DiMag out by a step.

In that game, incidentally, Lou Boudreau also took a hit away from DiMaggio by handling a hot shot up the middle — a play that most other shortstops could not have made.

DiMaggio's 56-game streak rubbed out the mark of 44 set by Wee Willie Keeler of "Hit 'em where they ain't" fame.

DIMAGGIO, TO BE SURE, also hit them where they weren't, en route to the record. During the streak, he blasted 15 home runs, batted .408 and drove in 55 runs.

DiMaggio's production during that two-month stretch in 1941 — his hits, homers and RBI — is a season's work for some pretty fair hitters by today's standards.

What is even more astonishing is that, after the streak was broken, DiMaggio hit safely in the next 16 ball games. So, conceivably, Joe's streak could have been 73 games, instead of 56 — if it weren't for Keitner and Boudreau.

No one has ever come close to DiMaggio's record.

When Pete Rose reached the 30-game mark Monday night, he became only the 11th player in baseball history to put together batting streaks of 30 games or more.

One of the others, by the way, happens to be Joe DiMag's brother, Dominic, who hit in 34 straight games for the Red Sox in 1949.

THE OTHERS ON THIS hitting streak list are George Sisler, 41 games in 1922; Ty Cobb, 40 in 1911; Tommy Holmes, 37 in 1945; Rogers Hornsby, 33 in 1922; Heinie Manush, 33 in 1933; Willie Davis, 31 in 1969; and Ron Le-Flore, 30 in 1976.

What I'm doing right now, as I submit this column to the C-E sports desk, is praying that Pete Rose's streak will still be alive when it hits print.

I'd hate to think I "scuzzied" the great, little hustler.

Baseball — LEO DUROCHER

Baseball legend steps down as Chicago Cubs manager.
Friday, July 28, 1972
Phil Ranallo: What's New, Harry?

IT APPEARS THAT THE STORMY baseball career of Leo Durocher — shortstop, coach, manager, umpire-baiter, raconteur, television color commentator, tough guy — is at an end.

If it is, the game of baseball is the loser — because Leo Durocher was perhaps the biggest part of the rapidly diminishing color that is left in the game.

Phillip K. Wrigley, the old gentleman who kept the game in the sunshine and watched Durocher make it pay off, finally surrendered to the Chicago Cub cry-babies and eased out the tempestuous and matchless "Lip."

Apparently Wrigley grew tired of giving Durocher votes of confidence. So Durocher, the greatest gum-chewer of them all, fell victim to the upstart gum-chewers that dot the Chicago lineup.

DUROCHER'S EXIT WAS THE culmination of three years of grumbling and open quarreling that began when the Cubs collapsed and blew the pennant to the Miracle Mets.

The grumbling and the quarreling developed into a festering boil that burst Tuesday, when the aging Wrigley finally yielded and squeezed the boil.

It was not easy for Wrigley to let Durocher go ... because the volatile Lippy worked wonders for the Cubs' owner — on and off the field.

When Durocher took over the Cubs in 1966, they had a 20-year-old lease on the second division — and they were bleeding at the gate.

"The Lip," in his second year on the scene, made contenders of the Cubs — and they remained contenders until this year.

DURING DUROCHER'S RE-GIME, Wrigley baled money. With "The Lip" doing his thing, attendance sky-rocketed from 635,000 to 977,000 to 1,043,000 — and to in excess of 1,600,000 the last three years.

Leo Durocher was the man who put all those fans in the stands ... so he must have been doing something right — despite what Ron Santo, the great grumbler, kept saying.

Durocher and his jawing and gesticulating and mimicking will be missed. Leo's departure leaves a hole in the game.

"The Lip's" career and what he accomplished boggles this mind.

Leo's endless rumbles with umpires and his front-page photos with beautiful women tend to obscure the fact that he managed to make at indelible mark on the game.

DUROCHER WAS, FOR EXAMPLE, the shortstop of the 1928-29 New York Yankees, when Babe Ruth and Lou Gehrig were the biggest bats in baseball.

He was a key member of the legendary Gashouse Gang of the St. Louis Cardinals and helped Pepper Martin and Dizzy Dean and Joe Medwick win the World Series in 1934.

He managed the Brooklyn Dodgers to the pennant in 1941, and was instrumental in helping Jackie Robinson break the baseball color barrier.

He was an integral part of the most dramatic moment in sports history, as manager of the New York Giants in 1951, the year of "The Miracle of Coogan's Bluff," when Bobby Thompson hit a home run to beat the Dodgers in a playoff for the National League pennant.

DUROCHER WAS THE FELLOW

who directed the Giants to a stunning
four-game sweep over the Cleveland
Indians in the 1954 World Series.

One man who will never forget Leo
Durocher is Jackie Robinson.

During the training season in 1947,
the year Jackie broke in, there were
rumblings among the Dodger players.
They threatened a boycott against
Robinson and were in the process of
getting up a petition attacking him.

Leo settled the racist bit in forthright
Leo Durocher style.

He got his coaches to wake up his
players in the middle of the night —
for an important meeting in the camp
kitchen.

AT THE MEETING, DUROCHER

got right to the point.

"Gentlemen," Durocher said, "I want
you all to know what you can do with
that petition of yours." Then Leo did
an about-face and went to bed — and
that was the last of the talk about
petitions.

Controversy followed Durocher all his
life. He was a bad loser — and a bad
winner.

But baseball will miss him.

Baseball — BOB FELLER

Pitching legend attends opening game as baseball returns to Buffalo.
Wednesday, April 18, 1979
Phil Ranallo: What's New, Harry?

MAYOR JAMES GRIFFIN had just done the honors — thrown out the first pitch. A fastball strike. And, with it, His Honor had demonstrated he is a southpaw who can really fog the ball — a guy who may be the best pitcher ever to come out of City Hall.

Now, Fred Breining, a tall and lean righthander, was on the mound for the Buffalo Bisons, and the long-awaited opener against the Reading Phillies — the match that marked Buffalo's entrance into the Eastern Baseball League — was under way in War Memorial Stadium.

As pitcher, Breining toiled and kept overpowering the Reading batters — a heavy-shouldered gentleman stood on the concrete apron, in the "box-seat area" behind the first-base line, and attempted to watch the proceedings.

The gentleman, Bob Feller, was not seeing much of the action.

Robert William Andrew Feller, the wondrous fireballer of three decades ago — the fellow who could throw a baseball as hard as anyone who ever breathed — was busy signing autographs for admirers and accommodating inquisitive sports writers.

"When this man was pitching," an admirer said to his son, as he introduced the boy to Feller, "he struck out everybody but Casey. Bob Feller rewrote the record book in the strikeout department — 18 strikeouts in a game, 348 strikeouts in a season."

A FEW MINUTES LATER, when the Reading team was retired in order in the second inning, Sam Jay, a man who played hooky from his wholesale novelty business to take in Tuesday's opener, approached Feller and said:

"Hey, Bob, did you ever strike out six guys in a row?"

Feller, scratching his head, thought a minute. "Gee, I don't think I ever did."

"Well, there's a kid who just did it," Jay said, pointing to Fred Breining, as the Bison pitcher was leaving the mound and heading for the dugout. "That kid, Breining, just struck out the first six Reading batters."

"Wait a minute," Feller said. "Once, in Philadelphia, I struck out 11 of 12 batters, so I must have done it. There's no way you can strike out 11 of 12 without getting at least six in a row, right?"

THE REVELATION MADE Feller feel better, since he is a man who cherishes his pitching feats — cherishes them so much, in fact, that whenever he makes a public appearance, as he did Tuesday, he brings along a stack of mimeographed "Feller Feats" sheets and distributes them to admirers.

Feller let it be known that it annoys him a bit to read that the no-hitter pitched by Houston's Ken Forsch on April 7 is described as "the earliest no-hitter pitched in baseball history.

"Forsch's no-hitter came in the second game of the season," Feller pointed out. "I pitched a no-hitter on opening day, in 1940, against the White Sox. Can I help it that the season back then didn't open in January, like it almost does now?"

That no-hitter in 1940, incidentally, was the first of three career no-hitters for Feller. Rapid Robert also compiled 12 one-hitters.

FELLER THEN SPOKE of his major league beginning, on request. "I made my first appearance with the

Cleveland Indians in 1936," he said, "in an exhibition game in St. Louis, against the Cardinals when I was 17 years old.

"I pitched the three middle innings — the fourth, fifth and sixth.

"I got the first guy on a little ground-out, on the first pitch. The next St. Louis batter was Leo Durocher. I threw nothing but fastballs. The first pitch sailed over Durocher's head and the second pitch went behind him.

"Then I blazed two strikes by Leo.

"When I was ready to pitch on the 2-and-2 count, I looked toward the plate, but Durocher wasn't there. He was in the dugout, hiding behind the water-cooler.

"Cal Hubbard, the umpire, hollered to Durocher, 'Hey, Leo, get out here; you've got another pitch coming.' And Durocher said, The hell with it; you take the pitch for me, Cal. I'm not coming out and face that wild, crazy kid."

"WHEN THE LAUGHING died down, Durocher came out and I struck him out. Then it was Frankie Frisch's turn at bat.

Frisch was the Cardinal manager. But Frisch never came up.

He sent a pinch-hitter to bat in his place — a guy named Stew Martin — and I struck him out.

"I struck out eight guys in the three innings that day. But the strikeouts didn't come in a row, because I walked a few.

But I showed the Indians enough to make them change their minds.

"Instead of sending me down to Fargo, as planned, they kept me with the Indians.

"In August, I made my first American League start against the old St. Louis Browns — and struck out 15. Three weeks later, in Philadelphia, I struck out 17 for an American League record."

HOW MUCH MONEY was Feller paid that first year?

"My salary, as a regular with the Indians, was $175 a month," Feller said. "At the end of the season, though, they got generous and gave me a $10,000 bonus."

And what kind of bonus had Feller received, when he originally signed his Cleveland contract?

"For signing, and I'm serious about this," Feller said, "the Indians gave me one dollar."

Baseball — HARMON KILLEBREW

Baseball legend hits the 500 home run plateau.
Friday, August 13, 1971
Phil Ranallo: What's New, Harry?

HE IS SO BALD THE Gettysburg Address could be crayoned in its entirety on the top of his head. He is constructed along the lines of a champion bar-room, brawler — the guy who picks up his antagonist and flings him over the mahogany and against the large mirror.

A broad derriere and a thick waist give him a squatty, hammered down appearance — although he stands six feet tall.

He has the biceps and forearms of one of those Russian weight lifters.

In his large meaty paws, a baseball bat — with which he has wreaked havoc on the diamond for 18 years — looks about the size of a toothpick in his hands of the Jolly Green Giant.

WITH THE POWER GENERATED by those massive arms, he has been hammering baseballs out of sight since he was 17 years old. He is slipping a little, his power is not as awesome as it once was, but he is still a valuable chunk of baseball merchandise — as evidenced by his American League-leading runs batted-in total.

He is not a perfect fielder, by any stretch of the imagination, but his shortcomings with the glove are offset by his drive and desire — and his barrel chest.

At first base and at third, he has stopped a thousand hot shots with that barrel chest, found the handle of the baseball and gotten his man.

HE IS A TOTAL TEAM PLAYER one who does not dictate where he will play in the field. He takes his position anywhere he is needed — at first, at third, in the outfield.

He is one of the games superstars, but he is a rarity in this money-mad age since he does not squabble with the boss over his salary ... or threaten to quit the game if he is not given his way.

He is described by manager, Bill Rigney, as "the damnedest player I have ever managed — totally unselfish, the complete team player.

He is gentle and kind and soft-spoken — characteristics that always stand out most in a man of extraordinary physical power.

This is Harmon Killebrew — "The Killer" — of the Minnesota Twins.

TUESDAY, KILLEBREW, THE most mild mannered killer ever to murder a fastball, became the 10th baseball player in creation to reach the 500 home run plateau.

It is a pleasure to applaud his achievement.

Although Killebrew's home run production has tallied off considerably this season — he has hit only 14 to date — he still ranks as the second most consistent home run hitter the game has known.

For his career he has averaged one for every 12.9 at bats, second only to the man himself — Babe, who lost a baseball every 11.8 trips to the plate.

Everybody else, Willie Mays and Henry Aaron, Mickey Mantle and Jimmy Fox, Ted Wiliams and Eddie Matthews, Mel Ott and Ernie Banks — ranks far behind "The Killer" in homers per at bats.

KILLEBREW IS ALSO NO.2 behind Ruth in number of "40 homer" seasons for a career. Harmon has reached the 40 mark eight times. Ruth did it 11 times. No other American

Leaguer has ever done it more than five times.

The National League champ in this department is Hank Aaron, who this season is attempting to do it for the eighth time.

"The Killer" though has never hit 50 in a season — and that is his only regret.

Twice he totaled 49 — in 1964 and 1969.

"I just wish one more homer one of those two years," he said with soft-voiced wistfulness the other night.

"THERE'S SUCH A HUGE gap between 49 homers and 50 homers, just as there is between a .299 batting average and a .300 one, or even between a 19-game winning year for a pitcher and a 20-game year.

"Any fellow who can hit 50 homers moves into a special category. Only 10 men have done it and I would have liked to have joined them."

There is such a huge gap between 499 home runs and 500.

Which makes last Tuesday night — Harmon Killebrew's night — so memorable.

Baseball — BILLY MARTIN

Baseball manager's legendary temper is always getting him into trouble.

Saturday, October 27, 1979

Phil Ranallo: What's New, Harry?

THERE HE GOES with the hands again.

Billy Martin, the fiery fellow who in his baseball career has had more fights than Muhammad Ali, has gotten into another jackpot because he can't keep that fierce temper of his under control.

He's beautiful, this Billy Martin.

Billy's the only guy I know who could start a fight, or a big argument, in the Vatican. Or in Buckingham Palace. Or in a monastery. Or anywhere.

Why, Billy, I think, could start a brawl while serving time in solitary confinement.

Martin, raised on the hard-bitten streets of West Berkeley, Calif., and Oakland, starting using his fists as a small child — took to muscle and swagger by way of survival.

And he's never stopped fighting.

BILLY MARTIN, if he'd chosen boxing over baseball, could have made it as middleweight champion of the world. In his baseball career, Billy has compiled a glittering boxing record.

Martin, with his fists, has pounded out victory after victory on the baseball field, off the field, in trains, planes, barrooms and on the street.

And Billy has never been too particular with whom he fights. He's taken on opposing ball-players, his own players, club officials, sports writers, innocent bystanders in bars — and not-so-innocent bystanders.

Clint Courtney, Jimmy Piersall, Jim Brewer, Howie Fox, Dave Boswell, Burt Hawkins, and sports writer Ray Hagar are among his TKO victims.

MARTIN'S BASEBALL "ring" record stretches back to 1957 when he — along with Whitey Ford, Yogi Berra and Mickey Mantle — was involved in the famous Copacabana fight.

That one cost Martin his spot with the Yankees, who traded him away because he was a bad influence on the Yankee players.

Although that incident failed to change Martin's ways, you'd think he would have learned his lesson three years later, in 1960 — when he punched out Jim Brewer.

Martin, then a player with the Cincinnati Reds, got the idea that Brewer, a Cubs pitcher, was throwing at him.

So Billy raced out to the mound, threw a roundhouse right — and broke Brewer's cheekbone.

THE BIG PUNCH cost Martin $50,000 plus lawyer fees — and it took Billy several years to pay it off. But it failed to get him to curb his terrible temper.

In 1966, while managing the Minnesota Twins, Martin kayoed Twins pitcher Dave Boswell with a sock in the jaw, and punched and kicked Minnesota outfielder Bobby Allison.

That same year, Billy punched out Howard Fox, then the club's road secretary, in a Washington hotel — in a dispute over room keys.

And age considerations have never slowed down the Martin temper, either.

In 1974, Martin, while manager of the Texas Rangers, slapped Burt Hawkins, his 60-year-old road secretary, in the face during an argument on a plane.

THEN, OF COURSE, there was the Nevada incident of last November in which Martin, while being interviewed by a Reno sports writer named Ray

Hagar, took umbrage at a question — and blackened Hagar's eye and knocked out one of his teeth with a flurry of punches.

Now, in this latest Martin fistic episode, Billy allegedly creamed a guy with whom he was talking baseball, in the bar of a hotel in Bloomington, Ind.

And no witnesses have come forward — publicly.

But a member of the Bloomington police force, Capt. G.J. Ruehle, said: "Undoubtedly, it was Martin, according to several witnesses."

ALL THAT'S KNOWN, for sure, is that the poor guy wound up on the floor of the hotel lobby, at Martin's feet, with a big gash in his lip — a wound that required 20 stitches to close.

Martin said that he and a friend, Howard Wong, were in the bar, having a drink, when two men came over and started talking to them.

"One guy was talking baseball," Martin explained. "I decided I didn't want to talk baseball anymore and left. As I walked through the lobby I heard a noise.

"I turned around and saw the guy on the floor. A security guard told Howard the guy fell and cut his lip. I left and went to my room. I'm sorry the guy got hurt."

IT'S EXPECTED that the guy with the fat lip will come out of the woodwork momentarily and make his pronouncement about the incident to the world — as soon as his lawyer clues him in.

Billy Martin, it seems, could be in extremely deep hot water — again.

He's a guy who appears bent on self-destruction.

His temper is destined to one day do him in.

Ironically, Martin has always regarded his temper as his most important attribute.

"My temper is my greatest asset," he once said. "It produced me. Without it, I'd be nothing."

Baseball — WILLIE MAYS

Phil recalls a stellar career and the day Mays made "the greatest catch in baseball history."
Saturday, August 5, 1979
Phil Ranallo: What's New, Harry?

HE WAS BORN on May 6, 1932, in Westfield, Ala., a little town near Birmingham. He began playing baseball — the game he was born to play — with the Birmingham Barons, a black team, when he was a high school freshman of 14.

When he matured, he wasn't big by athletic standards — only 5 feet 11 and around 185 pounds.

Others were bigger and stronger. Others hit the ball farther and ran the bases faster. But nobody did it all like this fellow — nobody put it all together like the "Say Hey Kid."

The Boston Red Sox were the first major-league club to have a shot at landing him, but declined.

The Brooklyn Dodgers, their arms twisted by Jackie Robinson, who told them the kid was one in ten million, sent a scout to look at him — but the scout was not impressed.

The Dodger scout reported that the kid could not hit the curveball — and never lived it down.

The kid, who was making $500 a month with the Barons, took a cut in pay to go to Trenton. But it was, for the kid, a chance of a lifetime, a dream come true — the opportunity to make the major leagues.

THE REST OF THE kid's story is now legend. And, today, in Cooperstown, the marvelous "Say Hey Kid" — Willie Mays — strolls into the Hall of Fame and takes his rightful place in baseball history.

The cold type in the record book supports Willie Mays' status as a Hall of Famer — 3,283 career hits, 660 home runs, 6,066 total bases, 1,903 runs batted in, 1,323 extra-base hits.

He led the National League in batting in 1954, with an average of .345. He batted better than .300 in 10 seasons — and over .315 in six of those 10.

He hit 40 or more homers in six seasons, with a high of 52 in 1965. He was the league's most valuable player twice — in 1954 and 1965.

But it is not the records or the statistics or the awards that distinguish him.

IT IS THE MEMORY of the way the man played the game — with a zest and a daring, with an excitement that is unmatched — which sets the wondrous Willie Mays apart.

If there is one word, one adjective, one description that fit Willie Mays, it is this — "Enthusiasm."

From boy wonder to "old man" in his 40s, Mays never lost his hunger for fun — that joy of dancing out from under his hat, that emotional pleasure of smashing a base hit in the clutch and then hearing the tumult and the shouting.

No man probably ever gave — and got — as much fun out of the game of baseball as Willie Mays.

He was one of those rare people in this life who make you smile every time — even when you simply think about them.

When Willie was out there, in uniform, and you were in the seats, he was thought of as a pal — even with those who hated the Giants.

"ANYBODY WHO EVER saw me play knows I loved what I was doing," Mays said the other day. "I didn't play for me. I played for the people who came to see me play."

Mays also spoke of the two plays in

his career from which he got his biggest charge — the impossible throw and the impossible catch.

He made the impossible throw, in a Giants-Dodger game, when he was in his rookie year. The Dodgers had men on first and third with one out, the score tied and Carl Furillo at bat.

Furillo laced a line drive to right-center.

Apparently certain to score no matter what happened, Billy Cox, the runner on third, played it safe and tagged up.

Mays, streaking over the outfield grass, trapped the ball with a frantic lunge. Then he spun around counter-clockwise and launched a throw home as he emerged from his spin.

THE BALL CAME to Wes Westrum, the catcher, as if shot from a cannon. It didn't bounce in. It came on the fly, a strike.

The astonished Cox was out by 10 feet.

"That," Mays said, "was the perfectest throw I ever made."

The impossible catch, of course, was the classic one on Vic Wertz of Cleveland in the 1954 World Series. The muscular Wertz blasted one over Willie's head in deepest center to the edge of the bleacher wall, 460 feet away.

Mays turned at the crack of the bat and ran and ran and ran. Presumably he had eyes in the back of his head. There is no other explanation.

Suddenly, Willie stuck his glove in front of him as he ran away from the plate. The ball darted over his shoulder and plunked into the glove.

It was the greatest catch in baseball history.

WILLIE MAYS left millions of baseball fans rich with memories. He was, as Jackie Robinson once said, "one in ten million" — one of the greatest ballplayers, and certainly the happiest, who ever played the game.

"If Willie Mays ain't in the Hall of Fame first crack," old Casey Stengel used to say, "they should burn it."

Well, Casey can rest in peace.

They won't have to burn it.

Wondrous Willie Mays walks in today.

Baseball — THURMAN MUNSON

The spectacular Yankee catcher dies in a plane crash.
Saturday, August 4, 1979
Phil Ranallo: What's New, Harry?

THE LIFE AND TIMES of Thurman Lee Munson, bring to mind an old, smash-hit tune the chairman of the board, Frank Sinatra, used to warble so beautifully back in the late '30s and early '40s — "I Can't Get Started with You."

You remember the lyrics, don't you?

"I've been around the world in a plane ... I've settled revolutions in Spain ... the North Pole I have charted ... but I can't get started with you."

Thurman Munson, like the guy in the tune, did it all. He did it all on the baseball diamond — with the catcher's glove and the bat.

But, because of his makeup, and because of little tricks fate played on him along the way, Munson was never able to get started with the fans, with the writers, or with some of his fellow ballplayers.

Dale Carnegie, with his teachings, never got to first base with Munson. Thurman, it seemed, was a fellow who did not believe in trying to win friends and influence people. That, in Munson's mind, was for phonies.

So Munson eventually became an unhappy warrior. An angry man. And, in a way, it was understandable. For Munson, when he wasn't being made the fall guy, usually was being dealt the short end of the stick.

EARLY IN HIS career in New York, when the Yankees were also-rans, the fans acquired the habit of picking on Munson. They booed and ridiculed him regularly — especially when he made a poor throw.

Instead of grinning and bearing it, when he heard the Bronx cheers, Munson often made his feelings known. Once, he went so far as to give the fans a "salute" — by making an obscene gesture.

In the 1976 World Series against Cincinnati, for example, Munson put on a virtuoso show of all the skills of a baseball catcher — a show which, had he been a bullfighter, would have won not only both ears, but also the tail.

IN THE SERIES, Munson batted .529, with nine hits in 17 trips. He finished the Series with six straight hits. He threw out five Reds attempting to steal — a record for a four-game Series.

It may have been the most brilliant performance ever turned in by a catcher in a Series.

Nevertheless, immediately after the game in which the Reds completed their sweep of the Yankees, Munson got it right between the eyes.

Asked by a writer to compare Cincinnati catcher Johnny Bench and Munson, Sparky Anderson, manager of the Reds, said:

"Hey, you don't compare anybody to Johnny Bench. Please, don't embarrass Thurman Munson or anybody by doing that."

THE NEXT YEAR, the Yankees acquired Reggie Jackson.

And, despite Munson's heroics in the Series — and the promise Thurman had been made that he'd be the top-paid Yankee — Munson wound up getting the shaft.

They gave Jackson more money than any Yankee in history, gave him the run of the town — and laid plans to name a candy bar after Reggie.

Thurman turned against the world. He pushed past autograph-seekers who approached him, and ignored the rest. He assailed the baseball writers, accused them of misinterpreting what he said. He gave photographers a tough time.

He went into a shell, and stayed in it — for the rest of his life.

TOO BAD. There is evidence the baseball world never got to know the real Thurman Munson. He was an athlete who rarely went out on the town. Where he went, at almost every opportunity, was straight home — to his wife and three children.

The ballplayers, though, were aware of the kind of family man Munson was, which is why they voted him "Father of the Year" among professional athletes two years ago.

"Thurman's a helluva nice guy," his wife, Diane, told a baseball writer a year ago, "but nobody knows it. But it's not the people's fault. Thurman just won't prostitute himself — and I'm proud of that.

"But I think his career has suffered for the way he is, and he knows that."

THURMAN MUNSON was a great baseball player, but not so great when it came to public relations. He'll be remembered not only because he played the game so well, but because he played it with such total commitment.

Munson, on the baseball diamond, never did anything but his best. He regarded it as stealing the fans' money to play the game any other way.

The only thing stolen from Munson were the years left to him when that plane crashed. It was too soon for anybody to go at age 32.

The one thing about Thurman Munson, though, is he always will be 32 years old in the memories of the fans — always able to smash those line-drive shots to all fields.

Especially with teammates on the bases.

Baseball — SATCHEL PAIGE

Baseball legend enters the Hall of Fame and breaks down the black barrier.

Wednesday, July 7, 1971

Phil Ranallo: What's New, Harry?

BASEBALL IS ABOUT TO DO as nice a thing as it has ever done, it is going to allow Satchel Paige to take his rightful place alongside Babe Ruth and Ty Cobb, Lou Gehrig and Walter Johnson, and the rest of the games greats in the Hall of Fame at Cooperstown.

Baseball has decided to scrap its plans for construction of a segregation barrier in the Hall.

The original plans called for Paige and all subsequent Hall of Fame inductees from the old-time black leagues to be enshrined in a separate wing at Cooperstown — away from the Ruths and Gehrigs.

The barrier would have served as a reminder of that horrible time — before Jackie Robinson was permitted to join the lodge — when racial inequality in this country extended to the baseball diamond and black players were kept out of the major leagues.

SEGREGATION IN THE HALL also might have given Cooperstown visitors the feeling that Paige and the other old-time black players were pathetic figures of the game's history — that there was true joy and fulfillment only in the white leagues.

That would have been an injustice.

The old-time black athletes were men devoted to laughter — despite the fact that a conspiracy of prejudice operated against them.

Baseball's decision to do away with the barrier is a wise one, an American one — and Bowie Kuhn, the game's commissioner, should be commended. It is the finest thing that Kuhn will ever do as leader of the sport.

KUHN WAS UNJUSTLY CRITI-CIZED when baseball announced last February that the old-time blacks had been made eligible for inclusion in the Hall of Fame — but would be placed in a separate wing when inducted.

The move had overtones of compromise and the finger was pointed at Kuhn — even though it had been the commissioner who had opened up the Hall by forcing it down the throats of the people who run the baseball shrine.

Had Kuhn insisted on all or nothing for the old-time blacks at that time, it would have been nothing.

Baseball has no connection with the Hall of Fame — aside from Kuhn being a member of the board of directors.

THE HALL IS RUN BY A FAMILY foundation deriving from Singer sewing machine money. Paul Kerr, the Hall president, is a stand-patter on rules — and one of them was that a player must have 10 years in the majors to qualify for nomination, which none of the old black-league players had.

So Kuhn had to agree to the segregation barrier.

The backlash that resulted gave baseball a black eye — a development that enabled Kuhn to show Kerr the folly of his ways and persuade the Hall boss to give full membership to old-time blacks who were inducted.

Kuhn convinced Kerr that rules can be changed just as laws can be changed — if the law is unjust. So the 10-year rule was changed in the case of old-time blacks.

NOW THERE IS ROOM IN the inn for Satchel Paige. There also will be room in the future for Josh Gibson and Cool Papa Bell and Cyclone Williams and the other old-time black greats, who because of prejudice, were forced to play the game in a ghetto of base-ball's making.

They rode the buses over rough roads. They played as many as three games on Sunday to make ends meet. They watched their white brethren operate in the majors and knew America and the national pastime for what it was and what it pretended to be.

They played in the back alleys of the game, in broken down parks in remote towns, far from major league stadiums.

Every once in a while they were permitted to walk on the same turf with the big leaguers, but never in formal competition.

Now, at last, they are being recognized as equals — at least in Cooperstown.

Baseball has righted a wrong.

Baseball — BROOKS ROBINSON

Legendary third baseman retires from baseball.
Wednesday, August 24, 1977
Phil Ranallo: What's New, Harry?

ANOTHER PIECE OF ART has vanished from the sports world. Brooks Calbert Robinson Jr. — "Mr. Vacuum Cleaner" ... "Mr. Third Base" ... "Mr. Nice Guy" — has put away his glove and called it a career.

Now, to be painfully honest about it, Brooks Robinson didn't exactly put away his glove.

The glove with the magic in it was wrenched from his hand by man's arch-enemy — "Time," the ravaging foe that marches on and on, relentlessly, and eventually catches up to everyone.

Sunday, in Minnesota, "Time" again got its man — caught Robinson in its clutches.

The very idea of Brooks Robinson, who was around almost forever, falling victim to "Time" comes as somewhat of a shock to me — and to a couple of generations of baseball addicts.

Why?

Because, suddenly, we realize it's getting late for us, too.

What's the march of time doing to us — the guys who grew up with Robinson, or who were still on the sunny side of 30 or 40 when Brooks first began making like a vacuum cleaner?

Nothing is as fleeting as time.

It seems like only yesterday that Robinson first came on the baseball scene — yesterday, when we were young and carefree. But now, it's today, and we're middle-aged — or older. And, for those who care to peek, there's tomorrow — dead ahead.

BROOKS ROBINSON BECAME

Baltimore's baseball darling the moment he stepped on the Oriole diamond in 1955 — as an 18-year-old straight out of high school in Little Rock, Ark.

Nineteen-fifty-five — the year Elvis Presley was being discovered ... the year Swaps won the Kentucky Derby ... the year the American Football League was still five years away ... the year Phil Dokes was born.

That's a long time ago.

Now, for the 40-year-old Robinson — after 23 baseball years and after making his mark as the best third basemen who ever played the game — it's all over. The sun has set on his career.

But what a career!

Especially for a fellow who once was labeled "too slow" to become a major-leaguer — and who once had doubts about his ability and feared he couldn't hit well enough to make it in the big leagues.

ROBINSON, IN HIS BOOK,

"Third Base Is My Home," reveals that in his high school days he was regarded as much more talented in basketball than at baseball — and that he had been offered a basketball scholarship by the University of Arkansas.

But he turned his back on basketball — and college — to give professional baseball a whirl.

"I couldn't help myself," says Robinson, who had dreamed of becoming a major league baseball player since he was a little kid — a kid who spent most of his waking hours behind his home in Little Rock, hitting pebbles out of sight with a broomstick.

Besides, there was "big money" in baseball — like the $4,000 Robinson received for his first year in the game.

That's right — Robinson signed his first contract for four grand, and didn't receive a dime in bonus money.

BROOKS ROBINSON GAMBLED on baseball, over basketball, and hit the jackpot. Before he walked away the other day, Robinson hit 268 home runs — more than any third baseman in American League history.

And he played in more American games, 2,896, than anyone but Ty Cobb.

The number of accolades he walked away with stagger the imagination — 16 straight "Gold Gloves" as the best third baseman in the business, 1960-1975, for example, plus 15 consecutive annual appearances in the All-Star game, 1960-1974.

He was the American League's most valuable player in 1964 as well as the MVP in the 1966 All-Star game and the 1970 World Series.

Robinson was "murder" in World Series play. In the 1970 Series, he batted .429 and spent most of his time in the field diving on line shots and throwing out guys from a prone position.

NOW, FOR ROBINSON, it's all over. And the man — who in 1969 was named Baltimore's favorite baseball Oriole of all time — went out with class.

Robinson retired because he was aware that the Orioles wanted to activate catcher Rick Dempsey.

"Our club," Robinson said, "will be a little stronger this way — with Dempsey available.

"I just wish I had 23 more years of baseball in me."

Robinson, incidentally, does not bow out as a man of means even though he commanded six-figure pay the last few years.

Last spring it was reported that Robinson's debts, following a bad investment in a shopping center, totaled $294,585 — and that the banks were foreclosing on his home.

Fortunately, the report was not completely accurate.

"IT COST ME A LOT OF money," Robinson said. "But I'm by no means broke. I never did lose my house. And I didn't come back to baseball this year, and take a cut, because I was desperate for money.

"I came back because I wanted to play."

Baseball — JACKIE ROBINSON

The man who broke baseball's color barrier passes away.
Wednesday, October 25, 1972
Phil Ranallo: What's New, Harry?

JACK ROOSEVELT ROBINSON.
The trail-blazer ... the gallant warrior who had the courage to invade the white world of major league baseball ... the man who changed the locks on the doors of sports — the most significant figure in the history of athletics.

Jackie Robinson died Tuesday morning.

He was 53 years old, a rather young age ... but into those 53 years he packed the fullest life possible, a life with impact — a life that made an indelible imprint on the face and the heart and the soul of America.

Jackie Robinson, in his 53 years of life, opened millions of eyes into the indecencies and outrages and humiliations inflicted upon him and his "brothers and sisters" because they were not white.

Jackie Robinson, in his 53 years, helped change America ... for the better — at least a little.

ON THE BASEBALL DIAMOND
Jackie Robinson was a living flame. He came on the baseball scene — as the first black man in the majors — in 1947 ... and he was cruelly treated.

Opposing players ripped him with racial slurs. Several of his Brooklyn Dodger teammates resented his presence on the club.

But Robinson, in those early years in the majors, had courage enough not to fight back.

He controlled his fierce temper for a reason.

He did not want to jeopardize the chances of other black players making it in the once all-white world.

He had opened the door — and he was determined to keep it open.

BLACK LITTLE BOYS IN THE ghettoes now were taking their swings at the ball with a new fervor ... and they were sleeping with their baseball gloves under their pillows ... and they were dreaming beautiful dreams — dreams of following in the footsteps of Jackie Robinson.

Jackie Robinson, a black man was a major leaguer. Black ballplayers all over America would have a place to play now ... and real money to make.

The black ballplayer — thanks to Jackie Robinson — had freedom at last.

That is why Robinson did not fight the bigots on the diamond with his fists in those early years.

He fought back only with base hits and stolen bases and electrifying plays with his glove in the field.

ONCE HE AND OTHER BLACK MEN were on firm footing in the majors, the real Jackie Robinson stood up — the Jackie Robinson who had spoken out and fought against racial prejudice and bigotry from his boyhood.

His diamond philosophy became art — eye for an eye and a tooth for a tooth.

The racial slurs stopped and Robinson was accepted for what he was — a great baseball player.

The kind of baseball player Jackie Robinson was, perhaps was described best by the late great dancer, Bill (Bojangles) Robinson.

"Jackie Robinson," Bojangles said, "is Ty Cobb in technicolor."

JACKIE ROBINSON HAD A FINE sense of humor. He even had it on the biggest day of his life, the most

frightening day — when he played his   warrior.
first major-league game against the
Boston Braves.

That day, as he was about to leave
his apartment for the park, he planted
a kiss on his wife's cheek and said to
her:

"Honey, when you get to the ballpark today, if you have any trouble
spotting me out there on the field, I'll
be wearing No. 42."

He was a man of principles — and
he never stopped defending them.

Once, during his World War II service days in the U.S. Army, he refused
to the dictates of a bigoted bus driver
on an Army post in the South.

The driver ordered Robinson to sit in
the rear of the bus.

Jackie refused.

THE DRIVER TURNED ROBIN-
SON in ... and Jackie was court-mar-
tialed — and won his case. A black
man — thanks to Jackie Robinson —
no longer had to sit in the rear of one
of Uncle Sam's buses ... in the South,
or anywhere.

Robinson was an outspoken defender
of civil rights to his dying day. He never stopped fighting for his people —
never stopped trying to show America
that black is as beautiful as white.

In his last public appearance — a
week ago in Cincinnati, at the World
Series, where he was honored on the
25th anniversary of the breaking of
the color barrier in baseball — Robinson is made a pitch for equal rights.

"I am extremely proud and pleased,"
he said, as he accepted a special award
from Commissioner Bowie Kuhn, "but
I will be more pleased the day I can
look over at the third-base line and see
a black man as manager."

Robinson will never see the day.

But the day will come thanks, most
of all, to Jack Roosevelt Robinson.

Eternal peace to the gallant black

Baseball — PETE ROSE

Rose might enter the Baseball Hall of Fame with a head-first slide.
Monday, May 1, 1978
Phil Ranallo: What's New, Harry?

A FEW YEARS BACK, a gentleman from Cincinnati who dabbles in thoroughbred racing, purchased a fashionably bred racehorse — one with all the looks of a real runner — and named the colt for one of his favorite people.

As a runner, however, it turned out that the horse, who cost a pretty penny, wasn't worth 10 cents. The only thing good about the plug was his appetite.

For the owner, it was too bad that the racehorse wasn't anything like the fellow for whom he was named.

What I mean to say is, had this colt been as good a racehorse as his namesake is an athlete, he would have won the Kentucky Derby, Preakness and Belmont Stakes. He would have been a horse they couldn't keep out of the winner's circle.

The racehorse's name, you see, was Pete Rose.

Pete Rose, the man, is one extraordinary guy. He's so extraordinary he's unique. And what makes him unique is the fact that nobody can quite figure out how he can be so good.

And that includes you.

Now, be honest. Does the name, Pete Rose, come to mind when you're baseball day-dreaming and listing the very best fielders in the business, or very best long ball hitters, or base runners, or throwers?

Certainly not.

The name, Pete Rose, comes to mind only when you're listing the very best baseball players, period.

See what I mean?

THE BEST WAY TO describe Peter Edward Rose is the way a toastmaster once did, when he was introducing Rose to a sports night audience.

"Now here's a fellow," the toastmaster said, "who can't run, can't throw, can't field, can't hit home runs — and can't miss making it into the Hall of Fame."

Rose, incidentally, topped the toastmaster.

"Hey, wait a minute," Rose said. "I've got some ability. Maybe I'm not the greatest runner, or greatest fielder, or greatest this or that. But you've got to admit I'm not too bad for a white guy."

Pete's right. He's not bad. He's marvelous.

At this moment, Pete Rose is about to crash the 3,000-hit barrier. Only 12 guys in history got more hits than Rose has amassed in his career. And all 12 are out of baseball action.

In fact, six of them are dead.

IF ROSE REMAINS physically sound and is able to play four more years, as he has planned, he stands an excellent chance of passing 11 of the guys ahead of him on the "most hits" list — all but Ty Cobb, the all-time champ with 4,191 hits.

And it's okay to mention Pete Rose's name in the same breath as Ty Cobb's.

Rose, during his career, has reached the 200-hit plateau in a season nine times, and is tied with Cobb for the all-time lead in that department.

Rose, in fact, would be the undisputed 200-hits-a-season champ if it weren't for the players' strike in 1972. That year, Rose rapped 198 hits in a season that was shortened eight games by the strike.

Year after year, Rose gets his 200 hits, scores his 100 runs, and drives in his 75 runs — as a leadoff man.

The guy is simply amazing.

ALTHOUGH ROSE IS a gifted athlete, it isn't talent alone that makes him a great baseball player. It's the intangibles he possesses — his matchless hustle, his esprit de corps, his dedication, his unselfishness.

Pete Rose is what the game of baseball is all about, or supposed to be all about.

He plays the game with the pure joy of a little boy — like a kid who goes to bed night after night and dreams his wonderful dreams, with his baseball glove tucked under his pillow.

He plays the game of baseball with the enthusiasm displayed by a kid standing at a candy counter, with his eyes popping, trying to decide what to get with the dollar he's clutching in a fist.

In 1963, the year he joined the Cincinnati Reds, Rose made "Rookie of the Year." Fifteen seasons later, Pete is still playing the game the same way — like a "Rookie of the Year."

Rose is 37 years old, going on 18.

AND ROSE IS NO prima donna.

He's a guy with a $350,000-a-year salary who, believe it or not, allows himself to be pushed around by his manager. Three times in his career Pete has moved over — switched to another position — to make room for somebody else.

And he has moved without moaning or groaning.

He came into baseball as a catcher, but was shifted to second base when a better catcher came along. Pete went on to make it as a National League All-Star second baseman.

Later he was transferred to left fielder — and became an All-Star outfielder.

Then, in 1974, when Sparky Anderson was trying to find a way to get George Foster into the lineup every day, Sparky's search was over after he chatted with Rose.

"Okay, okay, Sparky," Rose said, "I'll play third base."

Pete Rose's next move will be from third to the Hall of Fame. And when he enters the Hall, there's no question how he'll get in. He'll do it with a head-first slide.

Basketball — NATE ARCHIBALD

Archibald defeated poverty and gave back to his community.
Sunday, September 11, 1977
Phil Ranallo: What's New, Harry?

NATE ARCHIBALD IS A fellow who remembers well what he could have been if he had elected to run with the crowd instead of running up and down the court with a basketball in the playgrounds of his old South Bronx neighborhood.

Archibald, in his formative years, was surrounded by it all in South Bronx — the filth and the despair, the dope pushers and the ladies of the evening, the winos and the addicts, the "smart" guys with their big, shiny cars and big bankrolls.

It was all there, in the ghetto — and for some of Archibald's friends and acquaintances, it all served as a kind of spring training for their graduation into the big time of crime.

Many of them landed behind bars,and some of them are still in jail, including a couple of lifers.

But Archibald, the oldest of seven children in a fatherless family — a family held together by a mother who worked 18-hour days, as a homemaker and as a clerk in a department store — managed to avoid the pitfalls of the ghetto.

Archibald escaped, dribbled right out of the squalor and the despair — and demonstrated that a man need not necessarily live a demeaning life because of the demeaning circumstances that surround him.

"I WAS ONE OF THE fortunate few that didn't get into big trouble," said Archibald, the new Buffalo Brave. "Basketball helped to keep me out of trouble. But, really, ever since I can remember, my mind was made up that I wasn't going to be part of the street scene."

There also was, for example, the frightening sight of Ralph Hall, a gifted basketball player, collapsing and dying on a court in a Harlem playground from an overdose of drugs.

There was the experience of watching one of his younger brothers falling victim to the pushers and getting hooked, and staying hooked — until Archibald straightened him out.

And there were those "wonderful men" in the ghetto — the men who dedicate their lives to guiding and directing the ghetto kids.

ARCHIBALD MENTIONED one of the "wonderful men" — Floyd Layne, who overcame his involvement in the basketball fixes of 1950, when he was the star playmaker for the CCNY team that won both the NIT and NCAA championships.

"Mr. Layne got me off the streets and into the playgrounds," Archibald said. "He is the man who got me started in the game of basketball."

Thanks to Floyd Layne, Archibald was afforded a second basketball opportunity at DeWitt Clinton High School after Nate had been dropped from the squad in his junior year.

That second chance — which Archibald got after Layne twisted the Clinton coach's arm — proved the turning point in Nate's life.

Archibald, in his senior year at DeWitt Clinton — his first full season on the basketball team — made the New York All-City team.

THAT GOT ARCHIBALD out of the ghetto and sent him on his way — first to Arizona Western Junior College where he remained one year; then to the University of Texas at El Paso, where he gained collegiate stardom, and finally to the NBA, where he made it as a $400,000-a-year player.

Archibald, once a faceless and fatherless black kid who might have been pulled in by the cops if he had run with the crowd instead of running with a basketball, has made it.

He has escaped and he has made it big — because he refused to be pulled down by his environment and the depressing social conditions in which he was reared.

But Archibald has never forgotten the people who are still trapped in the squalid confines of those overcrowded tenements and overcrowded streets in the South Bronx.

Archibald returns to the ghetto every summer. He spends most all of his summer days there, in his old neighborhood talking to the kids, trying to guide them and give them a sense of purpose, and teaching them to play basketball.

ARCHIBALD IS ONE OF the workers with New York City's "Operation Sports Rescue" program. He is coaching two playground teams this summer, as he always does. And he has furnished his players with sneakers and uniforms, as he always does.

The main thing in the back of the minds of the kids in Archibald's old neighborhood is to become a professional basketball player, follow in Nate's footsteps.

"What I do is try to change their thinking a little," Archibald said. "I try to convince them that not everyone can become a pro.

"I tell them that the important thing is to prepare themselves for the rest of their lives.

"I tell them that even if they can't play in the pros, they can use basketball to get a scholarship to college — and that if they get a college education they can become anything they want to become.

"I TELL THEM THAT, with an education, they can become a lawyer or a writer or an artist or a phys-ed teacher — anything.

"I tell them that, with an education, they can become somebody."

Nate Archibald is some kind of guy. He's somebody on the basketball court — and he's somebody off the court.

Basketball — EMMETTE BRYANT

Bryant matches up against a young Pete Maravich.
Saturday, November 14, 1970
Phil Ranallo: What's New, Harry?

MUTTON CHOPS, CONNECT-
ED to a thick mustache, adorn his
fine-featured, ebony face. A sweat
band rings his head, an inch above
the eyebrows. The numeral seven is
stitched on his Buffalo Braves uniform. The seven is fitting. Emmette
Bryant is a natural.

On the basketball court, Bryant is
busy, busy, busy — so busy that when
the struggle is still very young his
jersey is sopping wet, as if he had just
hurried out of the shower.

Emmette Bryant is a dynamo. He is
always in motion.

On defense he stalks his man, bad-
gers him, pesters him, harasses him,
relentlessly. He never gives his man so
much as a second of peace.

In backcourt and in front court, he
is forever pressing his "victim," forever
thrusting one of his lightning-quick
hands at the ball.

Larceny is always on Bryant's mind
— and he commits the "crime" with
remarkable regularity. He is a superb
stealer of basketballs — a grand lar-
cenist.

If someone collected all the basketballs Bryant has stolen in his sev-
en-year National Basketball Association career and was able to transform
the air in the balls into helium, he
could launch the Goodyear blimp.

WEDNESDAY NIGHT, IN THE
AUD, Emmette Bryant went head-to-
head with the two-million-dollar kid,
Atlanta's Pete Maravich. Bryant gave
Pistol Pete four inches in height, 10
years in age — and one terrible pain in
the neck.

Bryant was beautiful!

Although Maravich showed flash-
es of basketball brilliance during his

17-minute stint, Bryant twice stole the
ball from Pistol Pete and three or four
times forced him into errant passes —
passes as sloppy as Pete's socks.

But Bryant had words of praise for
Maravich.

"Pete is a good basketball player,"
Em told a gaggle of sportswriters
in the dressing room. "He's going to
be all right in this league. There's no
question — Pete will hold his own.

"MARAVICH IS A VERY GOOD
dribbler, but he keeps the ball kind
of high. That gives his man a good
chance to steal it. Pete's got to learn to
dribble lower.

"No, Maravich will never average
in the 40s in the NBA, as he did in
college. After all, who does? No one
should expect him to do in the pros
what he did in college."

Bryant took a long sip of soft drink.
Then, on request, he talked about his
strong suit — defense ... and, especially, the art of relieving an opponent of
the basketball.

"I play a basic defense — tight. I
pick up my man immediately. I want
him to know I'm always there. I want
him to worry about me. I try to annoy
him by harassing him every second.

"Guys hate to be guarded closely, especially in backcourt. Sometimes they
get angry ... and that's good — because when they're angry they make
more mistakes.

"WHEN YOU TAKE ONE OFF
A guy — steal the ball — sometimes
it bothers him to the point where he
starts bringing the ball down court
with his back turned to you, in an
effort to protect the ball better.

"That's what you want. When his

back is turned, he does not get a full view of front court — and he may not see the open man."

Bryant would rather steal a ball than score a basket anytime. "Stealing the ball is like breaking a tennis player's service."

Bryant, who spent his first six years in the NBA with clubs that did considerable winning — the New York Knicks and Boston Celtics — said there was something special about the Braves' victory over the Hawks.

"THERE'S AN EXTRA MEA-SURE of satisfaction in winning, I guess, when you do things the fans don't think you can do — such as the things we did against the Hawks."

The enthusiasm displayed by the fans impressed Bryant. "The home court advantage is really something when thousands of fans are cheering — and when your wife and kids and friends are in the stands. It makes you play harder."

Did Bryant's family see him play that strong game against Atlanta?

"No, my wife, Barbara, and my 4-year-old son, Mike, were in New York. Barbara's a school teacher there. They come to Buffalo weekends, when the team is in town.

"But I'm bringing them here permanently, soon as I find a suitable apartment. What I'm looking for is an apartment with two bedrooms in the Allentown district.

"No suburbs for me. I'm the urban type. I've seen Allentown and it's for me. It's got atmosphere."

Basketball — ADRIAN DANTLEY

Dantley puts his entire future on the line to represent the U.S. in the Olympics.
Thursday, July 29, 1976
Phil Ranallo: What's New, Harry?

AT LONG LAST, a soothing breath of fresh air moves in and takes some of the sweat out of the long, hot summer — the summer in which Buffalo sports fans first agonized over the threatened departure of the Buffalo Braves, then watched O.J. Simpson run off into the sunset.

The breath of fresh air is a kid named Adrian Dantley, the Fighting Irishman from Notre Dame — the fellow who Tuesday night, in Montreal, was an unmasked marvel in sneakers as the United States regained the amateur basketball championship of the world.

Thanks, Adrian — we needed that.

Adrian Dantley is the kind of young man who makes you want to throw your hat in the air. Adrian, who is headed for the Buffalo Braves, is some kind of basketball player! And he's one tough cookie — and some kind of person!

In the Olympic basketball showdown with Yugoslavia, Dantley did it all, scored basket after basket and pulled down rebound after rebound under the most trying circumstances.

Dantley did it all, while a Yugoslavian "assassin" named Drazen Dalipagic was doing everything to him but pull out his fingernails.

YOU'VE HEARD OF basketball players who are referred to as hatchet-men? Jerry Sloan of the Chicago Bulls is one, for example. Well, Drazen Dalipagic does Sloan one better. Drazen is an axe-man.

Dalipagic, who is all elbows, spent the night ramming all those elbows into Dantley's chest and back, ribs and neck, face and arms.

And whenever Dalipagic missed with an elbow, he'd connect with a forearm to the chops.

But everything the "assassin" did to Dantley was for naught. Dalipagic, with his dirty work, even failed to get Adrian to change expression.

DANTLEY NEVER COM-PLAINED and never batted an eye — even when Dalipagic opened a gash over Adrian's right eyebrow, with a well-directed elbow, and the official had the audacity to call the foul on Dantley.

Dantley, on Tuesday night, wasn't about to allow anyone — or anything — to distract him, get his mind off his work. So Adrian just kept going about his business — swish! ... swish! ... swish!

Yes sir, on this night in Montreal, for which Dantley had made the supreme sacrifice and did it all — made it a night to remember for the rest of his life.

"THE SUPREME SACRIFICE?"

That's right. Dantley, while playing in the Olympics, was placing his lucrative professional basketball career on the line — was taking a million-dollar gamble, minimum.

Had Dantley been seriously injured, had the roughneck Dalipagic put Adrian out of business, there all the green stuff would have gone — right down the drain.

A million bucks!

Dantley, you see, was playing in these Olympics without first having signed a big, fat, no-cut contract with the Braves.

So he risked it all.

DANTLEY ELECTED TO make

the supreme sacrifice — play in the Olympics without the protection of a pro contract — because he's a kid who takes great pride in personal achievement.

Also, because those letters that are stitched on his Olympic jersey — U.S.A. — mean a great deal to him.

Only three other U.S. stars elected to take such a risk — Scott May, Quinn Buckner and Milton Kupchak.

The rest of the NBA first-round picks in the draft said, "No, thank you" — including, John Lucas, Robert Parrish, Leon Douglas, Richard Washington and Terry Furlow.

SO ADRIAN DANTLEY is some kind of guy — and some kind of basketball player! I'd certainly love to be his agent — his 10 per-center — and sit down with Paul Snyder and talk contract.

I'm sure I could get a terrific bundle for Dantley.

But I'd be completely fair in my dealings with Snyder.

To prevent a long, drawn-out negotiating struggle, all I'd ask for Dantley would be, say, a million bucks for three years.

But, for leaning backwards like that. I'd insist that the contract include a special clause.

THE CLAUSE WOULD read something like this: "Salary, $1,000,000, payable over a three-year period. However, salary figure is doubled, to $2,000,000, in the event the Braves' season-ticket sale reaches 5,000, or if the club's ticket revenue reaches $1,625,000 prior to the regular-season start in each of the three years."

Basketball — ERNIE DiGREGORIO

The Braves draft Ernie D. and he becomes the 1974 Rookie of the Year.
Monday, March 26, 1973
Phil Ranallo: What's New, Harry?

THE BUFFALO BRAVES, thanks to their pitiful won-lost record, will select third in the upcoming draft of college players ... and the commodity the club needs most is a penetrating guard, a backcourt man who can direct the offense.

Such a player is at large.

The Braves masterminds — Paul Snyder, Eddie Donavan and Jack Ramsey — should keep their fingers crossed. Their worries will be over as well as their long search, if this player is available when Buffalo's selection turn comes up.

The player is the sensational kid from Providence — Ernest DiGregorio, the six-foot whirling dervish who, even in defeat in the NCAA playoffs, has left his mark as a gifted guard, a 175-pound chunk of extraordinary basketball talent.

IN RECENT WEEKS, whenever the Braves bosses have been asked which college players they fancy most, they have started with the hardship possibilities, Bill Walton and Dave Thompson, then gotten around to fellows like Ed Ratleff, Doug Collins, Kevin Joyce, et cetera.

DiGregorio's name has rarely been mentioned.

Since the Braves' chances of landing either Walton or Thompson are nil, if they go hardship, the hope here is that their thinking has changed about DiGregorio.

Ernie D. is something. He has it all — grace, speed, reflexes, shooting touch. Few guards in the business have such control of the ball.

He appears to have the tools to become another Nate Archibald.

THE MOUTHS OF the Braves bosses should be watering. They should be desperate to get their hands on DiGregorio — because Ernie with his exposure on the tube in this NCAA Tournament, has given strong indication that wherever he goes in the pros he will be a box office magnet.

The name of the game in the NBA is money and DiGregorio is going to help fill some club owner's cash register — by filling a lot of empty seats.

Why not Paul Snyder's empty seats?

DiGregorio in his NCAA Tournament, failed to bring a championship to his school ... but he did bring the Friars farther than they deserved to go — to the semifinals — and he caught the eye of the basketball world.

ERNIE D. HAD THE NCAA customers screeching and howling and gasping, in wonderment with his dribbling, shooting and passing.

He can go left or right with equal facility and is a coach's dream as a shooter — but amazingly, the strongest part of his game is his left passing.

A few weeks ago, he destroyed Maryland with his brilliant shooting and with his pin-point passes of various lengths — long-long, long, medium and short.

And Saturday he almost pulled the rug from beneath Memphis State, a club whose personnel is far superior to Ernie D's fellow Friars.

Once, against Memphis State, Ernie threaded the ball through a thicket of arms and legs to a colleague for an easy basket.

ANOTHER TIME ON a fast break, Ernie, sensing that a giant defender would block his shot, dropped the ball back to a teammate and bingo — another basket!

This particular play was so startling, so breathtaking, that the cameraman blew all but a small piece of the action.

Houdini couldn't have managed any better.

The NCAA playoffs have lifted Di-Gregorio out of obscurity caused by the presence of Walton and the UCLA gang, Thompson and Collins and Joyce, et cetera.

The pros can no longer dismiss him as a fancy, nickel and dime gunner.

He is slick and exciting.

ERNIE D. SEEMS to be at his best in the big games. He can be counted on to direct the offense, ignite the defense and inspire his teammates.

Let's hope that the Braves bosses have the foresight to corral the sensational kid who hails from Providence.

Basketball — BOB LANIER

St. Bona basketball star is drafted by the Detroit Pistons in the first round.

Tuesday, March 24, 1970

Phil Ranallo: What's New, Harry?

STILL BEDDED DOWN IN Buffalo General Hospital, Bob Lanier, the St. Bonaventure All-America who was selected No. 1 Monday in the National Basketball Assn.'s draft of college players, tugged at a second blanket that covered his shoulders and huge chest.

"I feel lousy," Lanier said. "The nurses tell me it's warm in here, but I'm freezing. I must be coming down with something, or maybe it's just that I'm going batty from being in this hospital."

Lanier was congratulated on being plucked No. 1 in the draft by the Detroit Pistons of the NBA's Eastern Division.

"It is an honor, I guess," Lanier said, "but I can't fully appreciate it at the moment —being in the hospital, like this, and being in the middle of the arm-twisting and bickering over where I'm going to play and how much money I'm going to get."

THAT WAS LANIER'S WAY OF telling a visitor he has not reached a decision on where he will play as a professional — with the Pistons or with the New York Nets of the American Basketball Assn.

Lanier was asked if the report that he was leaning toward the NBA was false.

"No," Lanier responded, "That's the way I'm leaning — or, rather, that's the way I want to lean — but right now I don't know what I'm going to do ... because the Nets have made me an extremely attractive offer.

"I'm going to think about it at least a couple more days. I definitely won't make a decision until Wednesday, but maybe it'll be later."

Lanier, who'll become a millionaire-and-a-half the minute he takes pen in hand, tugged at the blanket again. "You got any information on the draft — where the other guys are going I mean?"

THE VISITOR NODDED, TOOK A sheet of paper from a pocket, and began reading aloud the names of the players who were selected in the first round of the draft.

When he had read nine or ten names, Lanier interrupted him.

"Where's Murph?"

"Lanier, of course, was referring to Niagara's All-America — Calvin Murphy.

Lanier was informed that Murphy was the 18th player selected in the draft — and that he had gone to San Diego in the second round.

"Eighteenth!" Lanier said, "I figured Murph would go in the top ten, for sure.

"Who'd the Buffalo team go for?"

"It was explained that Buffalo had traded first round picking positions with the Baltimore Bullets — getting guard Mike Davis of Baltimore in the deal — and had selected Princeton's John Hummer when its first turn came around, 15th in the draft.

"I'M SURPRISED THAT BUFFALO passed up Murph," Lanier said. But I'm sure the men who are running the Buffalo team know what they are doing.

"Which team did you say drafted Murphy?"

Informed that San Diego had selected Murphy, Lanier threw up his arms, laughed and said: "Do you realize what almost happened?"

The visitor shook his head.

"About four days ago," Lanier said, "they flipped a coin to decide which team would get first pick in the draft — Detroit or San Diego, and Detroit won the flip.

"If the coin had come up the other way, San Diego would have selected first — and if San Diego had picked me, Murph and I would be teammates with the Rockets.

"Wouldn't that have been amazing? It would have been great playing pro ball with Murph. We'd have showed them."

LANIER CHUCKLED, "THAT Murphy's lucky. He's going to be out there, in San Diego, in all that good weather, and I'm going to be back here in all this ...

"You'd better not write that, I don't want to get anybody sore at me.

"But that Murphy's lucky, I envy him."

Then Bob Lanier talked about the fellows who are closest to his heart, his Bona teammates.

"They did a tremendous job in the tournament," Lanier said. "For a long time a lot of people thought all Bona had was Bob Lanier. Well those people found out they were wrong. Those guys are talented, and they're a terrific team without me.

"Wasn't that Matt Gant something? This year he got better with each game. Watch him next year — he'll be All-American.

"And 'The Bub' — Greg Gary — really did his thing. What a hustler! And Billy Kalbaugh and Mike Kull. What a bunch!"

Basketball — BOB LANIER & LORRIE ALEXANDER

Lanier is mentored by a great man named Lorrie Alexander.
Thursday, March 26, 1970
Phil Ranallo: What's New, Harry?

THE BOY WAS 11 YEARS OLD, BUT already his dreams of becoming a basketball star were shattered. He was over-sized and clumsy and lumbering, about as graceful as a rhinoceros.

The neighborhood kids giggled whenever he tried to shoot or dribble a basketball.

Now he was discouraged and depressed.

Then a special man entered the disheartened boy's life — Lorrie Alexander, director of the Masten Boys Club.

Alexander saw something in the boy. He took the boy under his wing, became his personal martinet. He worked with the boy in private — out of the sight of the giggling kids.

Night after night, for more than two years, Alexander cleared the kids out of the Boys Club at closing time — 9 p.m.— then locked the door from the inside ... and put the boy through the Alexander regimen.

THE BOY BARELY TOUCHED A basketball during those nightly sessions. Under Alexander's watchful eye, he worked with weights to strengthen his arms and leg muscles. He climbed ropes. He crawled on the gym floor, first on his stomach, then on all fours.

The sweaty sessions were not wasted. The boy progressed slowly. He became less clumsy. He gained a measure of confidence. He began to dream his dream again. The boy was on the way.

That was 10 years ago.

Wednesday morning, the boy who was Lorrie Alexander's protege — Bob Lanier — became a millionaire.

The awkward kid who developed into one of the most agile big men in the history of sports signed with the Detroit Pistons of the National Basketball Assn. — in return for what was described as "the most lucrative contract ever given to a professional athlete."

LORRIE ALEXANDER WASN'T THERE Wednesday morning, in the doctors' dining room at Buffalo General Hospital, where the nation's newest millionaire faced a small army of sports writers and sportscasters — but Alexander wasn't forgotten.

Bob Lanier, on the biggest day of his life, remembered Lorrie Alexander first.

Clad in brown-and-white pajamas, and seated in a wheelchair, his right leg fully extended and encased in a huge cast, Lanier was wheeled before a battery of microphones.

Appearing a bit nervous, he raised his head, squinted in the glare of the television lights, then said, softly:

"To Lorrie Alexander, who started me off; my father, my coach, Larry Weise, and my teammates at St. Bona, and everybody who helped me ... "

Bob paused. Deep emotion showed in his strong face.

"All I can say is ... thank you."

HAD HE BEEN THERE, ALEXANDER, now at New York University, working toward his master's degree in physical education, would have been the proudest man in the large room — next to the newest Detroit Pistons scout.

The Detroit club's newest scout is Robert J. Lanier, Bob's father, who became part of the Piston organization — at a very substantial salary — the minute Bob signed the contract.

"My wife, Nan," Mr. Lanier said,

with a twinkle in his eye, is also working for the Pistons now — as Bob's secretary."

"No," Bob said, "my mother's too dedicated to her job — as a social worker — to take time off."

When the press conference was about 45 minutes old, Mrs. Lanier made an appearance. Asked how it felt to be the mother of a millionaire, she said:

"I'm just glad for my son."

WHEN BOB LANIER FIRST ARRIVED at St. Bona four years ago, he was not presented the key to the City of Olean.

But he did get the key to the home of Richard (Sugar) Alridge, 125 ½ N. 2nd St., Olean.

Alridge was there Wednesday.

"I just had to be here, on Bob's big day," Alridge said. "For four years in Olean, Bob's been like a son to me and to my wife, Esther. It was kind of Mike Abdo to give me a ride up here."

"For four years," said Abdo, sports editor of the Olean Times-Herald, "Sugar and his wife opened up their home to Bob."

"I guess Bob liked my wife Esther's cooking," Alridge said, smiling. "Bob ate anything Esther cooked ... and plenty of it — especially the soul food.

"We're going to miss Bob — especially our 11-year-old daughter, Lynn. She loves Bob. And Bob's nuts about her."

AN HOUR HAD PASSED — AND Bob Lanier was still obliging members of the media, still fielding their questions.

Someone asked Lanier if his exact height was 6-feet-11.

"No," Lanier replied, "I don't think I'm 6-11."

Ed Coil, general manager of the Detroit Pistons, stared at Lanier, then said:

"Now he tells us."

Lanier laughed. "I think I'm 6-11-½."

Everybody in the room looked at Ed Coil.

It was obvious Coil felt better.

Basketball — PISTOL PETE MARAVICH

"Pistol" Pete and the Atlanta Hawks face the Buffalo Braves.
Wednesday, January 20, 1971
Phil Ranallo: What's New, Harry?

THE TWO MILLION DOLLAR kid – Pete Maravich – feinted his defender dizzy and, from 25 feet, began to drive through heavy traffic toward the basket. As he took his second step, he was bumped hard by a Buffalo Brave.

Pistol Pete lost his footing and started to go sprawling.

An instant before he hit the floor, and with his body in a horizontal position, Maravich peered skyward — at the basket — then somehow got off a shot.

Swish!

It was a spectacular happening at once illustrating Pete Maravich's extraordinary body control, his split X-ray vision, and his remarkable ability to improvise ... even at the risk of losing his head.

THE 6,621 WITNESSES IN Memorial Auditorium — most of whom had started out against Maravich, goading him, daring him to show them — roared.

Pete Maravich was too much all night.

Those who had him marked down as being a pop gun now know better. Peter is a real pistol.

Maravich's outside shooting show — he rolled up 41 points, with most of his 13 goals coming from the distant ranges — was the best ever put on by a pro basketball player in the downtown hall.

It was a performance good enough to make the finest backcourt operators in the business envious — Jerry West, Walt Frazier ... anybody.

ALTHOUGH HE IS CONFORMING to the demands of the pro game, which frowns on individualism, there is still a healthy slice of showboat in Maravich.

There certainly isn't anything wrong with this. Pro basketball, after all, is entertainment.

Pistol Pete happens to be the game's No. 1 entertainer.

There was evidence Monday night that Atlanta Coach Richie Guerin and Hawk players — most of whom refused to warm up to Maravich when he first joined the club — are beginning to regard Pete as a brother.

Once, when Maravich was headed to the bench to take a short rest, Guerin greeted him with a fatherly pat on the posterior.

ON SEVERAL OCCASIONS, AFTER baskets by Pete, Hawk players gave Maravich some skin as they headed down the floor to man their defensive positions.

Harping on basketball officiating gets a bit tiresome, I know, but the horrendous job turned in Monday night by Jerry Loeber and Bill Rakel cannot go unmentioned.

Loeber and Rakel earned grades of 100 in inconsistency.

In addition to the numerous damaging calls they made against the Braves, one of the officials — Loeber — managed to hurt Buffalo by getting in the way.

IT HAPPENED WITH 6:10 LEFT, and the Hawks in front by a point, 103-102. Maravich flung an errant pass. The ball was headed out of bounds, right in front of the Buffalo bench.

But it struck Loeber in the area of the navel and stayed in bounds. Walt Hazzard scooped up the loose ball and immediately netted a jump shot.

Buffalo Coach Dolph Shayes, furious, yelled, "You," but stopped.

Loeber nevertheless called a technical foul against Shayes after having allowed Guerin, the Atlanta coach, to leave the bench several times and jaw and beef constantly over the officiating.

"ALL I SAID TO THE OFFICIAL was, "You", Shayes explained. "I never said another word."

Then Shayes smiled.

"But I did make one of those faces," the Buffalo coach said.

The face that Schayes makes when he does not see eye-to-eye with an official is a sight to behold.

It conveys a perfectly clear message to the official.

A thousand words are etched on that special face that Shayes makes, and most of the words are four-letter jobs.

Basketball — TONY MASIELLO

Column describes Masiello's last game with Canisius College.
Monday, March 10, 1969
Phil Ranallo: What's New, Harry?

So came the Captain with the
mighty heart;
  And when the judgment thunders
split the house,
  Wrenching the rafters from their
ancient rest,
  He held the ridgepole up, and spiked
again
  The rafters of the Home.
   — Edwin Markham

TONY MASIELLO, THE CANI-
SIUS COLLEGE captain with the
mighty heart — with his magnificent
performance Saturday night against
Niagara — took his place among the
great Golden Griffin basketball warriors of all-time.

The gallant young man truly belongs.

Tony Masiello, at 6 feet 4 inches,
spent three years in the basketball
"jungle" — the snakepit under the
backboards — and did battle with the
"Redwoods" of the sport, the athletes
who stand 6-feet-9 and taller.

And Masiello never backed off.

So Tony Masiello belongs among
the Canisius College players never
to be forgotten ... John McCarthy ...
Leroy Chollet ...Henry Nowak ... Bob
Gauchat ... John Morrison ... Johnny
Rybak ... Joe Niland ... Bill O'Connor
... Andy Anderson ... Bob MacKinnon
... Joe Cavanaugh ... Hank O'Keeffe.

SATURDAY NIGHT, IN THE
CANISIUS dressing room, Tony
Masiello, the West Side warrior who
jammed the finest 20 minutes of his
career into the second half of the Little Three struggle with Niagara, was
standing in front of his locker.

His left foot was planted on a bench.
His right foot was on the floor. He

was bent forward, resting his chest on
his left knee. The furiously contested
game had drained almost every ounce
of energy from his strong and wiry
body.

"I owed this game to my school —
Canisius," Masiello said.

"I owed it to my coaches, Mr. MacK-
innon and Mr. Markey. I owed it to
my teammates. I owed it to my girl,
Donna (Donna Abraham). She's the
girl I want to marry.

"I WILL ALWAYS THANK GOD
FOR giving me the strength to help
win this game. It meant so much to all
of us — because this team has always
been a better team than our record
showed.

"I am deeply moved by it all. I am
happy and I am sad — happy because
we won ... and sad because, for me, it's
all over. My basketball career at Canisius is over. I will never forget my four
years at Canisius."

Then Tony Masiello talked about his
future.

"I want a chance to play pro basketball," the Canisius captain said. "I
don't care where ... in the NBA ... in
the ABA ... in Europe — anywhere. I
just want a chance."

BOB MACKINNON, THE CANI-
SIUS COACH, was caught up in the
emotion of it all. MacKinnon, with
tears of joy welling in his eyes, first
made the rounds of the dressing room,
patting some players on the back and
shaking the hands of others.

Then, when MacKinnon took his
position in a corner of the room and
met the press, someone mentioned the
name, Tony Masiello.

"I'll tell you what kind of a fellow

Tony is," MacKinnon said.

"The first thing he said to me after the game was: 'Thanks for everything, coach.'

"Tony is one of the guttiest, most dedicated players I've ever coached. With Tony — from the first game he played for me and right through tonight — it's always been the same. It's been the team first and Tony second."

MASIELLO WAS 13-FOR-24 FROM the field, most of his goals coming on swishers from 15 to 20 feet out, and 9-for-10 from the free-throw line. With 15 seconds left, he broke a 79-79 tie with two free throws, then wrapped it up.

Two other seniors — Tom Pasternak and Tom Hardiman — and Gene Roberson and Roger Brown also came up with notable efforts. A field goal by Pasternak in the late stages was described by Niagara Coach Frank Layden as "the biggest basket of the game."

Hardiman was a wildcat in Canisius' zone defense. Tom, who seemed to be in at least three places at one time, forced the Purple Eagles into numerous errors.

A great play by Roger Brown, with six seconds left, shut the day on the Eagles. With six seconds left, and Canisius in front by 81-79, a jump ball was called at the Canisius end — between Roberson and Bob Churchwell.

CALVIN MURPHY, THE NIAGARA All-America, was left unguarded as the official threw up the ball. Churchwell won the tap and flicked the ball toward Murphy. The smart Roger Brown, anticipating where the ball would go, dashed in front of Murphy and intercepted the ball, flipped it to Pasternak who dealt it to Masiello.

Masielio was fouled. He stepped to the line and netted both free throws.

What a way to wind up a career!

Basketball — BOB McADOO

McAdoo deserves the National Basketball Association's MVP Award.
Tuesday, February 26, 1974
Phil Ranallo: What's New, Harry?

THE LAST COUPLE OF MONTHS, O.J. Simpson has been busy — busy picking up every chunk of hardware — every award — that has been handed out.

There's a chance, though, that one big prize won't wind up in O.J.'s jam-packed trophy case.

I firmly believe that O.J. will not be dealt the award that goes to the most valuable player in the National Basketball Assn.

My mind, in fact, is made up on the recipient of that coveted bauble.

If justice is served, that roundball MVP award will go to the young fellow who does his wondrous work garbed in the skivvies of the Buffalo Braves — the one and only Robert McAdoo Jr.

You disagree? You say the MVP should be Kareem Abdul-Jabbar, the smiler who does 90 percent of his shooting from six inches or closer?

NONSENSE! IF ABDUL-JABBAR were 6-feet-9, as Bob McAdoo is — instead of 7-feet-4 — and insisted on playing basketball, he'd be doing his thing in places like Delaware YMCA.

Bob McAdoo may be the finest outside-shooting big man in the history of the NBA.

If you have the audacity to disagree, think about it.

Try to name one guy, 6-feet-9 or taller, who ever played in this league and did most of his firing from 15 feet or further — and wore out as many basketball nets as McAdoo.

You've come up empty, right?

If McAdoo isn't named MVP, Walter Kennedy will have no choice but to launch an investigation.

IS BOB McADOO THINKING about the MVP award? "Not really," McAdoo said Monday afternoon as he took time out from playing with his 5½-month-old son, Robert McAdoo III, to chat on the telephone. "If it comes ... it comes."

He said he was pleased to learn that CBS had named him "Player of the Week" for the third time this season, during Sunday's telecast of the "NBA Game of the Week."

In three games last week — against Milwaukee, New York and Boston — McAdoo connected on 48 of 71 shots from the field, a percentage of .677.

Shame on Bob! He's slipping.

In his last seven games, he has "batted" .684, and here's the rundown: Boston 20-28, New York 13-20, Milwaukee 15-23, Houston 15-24, Capital 13-20, Detroit 15-23, Philadelphia 13-14 ... for a seven-game performance of 104-152 and a percentage of .684.

ONLY ONE THING SEEMS TO bother McAdoo and that's sitting on the bench. "What I want to do is play the whole game," he said. "I don't like to sit down ever — regardless of what the score is.

"I never get tired.

"I enjoy playing all the way — 48 minutes. I know that's impossible because we've got other guys on this team. But if I had my way, I'd play 48 minutes.

"It bothers me to be taken out of the game — unless I'm stinking up the court."

Then McAdoo spoke of the beautiful "New Brave World."

"The thought of no more 21-win seasons is wonderful," he said, " ... and I'm thrilled — really thrilled — about making the playoffs."

McAdoo goes back to work tonight, when Elmore Smith and the Los Angeles Lakers dribble into Memorial Auditorium.

"ELMORE AND I ARE GOOD friends, but we've never beaten the Lakers since I've been with the Braves — so it would be nice to win. I'm just going out there and do my best."

That's terrible news for the Lakers ... because McAdoo's best, especially of late, has been spellbinding.

The caller advised McAdoo to get a lot of rest.

Robert McAdoo Jr. said he'd rest by playing with Robert McAdoo III. "I enjoy rolling a ball to my son."

Bob plays with his son for hours at a time. But does he ever change the baby's diapers? "Only once in a while," he said. "That's a job I usually leave for my wife, Brenda."

Basketball — NIAGARA STUNS ST. BONAVENTURE, 87-77

Niagara University breaks St. Bonaventure's 99-game home winning streak.

Sunday, February 26, 1961

By PHIL RANALLO

OLEAN, Feb. 25 — They said it couldn't be done — but they forgot to tell Niagara's basketball team. The Purple Eagles blackjacked St. Bonaventure, the nation's No. 2 club, in a fantastic 87-77 upset tonight.

And Niagara did it in the Bona "execution chamber" — the notorious fortress of cold stone, the Olean Armory, where the mighty Brown Indians had butchered 99 straight enemies.

The Purple Eagles, inspired by the marvelous shooting of Al Butler, simply refused to face the facts. They simply refused to become the 100th successive victim in this mausoleum for visiting teams.

Niagara became the first team to escape with its life from the fabled Bona basketball bastille in 13 years, since 1948, four years before Dwight Eisenhower dug his first divot in the White House lawn.

Butler wielded the big axe, but he had plenty of help — particularly from Ken Glenn, Joe Maddrey and Don Jones — as the unbelievable Eagles made their record 15-4 and almost without question earned a spot in the National Invitation Tournament.

Butler Nets 25 Points

Butler drilled 25 points. This was the game of his life. He picked Niagara up by the bootstraps after Bona, which had trailed by 13 points, barreled back for a 51-51 tie. In the next four minutes, Butler scored five field goals and rifled a perfect scoring pass as the Eagles drew away to 76-67. Butler, with the burst, carved the hearts from the Brown Indians.

Glenn and Maddrey, the talented sophomores, combined for 45 points. Glenn meshed 23 and Maddrey 22 as Niagara became Bona's second conqueror. The Indians' only other loss in 24 games was a two-pointer to the nation's No. 1 team — Ohio State.

The triumph was Niagara's first in its last 10 games with Bona. The Eagles have been on an enforced diet of defeats in this series – for five straight years since 1956.

The Indians no longer can be identified as the world champion Purple Eagle eaters.

Greatest Win For Taps

The happiest man in the building was the Niagara coach, John (Taps) Gallagher. Taps said this was his greatest victory in 30 years as the Niagara boss.

The instant the buzzer sounded, Eagle followers gave Gallager an on the shoulder ride to the dressing room.

Eddie Donovan, the Bona coach, took it like the champion he is. "They played a great game," Donovan said. "They deserved to win."

All-America Tom Stith led the Bonnies with 33 points. Fred Crawford and Bob McCully each had 16. Glenn and Crawford went head-to-head and Glenn won his second straight decision over the talented Bona sophomore.

Niagara shot a brilliant 60 percent, netting 35 of 58. Butler was 11 for 19, Glenn 10 for 21, Maddrey 9 for 16, and Jones 4 for 8. Bona settled for 40 percent, 29 of 73. Stith was 10 for 25, Crawford 8 for 19, and McCulley 5 for 8.

Ron (Whitey) Martin was limited to three field goals by Butler.

Eagles Solve Press

The Eagles had the answer for the Bona half-court press. Whenever the Bona guards would press the Niagara player with the ball, Jones or one of the Niagara forwards would race to the top of the key and receive a lob pass.

On many occasions, the Eagle receiving the ball at the key would whirl and mesh a straightaway jump. Bona could not combat these tactics.

The Indians went into a full-court press when trailing by 9 points six minutes before the finish.

But the Eagles handled them cleverly, passing the ball adroitly. Four times in those last six minutes, the ball was whipped to a Niagara player under the hoop for an easy layup.

The tremendous leaping of Jones and Maddrey also was a major factor. These two did everything but jump out of the building. Jones grabbed 19 rebounds and Maddrey 11 as Niagara earned a 53-46 edge off the boards. Crawford led the Bonnies in this department with 41.

The lead changed hands 10 times in an extremely exciting first half. The Eagles were in front by five points, 41-36, at the intermission.

Eagles Extend Lead

Early in the second half, the Eagles moved out to a 51-40 lead, on the strength of an eight-point string – a side jump by Glenn, two baskets by Jones, and Glenn's conversion of Butler's pass on a fast break.

A bit later, Niagara built its advantage to 57-44. Then Bona charged back. The Indians netted eight in a row — a twister by Stith, Tom Hannon's set, another basket by Crawford. That made it 57-52, Niagara. But-

ler and McCully exchanged baskets before Maddrey made two free throws to build the Niagara bulge to 61-54. Then the Bonas tied it at 61-61 on a string of 7 — McCully's tap, Crawford's jump, Stith's hook, and a foul by McCully.

Eleven minutes remained — and the Bona partisans in the jammed crowd of 2,200 sat back and awaited the butchering of the Eagles.

But Butler grabbed the cleaver and began to slash. He potted a 20-foot jump. Crawford retaliated to tie it again. Then Butler drilled two in a row — a long jump and a short pop from the side on the business end of a fast break.

Crawford Cuts Margin

Crawford clicked from the pivot to reduce the Bona deficit to 67-65. Glenn took off the pressure with a 15-footer before Butler went to work again. Al drove the base line for a deuce and fed Maddrey a perfect scoring pass.

Stith interrupted with a driving basket. But Butler came back with another jump and Ed Ladley netted a foul to give the Eagles a 76-67 advantage.

Seven minutes remained, but the die had been cast. Bona began to scramble and make errors. The Indians never got closer than 7 points the rest of the way.

Two or three minutes before the game, the Bona fans chanted repeatedly, "We want 100 points; we want 100 points." They figured 100 points would fit the occasion of their heroes' 100th straight victory.

In the waning minutes of the game, the shoe was on the other foot.

The Niagara followers did the chanting. And it was the same chant – "We want 100 points; we want 100 points."

Basketball — ELMORE SMITH

Smith overcomes humble beginnings to sign with Buffalo.
Tuesday, April 6, 1971
Phil Ranallo: What's New, Harry?

THE YOUNG MAN AND HIS FOUR brothers and one sister — and their remarkable mother — have never had the world on a string. In fact, most of the time, in the years in Macon, Ga., and later in Orlando, Fla., they have not had the price of a piece of string.

They have had only one another.

They are well-acquainted with almost empty refrigerators ... and near-bare cupboards ... and confined living quarters ... and empty pockets ... and patched pants ... and darned socks ... and mended shirts.

They know well the tough, tough life.

Yet they have never been on the welfare rolls. Their remarkable mother — a 46-year-old woman of great pride — has seen to this.

This remarkable mother has managed to keep the bodies and souls of her loved ones together by toiling and sweating for 10 and 12 hour stretches over hot stoves and grills in restaurants as a cook.

NOW, THIS FAMILY'S HARD-SHIP and privation ... and the remarkable mother's worry and concern for her brood — and her long hours of labor — are at an end.

Monday afternoon the young man — Elmore Smith, a basketball player who stands seven feet one quarter inch — signed a contract with the Buffalo Braves and became a millionaire.

In a private conversation, following the press conference in the Buffalo Room of the Statler Hilton, Elmore Smith at first was reluctant to discuss the "tough, tough life."

Then he obliged — probably because he realized it was the best way he could pay tribute to his mother.

When listening to Elmore Smith speak of his mother, Emma, it is obvious that the 7-foot new millionaire regards her as being 10 feet tall.

ASKED WHAT HIS INNER FEELINGS were on this momentous occasion, Smith said: "The whole thing seems like a dream. I'm so happy for my mother."

Elmore Smith — shy, humble, courteous — pauses.

"Never again," he said, just above a whisper, "is my mother going to want."

The words were simple, but so beautiful.

Smith's bronze face creased into a warm smile. His face mirrored a special satisfaction.

"Tomorrow, I'll be in Orlando — and I'll take my mother shopping. I can't wait. I'm going to take her shopping for a house — for whatever house she wants."

The new Buffalo Brave said his mother doesn't know of his plans to buy a new home.

"I TALKED WITH MY MOTHER on the phone Wednesday," Smith said. "She's very unhappy with me because I hadn't called her for almost two months."

Was Mrs. Smith excited over developments — over the fact that her son was on the brink of instant wealth?

"No, she never mentioned money. If you knew my mother, you'd understand. My mother doesn't believe they pay people to play basketball.

"She told me that she'd read a couple of stories about me in the newspapers where a couple of professional teams were interested in me playing with them.

"Then she said what she always says to me:

"Take care of yourself, Butch ... and you stay out of trouble you hear?"

SMITH EXPLAINED THAT "BUTCH" is his nickname around home. But at school — Kentucky State — they call him "E," not "Big E" — as in Elvin Hayes — but just plain "E."

Someone asked Smith about the sizes of his four brothers.

"My oldest brother, Elbert, who's 23 and in the Army, is 6 feet 11."

How did Elbert get into the Army which has a height limitation of 6 feet 5?

"Elbert enlisted when he was 18," Smith explained, "and he was only 6-4 at the time.

"I've also got three younger brothers — Lonnie, Kenny and Keith.

"Lonnie is a high school senior. He's 6-8 — and he's going to enroll at my school, Kentucky State, next fall.

"Kenny is 16 years old — and he's 6 feet 6.

"Keith is the youngest, he's 14. But he's only 5 feet 11."

Basketball — RANDY SMITH

Buffalo's "Iron Man" is a product of the Buffalo State College basketball team.

Sunday, March 19, 1978

Phil Ranallo: What's New, Harry?

RANDY SMITH, THE wondrous Buffalo Brave — that "Iron Man" of the National Basketball Association who today, in Kansas City, plays in his 500th consecutive league game — can't kid me.

I mean, Randy would have one believe he's called "Iron Man" simply because he hasn't missed a basketball game since all of us were six years younger.

But I refuse to buy that.

I won't buy it because I've been watching this amazing fellow — this remarkable 6-feet 3-inch, 180-pound chunk of perpetual motion since he first raced off the Buffalo State campus and onto the courts in the NBA.

And I've long been convinced that this guy, Randy Smith, is an "Iron Man" more in a literal sense than in a figurative sense.

I mean, once the ref throws up the ball for the opening tap, Randy Smith seems to transform himself from mere flesh and blood into iron and steel — into a machine.

I'd swear that Randy Smith, the machine, runs on oil — and not on the red stuff that courses the veins of mere mortals.

Smith is a machine whose "on-and-off" button is locked in the "on" position. He's a machine that never stops running at top speed.

RANDY SMITH HAS been in the league seven years now, yet most of the poor guys on the other teams who draw the short straw — and "win" the assignment of guarding Randy — still don't know what color his eyes are.

Because all they ever see is a blur.

Yes, sir ... Randy Smith is a basketball machine — a running machine.

Take a good look at Smith the next time you get a chance, before the game starts — before Randy turns into a blur — and you'll see what I mean.

Physically, Smith is a specimen made to run and run and run.

His long calf muscles look like they were grafted on in a track shop. His narrow, muscular thighs could have been tooled in a piston shop.

What a machine!

THE GUYS WHO GO head-to-head with Randy simply can't believe he's real. They spend most of their time trying to figure out which way he went — or which way he came from.

To those poor guys, Randy looks like a fellow who just swallowed a thousand pep pills.

What makes Smith so extra-special is not only that he can run forever, but, that he also can shoot accurately from anywhere.

Smith is a scoring threat as long as he's in the building.

He drives opponents batty.

On offense, Smith fills the basket, repeatedly embarrasses his man by giving him "facials" — turning, leaping and firing the ball, while eye-ball-to-eyeball with his defender.

On defense, Smith's stamina enables him to stalk his opponent, relentlessly ... and his speed enables him to race from behind and pilfer the ball from a player who thinks he's home-free on a breakaway.

DESPITE SEVEN YEARS in the NBA, Randy Smith, the machine, shows no signs of any wear-and-tear. In fact, the machine is operating better than ever — to the point where Cotton Fitzsimmons believes Randy is the No. 1 guard in the league.

"There right," Fitzsimmons says. "Right now, Randy Smith may be the best guard in pro basketball. He's 29 years old and he's absolutely on top of his game."

Fitzsimmons is dead right.

Right now, Smith's court act could not be better. He is playing the best basketball of his career.

Secretariat or Seattle Slew or Forego never raced down a homestretch more spectacularly than Smith is streaking down the stretch of this NBA season — this long-lost Buffalo pro basketball season.

AS ONE OF THE TOP backcourt operators in the NBA the last few years, Smith has set a standard that can't be lived up to every time out. Sometimes, after all, Robert Redford doesn't get the girl — or Rodney Dangerfield doesn't get a laugh.

Sometimes, though, guys who set such standards exceed themselves, as Randy has done in his most recent games — matches in which he has left himself and everyone else breathless.

In his last three games, for example, Randy has done everything but keep score. In the three games, he has scored 107 points, amassed 30 assists, and grabbed 16 rebounds.

Randy has been so brilliant in those last three games that he has surprised himself.

"NOPE, I'VE NEVER before had three games in a row that good," Randy said the other night, after drilling 31 points in the victory over Milwaukee.

Then Smith grinned and added, "you know, after three games like that — 38, 38 and 31 — I'm beginning to think my production potential is unlimited."

Randy Smith takes his role, his im-age, his status — as the "Iron Man" of the NBA — very seriously.

"I regard that title, 'Iron Man,' as an honor," Randy said.

"To me, it's prestigious. I know Jo-Jo White felt good about it, when he had the 'Iron Man' title.

"Now that I've got it, I feel good, too. In fact, better than good — feel great."

Now basketball fans, you're probably dying to find out what the NBA record is for "consecutive games played." Right? Well, it's 844 and it's held by Johnny Kerr of the old Syracuse Nats.

Which means that Kerr's record has only four years to live.

It'll die late in 1982, when Randy Smith, the "Iron Man," plays in his 845th straight game.

Bowling — TOM BAKER

Bowler from Buffalo's Riverside neighborhood makes it big on the Pro Bowlers Tour.

Sunday, August 17, 1980

Phil Ranallo: What's New, Harry?

WHEN TOM BAKER joined the Professional Bowlers Association tour in 1976, the skeptics predicted he'd fall on his face. After all, down through the years some really talented Buffalo bowlers had given it a whirl on the pro tour — and failed.

Why, the skeptics reasoned, should Tom Baker be any different?

Another thing, isn't this Tom Baker the fellow who couldn't even win with any consistency on that local television bowling show, "Beat the Champ?"

Sure, he is. So what chance did he have against the best bowlers in the world?

Poor Tom Baker, the crepehangers concluded, would be eaten alive by the pros, and would be back in his old stamping grounds — the Riverside section of Buffalo — before anybody could say "Earl Anthony."

Well, the skeptics could not have been more wrong.

Tom Baker has definitely made it as a professional bowler — big. And the thing about the guy is, he seems to be getting better by the minute.

THIS SEASON, HIS fifth on the tour, Baker is averaging a red-hot 215 — a mark topped only by Earl Anthony and Mark Roth — and is making money faster than all but seven pros.

So far this season, Tom has won $51,800, not much by the financial standards of other sports — but a hefty figure for a pro bowler.

And success has not spoiled Tom Baker.

"I'm doing better than I first thought I'd do," said the modest Baker Saturday, as he awaited the start of the PBA Sunkist Open Tournament at Thruway Lanes.

"I always thought I'd make money as a pro bowler, but I didn't believe I'd be where I am now," he added, alluding to his 1980 money earnings and his high-ranking 215 average.

BAKER, WHO FIVE weeks ago made the big breakthrough — by winning the $80,000 Northern California Open at Fremont, Calif. — also confessed that he "didn't believe my first PBA championship would come this soon."

But come, the championship did, on the strength of some spectacular stretch bowling in which he averaged 239 for his final four games, so Baker now qualifies for a PBA name banner.

The banner, though, is not gracing the Thruway Lanes in this tourney.

"They haven't delivered it yet," Baker said.

"They're making it." His banner will be red, with black letters. "They're my favorite colors," he offered. "My car's even red and black."

Baker, who'll celebrate his 26th birthday on Sept. 12, has been "a bowling nut" for half his life.

"WHEN I WAS 13, I WAS averaging 186," Baker said, "and when I was 15, I was up there around 200."

Baker disclosed that he had a burning desire to turn pro when he was 18, but couldn't — due to lack of money.

"And I couldn't get anyone to sponsor me. Three years later, Fred Saia came along and gave me my pro chance — by sponsoring me on the pro tour.

"Saia gave me the money to get started in 1976, and I did well enough that year — and thereafter — that Fred's never had to go into his pocket again."

Baker said that first season, after bowling several weeks with the pros, he knew he possessed enough talent to be a professional bowler.

"A guy's got to average about 210 to have a chance to make it as a pro."

ASKED TO GIVE once-a-week bowlers a tip that might add a few pins to their average, Baker said he'd advise them to be sure to have a ball that fits properly — and to buy a new pair of bowling shoes, if they happen to be shoe-renters.

"Some people bowl with the same ball for 10 years and longer," he said. "Your hand, your grip, changes with the passing of time. The right ball and good shoes could add pins to their game."

Baker credited two older brothers with part of his success. "My brothers worked the counter at Voelker's Lanes when I was a kid, so I bowled there a lot."

Then he smiles. It was obvious that Tom bowled at Voelker's "a lot" because, with his brothers working the counter, the price was right.

WHILE ON THE SUBJECT of Baker's family, I'd like to point out something that most of today's parents — those with children in their high teens and early 20s — will have difficulty believing.

Tom Baker, who's 25 — and rather successful — hasn't even moved out of his parents' home yet.

That's right! Baker lives with his parents, Hank and Clara, in their home on Roesch Street, in Riverside.

"Sure, I live with my parents," Baker said. "After all, I'm still single."

Boxing — ALI-FRAZIER: THE FIGHT OF THE CENTURY

Heavyweight Champion Frazier defends the heavyweight title against Muhammad Ali.

Wednesday, March 10, 1971

Phil Ranallo: What's New, Harry?

"IT WAS BILLED AS 'The Fight of the Century,' Sam," Honest Harry said, "But now that it's over — now that Joe Frazier is officially greater than 'The Greatest' — we know that the billing was nonsense.

"The Frazier-Muhammad Ali match was such a smokin' go, such a beautiful brawl, such a box office smash, that almost everybody realizes — especially promoters Jack Kent Cooke and Jerry Perenchio — that 'The Fight of The Century' has yet to be fought.

" 'The Fight of the Century' lies in our immediate future, Sam.

"It will be fought in the house that Jack Kent Cooke built — the Los Angeles Forum — when Frazier and Ali go at one another in the rematch.

"FOR THE REMATCH, I'M sure the promoters, Cooke and Perenchio, will correct the multitude of mistakes they made in the promotion and presentation of Monday's fight. Cooke and Perenchio have lived and learned.

"First, the promoters learned that the ticket price scale for Monday's go in Madison Square Garden — from $75 to $150 — was utterly ridiculous.

"The 20,000 ducats were gobbled up and gone, long ago, a day or two after the Garden opened the ticket wickets.

"The ticket scalpers had a fantastic ball, they say, reportedly getting as much as $700 for a $150 ticket.

"Since Cooke and Perenchio are very sharp chaps, it must have dawned on them that if the scalpers can get $700 a ticket illegally, they can get that price, too — and legally.

"SO, FOR THE REMATCH, SAM, look for the ticket price scale to range from, say, $300 to $1,000. After all, the Los Angeles Forum has 2,000 fewer seats than the Garden.

"The promoters also learned that the prices they charged for the closed-circuit television were much too low.

"Right here in town, at Loew's Buffalo Theater, they had a standing room crowd — at what was it, $12.50 a pop?

"The closed-circuit teevee loaded cash registers in theaters across the land, according to early reports.

"For the rematch, those teevee prices should be doubled, at least.

"THE THING THAT THE promoters must straighten out — to guarantee gross receipts of $100-million for the rematch — is this news coverage bit. For Monday's bout, Cooke and Perenchio tried to restrict news coverage of the fight — but failed.

"The promoters attempted to prevent the wire services — the Associated Press, United Press International and Reuters — from issuing reports on the progress of the fight.

"The wire services paid no attention.

"What the wire services did was expose Cooke and Perenchio as rank amateurs when it comes to placing embargoes on news.

"Before the rematch, Cooke and Perenchio had better get some advice from Washington.

"I CAN ALMOST SEE IT now, Sam — the Frazier-Ali rematch, I mean. A ringside ticket priced at one grand; a ticket for theater teevee at 50 bucks.

"And if Cooke and Perenchio get their way — if they're allowed to put handcuffs on the wire services and restrict the news — nobody in the outside world will know who wins the rematch, say for 48 hours.

"Imagine Sam, for two days after the final going, the news service can't transmit the result, the spectators aren't allowed to leave the Los Angeles Forum, and the closed circuit teevee customers can't leave the theaters!"

"I can't imagine it, Harry," Sam the immigrant said. "After all, the promoters — Cooke and Perenchio — have their rights, don't they?"

Boxing — MUHAMMAD ALI
(AT BUFFALO STATE COLLEGE)

Ali talks about having a purpose in life.
Wednesday, March 29, 1971
Phil Ranallo: What's New, Harry?

AN HOUR WITH MUHAMMAD ALI.

A few minutes past four Sunday afternoon, "The Greatest" — Muhammad Ali, also known as Cassius Clay — walked into a conference room in Union Social Hall on the Buffalo State College campus and met the press.

Ali, an imposing figure, was attired in a gray herring-bone suit of Madison Ave. cut, a light blue shirt, dark blue-and-white striped tie, and black socks and shoes.

He settled in a chair, behind a battery of microphones and in the bright television lights — and deftly fielded all questions.

The one thing Ali never said, as members of the media and Buffalo State Student Council fired away, was: "No comment."

It was mentioned to Ali that Wilt Chamberlain, the 7-foot 1-inch basketball giant of the Los Angeles Lakers, had voiced interest — before the Joe Frazier bout — in fighting Muhammad.

WOULD A FIGHT ACTUALLY HAVE been set up with Chamberlain if Ali had defeated Joe Frazier?

"Maybe," Ali replied. "I could have had Wilt if I wanted him — and I think the fight might have been held in the Houston Astrodome. But it still can be set up — if Chamberlain insists."

Would Ali like to fight Wilt?

"Sure, I would."

"Why?"

"Because there are almost no people in the boxing world left to fight."

Ali grinned.

"They've asked me what would happen if I did fight Chamberlain, and I've given them a straight answer. I've said the first-round bell would ring, I'd come out and throw a couple of quick punches, and if one of them landed, they'd hear the referee say two words: "T-i-m-m-m-m-n ... b-e-r-r-r-r!"

YOU, MUHAMMAD ALI, HAVE been quoted as saying you believe you won the fight with Frazier. Were you quoted correctly?

"Yes. I know I won. But I just didn't get the decision. Joe Frazier just got the decision and, as you know, he also just got out of the hospital — because it was so rough on him.

"Three fights like that — like the one he had with me — and he'll have to retire. Too much damage, too much wear-and-tear, on the brain and body."

Why do you think the decision went against you?

"I think the draft had something to do with it — also my religion and me being black ... and also the New York Boxing Commission, which was first to take my title away unjustly. The Commission had control of all the judges and the referee.

"IN THE RETURN FIGHT WITH Frazier, I'd like to see international officials in charge — maybe a judge from England and, say, a referee from Germany, and maybe another judge from Scotland.

"I'd like officials who aren't wrapped up in what happens in America and the people in this country. They'd judge the fight solely as a boxing match — the punches landed, the bruises, the cuts, the rounds won."

Are you saying you didn't get a fair shake?

"I know I didn't. But I'm not protesting. I'm just saying that people who know boxing agree with me. They look at his face and look at mine — and they know I won.

"They know that Frazier took a terrible whupping. He was hit with every punch in the book — ripping, tearing punches — and his face was a mess."

DO YOU AGREE THAT BOXING is a dying sport?

"Yes. It's dying because they don't have enough white hopes. They need more white fighters. There are hardly any white fighters on the scene in any of the divisions."

How good is George Foreman?

"He's good. All he needs is another year of experience. He's right in line. We've got to run into him — Frazier and I — if we keep fighting."

Do you have any Presidential ambitions — say, to run against Richard Nixon in 1972?

"No."

Ali grinned again.

"But if I ran for vice president, it would be good insurance for the President — because it would give the Nixon ticket good balance."

WHAT WILL THE GENERAL TOPIC of your speech be tonight (Sunday night) when you address the Buffalo State students?

"The purpose in life."

What is your purpose in life?

"Since I was a little boy I wanted to be popular, a world figure — and I wanted to help lead my people to freedom and equality without being an Uncle Tom and without selling out.

"I wanted to take a stand, one thousand percent, for my people — regardless if I got shot or was put in jail.

"I just want my people to say, 'There goes a black man who didn't go off and marry a white woman, who stayed with his own, fought for his own and

didn't give a damn about the money or the price he had to pay.'

"If they say to me tomorrow that I'm going to jail for five years, I'll say 'Good, let's go see what jail's like — because it's part of my purpose in life.'

"Some people die for their purpose. Some boys in Vietnam are dying for what they believe in — and a lot of them are dying for what they don't know."

MUHAMMAD ALI, DO YOU HAVE any special poetry for Buffalo?

That had to be a planted question — because Ali answered instantly:

"Well, I like your school,
"And I like your style,
"But your pay is so cheap
"I won't be back for a while."

Boxing — MUHAMMAD ALI: THE GREATEST

The column says it all — Ali was "The Greatest."
Tuesday, June 29, 1971
Phil Ranallo: What's New, Harry?

IT IS A STRANGE WORLD — also a rapidly changing one. Take the case of Cassius Clay, the man who is also known as Muhammad Ali. Four years ago, when he refused to take that one step forward, the people in this country turned against him — almost unanimously.

Cassius Clay was condemned as a low-life, a coward, and his claims and pronouncements as a conscientious objector were ridiculed.

Cassius was labeled a cad, a man beneath contempt — and the race to cast the first stone was on.

Ed Dooley, chairman of the New York State Boxing Commission, and the ring game's other overseers — prodded by patriotism and flag-waving politicians — fixed Clay by stripping him of his heavyweight title and his boxing license.

Dooley and Co. were cheered as heroes — even though their action against Clay seemed somewhat un-American, since it deprived Cassius of his livelihood while still waiting for the court's ultimate disposition of his case.

THE ULTIMATE DISPOSITION came Monday, when the Supreme Court, by a unanimous vote of 8-0, overturned Clay's five-year conviction, thus freeing him for his next fight — against Jimmy Ellis on July 26.

Although the climate in this country has changed considerably since Clay refused to accept induction into the armed services more than four years ago, there will always be few neutrals as far as the former heavyweight champ is concerned.

One group will always detest him as a draft dodger.

Another group will always admire him as a man of high principle — a man who sacrificed the heavyweight title and the millions of dollars that go with it to stand up for his beliefs.

THERE IS LITTLE DOUBT that in the intervening years, the latter group — the admirers of Cassius Clay — has swelled.

Since Clay first delivered his un-grammatical utterance against the war in Vietnam — "I ain't got no quarrel with them Vietcong" — officials in lofty places, including Presidential hopefuls, have denounced the war in angrier and more persistent fashion.

Surprisingly few public voices were raised in Ali's defense however, despite the unpopularity of the war and the hungry political quest for student support and black votes.

Cassius Clay was left to stand up for his principles alone.

AT FIRST, CLAY'S SINCERITY was suspect. Then, as the months and years rolled by, the suspicion was gradually chipped away. It had to happen.

After all, here was a man who, at the height of his earning power as a champion, had given it all up to stick to his principles.

Another thing ... had Clay not refused to be drafted, he most assuredly would have been a privileged soldier — one who would have played a non-combatant role as a special service entertainer.

Also, how much deeper can a man feel about something than to fight it in the courts for four years, as Clay did, and express a willingness to go to jail for five years if he lost his fight?

NOW, THE FIGHT IS OVER —
and the right arm of Cassius Clay, who
looked like a 10,000-to-1 shot when he
began the lonely fight four years ago,
has been raised by the Supreme Court
... and without a dissenting voice.

But Cassius Clay paid a big price to
win his fight.

It cost him 3½ years of boxing at
the height of his career. Although the
court has declared him innocent, there
is no way those 3½ years can be given
back to him.

I was a Cassius Clay knocker four
years ago. Now, I regard him as sort
of a Gunga Din — a better man than
I am.

Boxing — ALI-FOREMAN:
THE RUMBLE IN THE JUNGLE

Undefeated Heavyweight Champion George Foreman faces Ali in Zaire.

Thursday, October 31, 1974

Phil Ranallo: What's New, Harry?

BEFORE THE "GREAT MATCH" began in Kinshasa, Zaire, Muhammad Ali danced around the ring and shadow-boxed and constantly glared at the heavyweight champion of the world, George Foreman.

Foreman, seated on his stool and still clad in his robe, paid no attention.

Then, when it was time for the introductions, Foreman stood up and removed his robe. The sight of Foreman's upper body drew gasps from the ringside fans and the viewers on closed-circuit television.

Foreman's chest appeared to be 40 feet wide. His arms looked like a pair of oak tree stumps.

Muhammad All, a 3-to-1 underdog in betting circles, looked more like a 100-to-1 shot — a sacrificial lamb — once the teevee camera zeroed in on Foreman's incredible body.

The religious had to say a prayer for Ali — a prayer that he would survive this night, escape with his life.

THE BELL FOR THE FIRST ROUND sounded, and Foreman immediately went to work with those arms that resemble battering rams. Ali, however — a true master of the "Sweet Science" — somehow managed to keep his chin off the bullseye, sometimes by dancing away, but mostly by lunging at Foreman and tying him up.

This relentless assault by Foreman went on for almost three rounds. It seemed inevitable that one of Foreman's dynamite-laden fists would explode on Ali's jaw and tear his head off.

With about 20 seconds left in the third round, though, a startling thing happened. Ali switched from defense to offense and stunned Foreman to the soles of his feet with two gorgeous right-left combinations.

In those 20 seconds, the seeds of a spectacular upset were sown. At the bell, the dazed Foreman was heavy-legged as he returned to his corner.

The tide of the "Great Match" had turned.

THEY SAY SEEING IS believing, but I still can't believe what I saw Ali do, starting with the fifth round.

It was rationalized by the experts that Ali had no chance in this fight unless he was able to hit-and-run — jab and retreat.

Let Foreman pin Ali in a corner or against the ropes, they said, and for Muhammad it would be, "Good night, sweet prince."

Well, for the first two minutes of the fifth, Ali used a ploy that flouted every preconception of what he had to do to win.

Muhammad voluntarily backed against the ropes, stood there flat-footed, went into a shell — covered up like a kid who has been cornered by the big bully on the block — and allowed Foreman to flail away. In the final seconds of the round, Ali came out of his shell and tattooed the champ with a volley of sharp shots.

THIS WENT ON FOR TWO MORE rounds, the sixth and seventh — Ali standing there in his shell, permitting Foreman to punch, punch, punch, then suddenly coming to life and rapping two base hits off George's chin in the waning seconds of each of the rounds.

Now, it was clear that Foreman was a beaten fighter.

Foreman, at Ali's invitation, had punched his way to defeat. George's compulsion to throw punches proved his undoing.

The punches Foreman threw at the stationary Ali in those sixth and seventh rounds wouldn't have broken a pane of glass, wouldn't have fazed anybody's grandmother.

Foreman might have said to himself, through those rounds, "Please move away from the ropes, Muhammad, and give me a break — because I'm too pooped to punch you anymore, and it's embarrassing."

IN THE EIGTH ROUND — the Waterloo round for Foreman — Ali changed his style and became mobile. He peppered Foreman at will. Late in the round, Ali hit a triple off George's chin — and Foreman began to reel to his right.

Ali followed up with a devastating right — a home run shot. And the savage blow sent Foreman sprawling in the opposition direction.

That was it. The lights went out for Foreman.

Muhammad Ali is the fistic wonder of the world.

He knows how to win — every way possible.

On this night in Zaire, Ali won the way they claimed he couldn't win. Without dancing, without giving an elegant exercise in choreography, he left his man for dead.

He made Foreman look like just another mortal, just another human being, just another guy with boxing gloves on.

He refused to allow a manual laborer to beat an artist.

In Zaire, Ali, the artist, reached deeply into himself for the courage and the will to endure — and the artist with the courage and the will is a true champion.

"Ali! Ali! Ali!"

Boxing — ALI-FRAZIER: THE THRILLA IN MANILA

Ali defends his heavyweight title against Smokin' Joe Frazier in Manila.

Thursday, October 2, 1975

Phil Ranallo: What's New, Harry?

IN THE 10TH ROUND of Super Fight III, a spectacular brawl that lived up to its billing — "The Thrilla in Manila" — Muhammad Ali's days, or minutes as heavyweight champion of the world, appeared to be numbered.

Relentless, rough, tough Joe Frazier, with one of those pile-driving fists of his, had just hit the "bullseye" — Ali's chin.

It was a devastating left hook, a crusher of a blow.

It all but lifted the champion right out of his hosiery.

Ali felt the savage punch down to the soles of his feet. It made his legs quiver — sort of like soft jello in a bowl that's being carried by a fellow with a severe case of delirium tremens.

Time — Ali's 33 years — and Frazier's fists, it seemed, had the final grains of sand running out of Muhammad's hour-glass.

PAIN AND ANGUISH AND frustration were etched on Ali's countenance. Frazier was Smokin' Joe. He was piercing his foe's defenses — and Ali resembled a guy destined to be carried off on his shield.

Ali appeared to have reached the end of the road. He looked like just another mortal, just another skidding and aging prize fighter.

But the look was deceiving.

Somehow, Muhammad Ali survived and lived for another "day" — the 11th and 12th rounds.

AND IN THOSE TWO rounds, the champion not only managed to muffle Frazier's assault, but actually began to take the initiative — with some patented Ali sharp-shooting.

Then the bell rang for the 13th round, and Ali proceeded to prove that when two men of near-equal ability are pitted against one another in combat, the man who reaches most deeply into himself — for courage and the will to endure — is a true champion.

Early in the 13th, Muhammad Ali summoned up the strength to detonate a pair of bombs, left-right — and both bombs exploded on Frazier's jaw.

FRAZIER'S LEGS WOBBLED. His legs went bow-legged — bore the appearance of a fellow who has spent his lifetime as a cowpoke. Ali kept bombing away, and none of the bombs seemed to miss the target — Frazier's iron jaw.

When the bell sounded, ending the 13th, Frazier wobbled to his corner like a drunk walking against a high gale.

The 14th was worse — for Frazier. Ali hit him with everything but a cream pie — or a cement pie.

When Frazier arrived at his stool and planted himself on it, and trainer Eddie Futch took a look at him, Futch did the compassionate thing — told the ref to stop the fight.

FRAZIER HAD FOUGHT the good fight. A couple of rounds before his "waterloo," he had turned Ali into a near disaster. But "near" wasn't enough.

The matchless Ali had managed to pull off another miracle — comparable to the one he had pulled off a year ago in Zaire.

Ali, from the brink of defeat, had fought back and pulverized Frazier in those last two rounds — turned Joe's face into a caricature of himself.

From the neck up, every part of Frazier was swollen and bruised — even his forehead.

Muhammad Ali is a remarkable fist-fighter.

TUESDAY NIGHT, in Manila, when Joe Frazier got to "smoking," it seemed to be all over for Muhammad Ali, the fellow with whom the world has carried on a love-hate affair for a dozen years.

It seemed to be all over for the man who in his lifetime has done everything — win the Olympics, become heavyweight champ, defeat poverty, join a religion despised by many, defy the government, get sent into exile, have his defiance of the government upheld by the Supreme Court, then come back again and win the title.

It seemed to be all over for him.

But it wasn't.

It wasn't because Muhammad Ali, love him or hate him, is a rare bird, a man able to summon a reserve from deep within himself in the most dire of circumstances — when the writing appears to be on the wall and his number seems to be up.

Boxing — DON ELBAUM

Boxing promoters car is blown up in a motel parking lot.
Monday, January 31, 1972
Phil Ranallo: What's New, Harry?

DON ELBAUM, THE CHUNKY BOXING promoter who blew a bundle of money in a futile attempt to revive the ring game in Buffalo, is at wits' end trying to figure out why anyone would bomb his automobile — which somebody did 10 days ago in a suburb of Cleveland.

"It's bothering me, really gnawing at me," the shaken Elbaum confessed Sunday night on the telephone, from a hideout in Cleveland.

"I've got the willies. Every night now, before climbing into the sack, I check the clothes closet and the bathroom, look under the bed, see that the windows are shut and locked, and place a chair against the door.

"But it doesn't do any good. I can't sleep, I haven't slept 40 winks in 10 days."

Elbaum's car was bombed on the morning of Jan. 21 — at 2:35 a.m., to be exact.

THAT MORNING, ELBUM ARRIVED at the motel — the Highlander Motel, which is in Warrensville Heights, a suburb of Cleveland — at about 1:45 a.m. He parked the car and entered the motel restaurant, where he had a bowl of chili.

"Then I went straight to my room and got into bed," he explained. "At 2:35 — b-o-o-o-o-m! I thought World War III was under way — and that the Russians or Chinese had launched a sneak attack.

"I ran to the window, glanced out and couldn't believe what I saw. Half of my car was missing. Maybe even a little more — say, 60 percent.

"I'd parked the car in front of another guy's room, fortunately. The blast tore down the guy's motel door and blew in all his windows — and almost blew the poor guy right out of his underwear."

AFTER THE POLICE ARRIVED AND investigated, one of the lawmen told Elbaum that the explosion had been caused by six sticks of dynamite that had been placed under the right fender of his car.

"The cop told me that a chunk of the fender had been blown over two apartment buildings," Elbaum said, "and when he said that, he seemed to be very impressed — so I asked him if that was a record for right fenders on 1967 Pontiacs."

Elbaum said that the FBI and the Intelligence Division of the Cleveland Police Dept. have told him the bombing was a warning. "I'd certainly like to know what I'm being warned about.

"I didn't get a call before or after the bombing — so I can't buy that warning bit."

Elbaum is disturbed by the talk that the bombing was the result of his connection with boxing.

"Boxing's my love," he said, "and it bothers me when people think that way."

ELBAUM ADMITTED HE'S BEEN taking a pretty lacing in the boxing promotion business lately — and if anyone wanted to come in as a partner with him, it wasn't necessary to blow up Don's car,

"All the guy's got to do is walk through the door, say he wants to be a partner and I'll tell him, 'Great, just put up some money and let's go.' "

Then Elbaum, who has lost a lot of sleep recently — but none of his sense of humor — talked about his car.

"It was a 1967 Pontiac — the dirtiest car you ever saw. I hadn't had it washed since about 1969, and there must have been a million fight-posters and newspapers and junk in the trunk and on the back seat and floor.

"Maybe the bomber was a guy who's got a 'thing' about dirty cars."

ELBAUM SAID THE BOMBING could not have been the result of his financial condition. I owe a few bucks — $3,000 here, $1,500 there, and so on — just like most everybody else. But nothing to get excited about."

Then Elbaum laughed loudly.

"Maybe this is a good thing. I'm sure my creditors won't be dunning me for awhile — because anybody who pushes me for payment now will become a prime suspect."

Fear, Elbaum says, is beginning to get the best of me.

"Ever since it happened," Elbaum said, "I haven't had a bite to eat — without somebody first tasting my food.

"A couple of days ago, somebody knocked on my motel door. I peeked out the window and saw this guy — in a postman's uniform — holding a good-sized package. So I did the logical thing. I fled — through a rear window."

ELBAUM SAID HE HAS BEEN forced to do a lot of walking the last 10 days. "Nobody will lend me his car. A few days ago, I sent a telegram to a friend of mine — Nick Mileti, owner of the Cleveland Cavaliers — asking him for the loan of his car for the weekend, and Nick didn't even pay me the courtesy of a reply.

"People have been asking me if I'm going to hire a bodyguard and I tell them, no, what I'm going to do is hire a chauffeur — a guy who will get in

and start my car while I'm about 100 yards away, standing behind a tree, or something.

"Sort of like what that character in Jimmy Breslin's book, 'The Gang That Couldn't Shoot Straight,' used to do — lie down on the kitchen floor every morning, with his hands clamped over his ears, while his dutiful wife was out in the garage starting his Cadillac.

"Seriously, though, I think the bombing was a mistake — or maybe the work of a prankster.

"I hope."

Boxing — SUGAR RAY LEONARD & ROBERTO DURAN

Leonard defeats Duran in the "Little Men's Fight of the Century."
Sunday, June 22, 1980
Phil Ranallo: What's New, Harry?

WELL, NOW THAT they're busy counting that mind-boggling $30 million take from last Friday night's fistic extravaganza in Montreal – "Beauty versus the Beast" — there's one thing that's perfectly clear.

Sugar Ray Leonard is definitely not a carbon copy of Sugar Ray Robinson.

A facsimile, perhaps, but a carbon copy, no.

Like the one on whose sweet sobriquet he drew, Leonard is courageous and persevering, willing and tireless — but there the similarity ends.

Unlike Ray Robinson, Ray Leonard, in the biggest fight of his life, was unable to rise to the heights.

Roberto Duran, the mean street-fighter from Panama, won the fight on brute strength.

Roberto was the clear winner. His margin of victory — in the eyes of the fight writers and other experts — was considerably greater than the ballots of the judges deemed it to be.

Duran won it on brute strength — on merit. Since he is a true lightweight — and not a true welterweight — Roberto showed he very well may be the best fighter in the world, pound-for-pound and punch-for-punch.

ROBERTO DURAN'S modus operandi — his rushing, his lunging, his relentless aggression — cancelled out Leonard's speed of hand and foot, and constantly kept Sugar-Ray's offense out of sync.

Duran's "game plan" kept Leonard's ace in the hole — sharp-shooting — mostly in the hole.

Duran, with his victory, earned a special niche in ring history and won a place alongside two great fighting machines of yore, Henry Armstrong and Barney Ross, as the only fistic warriors ever to win both the lightweight and welterweight championships.

Leonard displayed he's capable of giving the world's best fist-fighter almost as much as he can possibly handle — and that there are things he has yet to master.

The fight In Montreal, without question, was "the best of Roberto Duran."

AT 29 YEARS OF age, there's no way Duran can get better. On the other hand, Sugar Ray Leonard, still a kid at 24, figures to improve from the schooling he received at the hands of Duran.

So there is a chance that, from Leonard, the best is yet to come.

But right now, the best that can be said of Leonard is that he's a facsimile of Ray Robinson — not a carbon copy.

Booked as the "Little Men's Fight of the Century," it turned out to be a bout more menacing in anticipation than in reality.

THE FINANCIAL figures for this fight are hard to believe. The estimated $30 million gross gate surpasses by $12-million the previous record of a fight — the $18 million gross by the first Muhammad Ali-Joe Frazier fight in 1971.

Just in the Los Angeles area, where they have pay-television on cable, people paid $1.3 million to watch this fight.

That's right, 130,000 Los Angeles homeowners ordered the fight by telephone — at $10 a pop.

It's believed Sugar Ray Leonard's end of the gate will approximate $12 million — and make him the second richest fighter in history, next to Muhammad Ali.

And Duran will get a guaranteed $1.5 million, tax free.

The sweetest thing about all this, from the viewpoint of Leonard and Duran, is that they'll one day soon do this all over again in a rematch, with Roberto getting the big end, of course.

Boxing — ROCKY MARCIANO

The undefeated heavyweight boxing legend passes away at age 45.
Wednesday, September 3, 1969
Phil Ranallo: What's New, Harry?

ROCKY MARCIANO.

The name had a ring of strength and power — and the name fit him perfectly. With his destructive fists, "The Rock" gouged a huge hole in the tenet that only masters of the sweet science — the science of boxing and the art of self-defense — can be masters of the ring.

Rocky Marciano was not a boxer. "The Rock" was a brawler. He annihilated masters of the sweet science. He demolished them with as ferocious an offense as ever was witnessed in the ring.

He was a super hitter. He was the Babe Ruth of the fist-fighting world.

Those who saw him only outside the ring, in his street-clothes, found it almost impossible to believe that "The Rock" could whip any man in the world.

ROCKY MARCIANO WAS NOT constructed along the lines of the classic heavyweight. He stood only 5 feet 10 inches. He weighed only 185 pounds. His calves and his thighs and his torso were thick. His arms were short.

But a classic heavyweight, he was — thanks to his courage and his heart, his desire and his dedication.

The ring was Rocky Marciano's jungle — and he was king of his jungle. And, like the king of the wooded jungle, the lion, "The Rock" was most dangerous when he was wounded.

In many of his 49 professional fights, Rocky's eyes were blackened, his brows were gashed, his large nose was ripped. But every time, at the finish, there he was ... standing with his foe crumpled on the canvas.

THE GREATEST FIGHT OF the Brocton Blockbusters career was the one in which he won the championship — from the extremely gifted and ageless Jersey Joe Walcott — in Philadelphia on Sept. 23, 1952.

This one pitted a master of the sweet science, Walcott, a superb boxer, against a crude, pier-six brawler, Marciano.

Walcott, a few years earlier, had almost wrested the crown from Joe Louis, at the height of the Brown Bomber's career. Jersey Joe was denied the title when Louis was awarded a highly controversial decision.

In the memorable Philadelphia fight, it appeared that Walcott, the master boxer, would make short shrift of his crude, wild-swinging opponent.

WALCOTT TOOK CHARGE IMMEDIATELY. In the first round, Jersey Joe hit the bullseye — the point of Rockey's jaw —with a savage left hook ... and Marciano went down for the first time in his life.

Marciano got up at the count of four.

Then Walcott proceeded to give Marciano the boxing lesson of his life.

In the fifth round, Walcott landed another damaging left hook — and the blow tore open a big gash on the bridge of Marciano's nose.

Between rounds, Marciano's corner cut-man doused the gash with medication to stem the flow of blood.

This almost proved to be Marciano's undoing.

SOME OF THE MEDICATION SEEPED into Rocky's eyes, and, for the next three rounds, Marciano was almost blind and fought Walcott by feel.

In the ninth round, Marciano's sight began to return but he continued to take a thorough lathering as Walcott kept sticking him from long range.

After the 12th round, Marciano, while on his stool, asked his manager, Al Weill, how he was doing.

"You're way behind, Rock," Weill said. "There's only one way. You've got to knock him out."

In the 13th, Marciano delivered. As Walcott bounced off the ropes, inadvertently, Marciano exploded a straight right on Jersey Joe's chin-and for Walcott, the lights went out.

The crude, wild-swinger was heavyweight champion of the world.

OUTSIDE THE RING, MARCIANO was gentle and kind and soft-spoken — and, most important of all, he lived the clean life. He was a family man. His devotion to his wife and children and parents prompted his premature retirement from the ring.

Rocky's loved ones asked him to quit.

So Rocky quit.

"The Rock" was a champion from Sept. 23, 1952, until the last day of his 45th year — Sunday night, when tragedy struck on that farm near Des Moines, Iowa.

Boxing — JIMMY RALSTON

Phil considered Ralston one of the greatest fighters ever to lace the gloves.

Friday, June 28, 1968
Phil Ranallo: What's New, Harry?

THREE-AND-A-HALF YEARS AGO, Jimmy Ralston, the handsome fist-fighter, grew discouraged and hung up the gloves — despite the fact that he had won 13 of 14 bouts as a professional.

Ralston packed it in because he couldn't get a break. His fights were too few and too far between. He had a wife and a son ... and couldn't make a living with his fists. So he quit and went to work.

A year ago or so, Ralston's employer and new manager and friend, Pat Giordano, a portly and pleasant man who is in the contracting business, persuaded Jimmy to give the ring another try.

Ralston reached for the gloves for a reason. He wanted to supplement his income.

NOW, TODAY, JIMMY RALSTON, the dark-haired and swarthy Buffalonian with dynamite in his fists, is dreaming a wonderful dream. He believes that one day he will be light heavyweight champion of the world.

Ralston is 27 years old ... but his dream is only seven weeks old. The dream started early last month, at Grossinger's, where Ralston was supplementing his income by toiling as a sparring partner for Bob Foster.

Foster, at the time, was preparing for his championship bout with Dick Tiger — the fight in which he wrested the crown from the aging Nigerian.

"THE FIRST TIME I WENT at it with Foster, I was pretty nervous and not too confident, to put it mildly," Ralston said Thursday afternoon, at Michele's Restaurant in Fort Erie, where he and Canadian light heavyweight champ Al Sparks signed for their 10-rounder Tuesday night in the Fort Erie Memorial Arena.

"I was waiting for the bomb from Foster — but it never came. After boxing a few rounds with Bob, I was inspired. I had a new feeling ... a new outlook. I was confident — because I proved to myself I could stand right in there with him and go toe-to-toe."

"Jack Dempsey was there at the camp," Pat Giordano broke in, "and Dempsey, after watching Jimmy work, paid him the supreme compliment. Dempsey turned to me and said: 'The Buffalo boy has Slattery's moves ... and my punch.' "

THE SOFT-SPOKEN RALSTON said he boxed 30 rounds with Foster. "I learned more in those 30 rounds than in all my 10 years of boxing."

The proud Giordano pointed out that Foster had several sparmates when he started training, but worked exclusively with Ralston the final week.

"Foster settled on Ralston," Giordano explained, "because Jimmy was hard to hit. Foster figured working with Jimmy would make him sharper for Tiger ... which it did."

How does Ralston think he would fare against Foster?

"I HAVE GREAT RESPECT for Foster," Ralston said. "He's a good puncher. I don't want to sound immodest, but I know how to fight him and I am confident I could beat him."

"And there's a chance," Giordano broke in again, "that Jimmy will fight Foster in the fall, in Buffalo — in a non-title bout. We have a tentative agreement with Foster.

"And we'll fight for promoter Don Elbaum. Don and I have ironed out our problems. Our relationship is a happy one again."

Then Giordano paused. Then his eyes twinkled.

"Wouldn't it be something," he said, "if Jimmy Ralston became light heavyweight champion of the world ... right here in Buffalo?

"That's our goal ... our dream."

Boxing — BARNEY ROSS

Boxing champ, Marine and WWII hero passes away.
Friday, January 20, 1967
Phil Ranallo: What's New, Harry?

"YOU HEAR ABOUT THE mugs and the hoods and the creeps that infest boxing, Sam," Honest Harry remarked, "and you draw a big X through the game. You mark it down as a racket rotten to the core."

Then you hear about Barney Ross.

"Barney Ross, reared in the slums of New York and Chicago, and exposed to the foul elements of a society that included Al Capone, never went wrong.

"He was an extraordinary fist-fighter and an extraordinary man. He had class and character, and he never turned his back on his responsibilities.

"WHEN BARNEY WAS in his early teens, his father, who ran a little grocery store, was murdered by two young hoodlums. The tragedy broke up the family.

"The three youngest members of the family — two of Barney's brothers and a sister — were placed in an orphanage. Barney vowed to make a new life for them some day.

"A few years later, when Ross made his first financial strike as a fist fighter, he kept his promise. He took his brothers and sister out of the orphanage and moved them into a large and luxurious apartment in Chicago.

"IN 1941, WHEN THE Japs bombed Pearl Harbor, Barney Ross was 32 — too old for service. But it didn't stop him. He talked the authorities into giving him an age waiver — and he enlisted in the Marines.

"When he arrived at Parris Island for boot training, the Marine brass greeted him with open arms and told him they had just the spot for him — as a Marine boxing instructor.

" 'I don't want to teach boxing,'
Ross told the Marine officers. 'I enlisted because I want to help win the war — and the war, for the Marines, is in the South Pacific. So that's where I'm going.'

"AND GO TO WAR, Barney Ross did — to the jungles of Guadalcanal, where he won a Silver Star for his heroics in a fox-hole one night, when he defended three wounded buddies by killing a swarm of Japs.

"Barney Ross contacted malaria during his tour of duty in the South Pacific — and then fell victim to the morphine used to ease his pain. He became addicted — a drug addict.

"And he was man enough to beat the dope.

"Barney Ross was extra special, Sam — as a fighter, as the head of a family, as an American.

"May he rest in peace."

Column Characters — JULIE DOBOZIN, "JULIE POTATOES"

Everything Julie Potatoes and his wife Norma do is for their son, daughter and dog.

Tuesday, March 21, 1971

Phil Ranallo: What's New, Harry?

JULIE POTATOES IS A MAN whose nickname fits. He has peddled potatoes all of his life. He buys from the farmer and sells to the retailer. Once, it was a very good business, but not anymore.

Julie is one of the middle men who have been knocked out or made unessential by the march of time. Now, the supermarket chains deal directly with the farmer. They don't need Julie's potatoes.

Julie nevertheless keeps hanging in there.

He keeps rising at 4 a.m., keeps driving his 10-year-old truck long distances to the farmers, keeps loading the truck with 50-pound sacks of potatoes ... and somehow keeps finding a retailer who will buy his load, or at least part of it.

Loading and unloading 50-pound sacks of potatoes is bull work, especially for a man approaching 60, but Julie whistles as he toils and sweats because it's all for the benefit of his wife, Norma; his daughter, Diane; his son, Bruce and his dog, Alfie.

JULIE DOES NOT WASTE MONEY on himself. The Sunday suit he owns, for example, has been worn a thousand Sundays. He can't remember the last time he bought a tie, but the ties he owns are back in style-because they're 10 inches wide.

Julie's wife, Norma also practices self-denial unconsciously. Everything Julie and Norma have, everything they do, is for their son and daughter.

"My son, Bruce," Julie says proudly, "is going to be somebody — a doctor or a lawyer or maybe a scientist. Bruce is going to be somebody — not like me."

The irony of it is that it will be considerably easier for the son to be a doctor or a lawyer or a scientist than to be like his father.

People such as Julie Dobozin, 23 Shoreham Blvd., seldom come in pairs.

If Alfie, the Dobozin's dog, could only talk!

ABOUT TWO WEEKS AGO, JULIE noticed that Alfie, a 4-year-old dachshund, was hobbling a bit. As the days went by, Alfie got progressively worse-to the point where he could not stand on his hind legs.

Julie took Alfie to a veterinarian. The vet informed Julie that the dog had a spinal disorder and required surgery.

The vet said he could perform the surgery, but did not have the facilities to give the dog the post-operative care and therapy he would require, and therefore recommended that Julie have Alfie put to sleep.

Julie went aghast at the suggestion.

"Isn't there anybody who can do it?" Julie asked the vet.

"Not in this area."

"Where then?"

"THEY HAVE THE FACILITIES at Cornell University," the vet said, "as well as one of the finest spinal surgeons in the country, a Dr. George Ross, but that would cost you a lot of money."

"Thank you doctor," Julie said.

The next day Julie took off from work. He and Norma placed Alfie on the back seat of their car, made the dog as comfortable as possible and made the 150-mile trip to Cornell.

Dr. Ross examined Alfie.

Yes, he could make the dog as good as new, but it would cost $50 for the operation, $20 for the x-rays, and $4-a-day for the post-operative care that Alfie would require for at least a month. Julie's ruddy face wrinkled into a relieved smile.

"FIX UP OUR DOG, DOC," Julie said to Dr. Ross. "We love him."

The next day, Dr. Ross performed surgery on Alfie. That night, Julie phoned the vet and learned that the dog was doing fine.

"Phone me again in about three weeks," the vet said to Julie, and I'll tell you when you can come and get your dog. I figure he'll be okay to go home about April 15th."

"April 15th is a long way from now," Julie said, "so tell me, doc, when is visiting day?"

A visit — which requires a drive of 300 miles, round trip — was arranged.

These days, Julie potatoes is lifting those 50-pound sacks of Spuds as he did in his twenties. Alfie is on the mend and life for Julie Potatoes is full and beautiful again.

What a lucky dog Alfie is!

Column Characters — LOUIS VALVO, "LOOSE LIPS LOUIE"

Phil's dear friend and column character passes on Christmas day.
Saturday, January 4, 1969
Phil Ranallo: What's New, Harry?

LOUIS VALVO, AN EFFERVES-CENT lover of life whose unique experiences — on and off the racetrack — have been noted in this space for more than a decade, died Christmas Day.

His alias was Loose Lip Louie.

Those who knew Lou Valvo do not regard it as pure coincidence that this warm, always joyful fellow took his last breath on that very special day.

He lived 59 years and enjoyed every minute.

When Lou hit 59, he regarded it a handicap. "Now, when I go to the trots," he said shortly after his last birthday, "I can't play my age in the double."

THEY CALLED HIM "LOOSE LIP" and "The Doc." There was a reason for the latter nickname. Whenever Lou learned that a friend was hospitalized or ill at home, there he'd be the next day — at his friend's bedside.

"The Doc" made more sick calls than a dozen busy physicians. And he always made his visit bearing a gift — usually a fresh racing form.

Lou Valvo also had a remarkable attendance record at wakes and funerals. Lou paid his respects even if he only suspected he knew the deceased.

ONCE, A COUPLE OF YEARS AGO, I asked Lou if he knew that a mutual acquaintance had died.

"I know it," Lou replied. "I went to the funeral ... and I'm glad I went — because there was hardly nobody there."

Although Lou Valvo was not an English major, he was an extraordinary person.

He was the only man I've known who could approach a friend unexpect-edly from the rear, greet him with a resounding slap on the back — and get away with it.

If it wasn't a slap on the back, it was a bear-hug or a headlock.

LOUIS VALVO WAS WILD ABOUT people and horses — in that order — and he had the gift to make grouches smile. He was an assistant foreman in The Courier-Express mail room.

Every night, between editions, he paid visits to the newspaper's Editorial Dept. — which is extremely dangerous territory, inhabited by scowlers and growlers.

Lou Valvo, the miracle worker, though, usually drew chuckles from the reporters, copy-readers and re-writemen who, when toiling and fighting deadlines, almost hate themselves.

A cub reporter would look on aghast as Lou bear-hugged the managing editor.

LOUIS VALVO KNEW HOW TO MAKE a buck — and also how to lose it. A few years back, when the price of a cup of coffee jumped to 15 cents (17 cents to take out), the mailers who sent out for coffee regularly were incensed.

"I don't blame you guys," Lou said. "Sending out for 25 cups of coffee a couple of times a night and paying 17 cents a smash is ridiculous. I'm so hot about it, I'm going to fix those restaurant people."

And Lou Valvo did.

The next night, when Lou reported for work, he staggered in with a giant coffee urn, three two-pound cans of Maxwell House, a five-pound sack of sugar, a gross of paper cups and a bag of plastic spoons.

"We'll fix those restaurant people," Lou said to his colleagues. "From now on, you guys can get your coffee from me — for 10 cents a cup."

AT THE RACETRACK, LOU VALVO was something else. He always had from 5 to 25 partners in the daily double — on endless combinations — and usually lost money ... even if he caught the double.

And he made the strangest bets — $23 to win, or $17 or $31. Always an odd number.

One day, when he jumped for joy at the conclusion of a race and announced he had $51 on the winner's nose, I asked him how he could bet $51.

"I got three $10 tickets, three $5 tickets and three deuces on the horse, dummy," Lou said.

Without Lou, the Fort Erie Jockey Club and Buffalo Raceway and Batavia Downs and, most of all, The Courier-Express, will never be the same.

Lou Valvo was one of a kind.

Courier-Express — JOE ALLI

Longtime Courier-Express sportswriter retires.
Sunday, April 29, 1979
Phil Ranallo: What's New, Harry?

THIS MORNING, I FEEL like the last of the Mohicans. Everybody else is gone.

I mean, all my longtime sidekicks — all the guys who comprised The Courier-Express sportswriting team when I first cracked the lineup almost 40 years ago — have made their last trots around the reportorial bases.

And it was some kind of lineup.

All long-ball hitters, guys who feasted on the curve ball, guys who hit a ton with their daily reports on the latest in sports.

Billy Kelly ... Bill Coughlin Sr. ... Jack Laing ... Ray Ryan ...Mike Kanaley ... Charley Bailey ... Joe Alli.

Joe Alli, the little fellow with the big cigar — the friend who began a labor of love for this newspaper when President Roosevelt was still serving his first term, 43 years ago — called it a career Friday.

This morning, in reflecting on Joe Alli's newspaper career, the best tribute that can possibly be paid Alli is to tell you this.

Friday night, when Joe Alli said goodbye and walked away, he departed in possession of the greatest honor a man can earn in his lifetime — total respect.

IN JOE ALLI'S CASE, it's the respect he commanded as a newspaperman — the respect of every newspaperman who worked with him, or ever worked with him, or ever knew him.

Of all the newspapermen I've known, the work Joe Alli turned out, during his 43 years as a reporter, perhaps best exemplified the qualities that are the hallmark or this business — accuracy and objectivity.

When Alli sat down at the typewriter and went to work on a news item, he told the story, told it well, and told it right.

When Ali wrote it, it was never fiction — it was fact.

When Alli wrote it, the readers could take it straight to the bank.

FOR YEARS AND YEARS, Alli pounded the baseball and boxing beats — in the days when the baseball Bisons and the weekly fight cards in the Aud were the biggest sports shows in this town.

Alli bothered to scruple about writing and people.

He lived his professional life, in the baseball world, with the kind of jock who often is bitter for being in the minors — and who takes factual reporting on his play, when it isn't positive, as a personal attack.

In boxing, Alli existed with many side-of-the-mouth characters, guys who had their offices in their hats — and specialized in selling boxing writers bills of goods.

The baseball players never succeeded in their attempts to persuade Alli to "write nicer and lie a little."

JOE ALLI WAS flintly honest.

For several years, he served as the International League's official scorer for Bison home games — a chore which gave Alli the final say, for example, on whether a grounder deep in the hole was a base hit or an error for the shortstop.

Alli's official decisions constantly boiled Bison players.

Whether Alli was a friend of the player made no difference.

The Bison batter never got a hit, if Alli thought it was an error — regardless of how debatable the play might be, or regardless of whether the call would cost the player the league batting title.

No, sir; if Alli saw it as an error, there was no way he'd call it a hit — even if the batter happened to be his mother.

AND THE BOXING promoters never made a "sale" with Joe. When a new fighter was booked for an Aud bout, for example, the promoter — more often than not — would give the boxing writers a phony record of the guy's recent fights.

The phony record, which made the guy out to be a much more able ringman than he was, never made its way into Alli's boxing story.

Alli, somehow, would dig up the guy's true ring record and print it — much to the chagrin of the promoter, who, in some cases, might be a fellow with connections among "hit men."

Joe Alli didn't scare easily. Understandably. I mean, how do you scare a guy who spent more than a couple of years of World War II with the U.S. Marines, in the South Pacific — serving as a combat correspondent?

FOR THE LAST several years — after the death of the baseball Bisons and the death of boxing in Buffalo — Alli toiled on the copy desk in this newspaper's sports department.

A copy reader, for the uninitiated, is a person who edits reporters' stories and prepares them for the type-setters.

And Alli, as a copy reader, was as efficient as he was as a reporter. So efficient, in fact, that in the last 10 years, I'd venture to guess he saved me a million times — by correcting a million of my mistakes.

I wish Joe Alli, in his retirement, happy days.

Courier-Express — CHARLEY BARTON

Courier-Express hockey writer passes away.
Sunday, May 21, 1972
Phil Ranallo: What's New, Harry?

SOMEHOW OR OTHER IT SEEMS appropriate that the hockey season is over — that Gil Perreault and Bobby Orr and Jean Ratelle have finished their work for the year — so that the people who knew Charly Barton can mourn their great loss.

Charley Barton, the quality hockey writer for The Courier-Express, a fellow typewriter pounder and a pal, is dead — and I find myself gripped by a strange emptiness.

Yet Charley's death isn't all sadness. He is at last free of the torture of illness that he bore in recent months.

For this, his friends give thanks.

No nicer fellow ever dignified our craft — and no better hockey writer.

Charley Barton wrote hockey from his heart and from his soul — because the game was his lifeblood.

WHEN HIS FINAL ILLNESS struck him a few months ago and he began to fear for the worst, he thought first of hockey.

"I waited 20 years for Buffalo to get into the NHL," he told his dear friend Punch Imlach ... and now this.

"I didn't get enough of an opportunity to enjoy it, Punch — to savor it ... to really taste it."

Imlach grieves the loss of Barton.

"Ours wasn't a reporter-coach relationship," Imlach said Saturday. "It was friend-friend — actually closer than that. I was nuts about Charley. It will never be the same without him.

"I know I'll never be able to forget him."

In the world of newspaper reporting, the qualities most widely honored are integrity and fairness. And both integrity and fairness were Barton's trademarks.

FIERY INDEPENDENCE IN HIS reporting of the game of hockey and fierce loyalty to his newspaper were other Barton attributes. The Courier-Express was Charley's private newspaper. Had he owned it, he could not have been more dedicated to it.

In his 20 years as a reporter, Barton came up with more scoops — more firsts — than any other newsman who ever toiled in this town.

His scoops were the fruit of his countless contacts that were spread the length and breadth of this continent — wherever a reporter pecks out a hockey story; wherever a hockey player, from junior league and up, laces on a pair of skates.

He was an expert at writing the game.

He missed few nuances on the ice. More often than not, his reports were masterpieces of insight and analysis, spiced with pungent comments and keen observations.

BUT IT WAS NOT ALONE THE accomplishments of his reportorial life that set him apart from other hockey writers. His chief contribution to the newspaper world was his personality.

Charley was a softie. He was wonderfully kind. He was pleased by small things, just like a big kid.

When Charley was on hand, the day in the newspaper office or in the press box was certain to begin with a friend at the next typewriter.

Charley Barton had a handsome face and when he smiled, his eyes twinkled. Without even trying, he won people over with his overwhelming charm and appeal.

And with his generosity.

He was a walking loan company for his friends, continuously bailing them out whenever they were financially strapped. Unlike the banks, though, Charley's price was right. He charged no interest.

Once, several years ago, he loaned a friend what almost amounted to his life saving — $11,000 — without so much as an IOU.

CHARLEY BARTON WAS A MAN of principles and ideals and loyalties — and he clung to them throughout his life, 52 years, because that is the way his character was shaped.

He loved his family, his home, his God, his two countries (Canada and the United States), his newspaper, and the Buffalo Sabres, perhaps in that order.

He could laugh as loudly as anyone at a joke. But there were some things that he could not joke about — one of them was any defeat by the Sabres, or the old Bisons. There was nothing funny about losing.

There was a side of Charley that not many people are aware of — his relationship with his mother.

When he lost his father about 30 years ago, he vowed that his mother would never want, never be alone — and he kept his vow.

He bought his mother a home in St. Catharines, Ont., in the city she loved, and in that home Charley and his mother lived happily ever after.

CHARLEY WAS A LOVER of children. He often babysat for friends — just to be near the children. He longed for children of his own, but never had that longing fulfilled ... since he never married because of his dedication to his mother.

"I'd love to get married and have children," he said to me once, baring his soul, "but I can't. I just can't take that chance. Ma means too much to me. If I got married and my wife and my mother didn't get along, it would be the end of the world for me."

Punch Imlach will never forget Charley Barton and neither will I.

I can see Charley now ... and always will see him ... sliding into his seat in the Auditorium press box, setting himself behind his typewriter, his spectacles lowered to the tip of his nose – waiting for the hockey battle to begin.

THE BEST TRIBUTE I can pay him is to inform the thousands and thousands of hockey fans who read him daily — and delighted in devouring his stories on the Sabres — that people who knew Charley Barton best will weep at his funeral today.

Courier-Express — LEONARD FELDMANN

The legendary Buffalo Courier-Express managing editor passes away.
Wednesday, December 6, 1972
Phil Ranallo: "A Beautiful Boss"

BAD NEWS DOES NOT OVERLY DISTURB newspapermen. They take bad news in stride, generally. They become immune to it, in a way. This is not due to a lack of compassion, but rather to the nature of the profession since bad news is so much a part of the newspaper business.

It was different late Monday night.

There was bad news and it chilled every room of The Courier-Express ... and the bad news had an impact that reached into, and tore at, the hearts of everyone ... every reporter, every copy editor, every copyboy, every printer, every mailer, every stereotyper, every pressroom man.

Leonard G. Feldmann was dead.

Leonard G. Feldmann — one of the most admired and beloved managing editors ever to grace any city-room of any newspaper; the man who for 25 years was the heart and the soul of The Courier-Express.

Everybody's friend — the beautiful boss — was gone.

COPYBOY ... REPORTER ... FINANCIAL editor ... financial columnist ... managing editor Len Feldmann touched all the bases of his craft. He toiled as a newspaperman for 46 years of his 63 years — and it was a labor of deep, deep love.

The facts concerning Len's career are not hard to uncover. As a Courier-Express man, he rose to a position of great influence as a writer and public speaker and leader of newspapermen.

For long years, Len Feldmann was part of the conscience of the community.

In his 25 years as managing editor, Len Feldmann "put to bed" perhaps 25,000 editions of The Courier-Ex-

press ... and every one of them — every single edition — had soaked into it some of Len's sweat, some of his lifeblood.

Page One was Len Feldmann's "baby" ... and he treated his "baby" tenderly, selecting the Page One stories with special care — always keeping uppermost in his mind that his 'baby" had to have the face of a family newspaper.

LEONARD C. FELDMANN WAS A MAN of extraordinary makeup. A friendly, oversized bear of a man, Len Feldmann was one of the few people of stature I have known in my lifetime who never looked down at anyone.

Len was a man of humanity. He treated everyone as his equal — the copyboy, the cub reporter, the janitor, the switchboard operator.

And what a newspaperman!

He was a marvel in the heat of a newspaper night when big stories were breaking at the 11th hour ... when the deadline was but a few sweeps of the second hand on the clock away.

With the pressure on, he was an icicle — but a remarkably warm one.

He issued orders in a low calm voice — and they came across to his men more as requests for personal favors than as orders.

DURING THOSE DEADLINE STRUGGLES, Len corralled the copy as it flowed from the typewriters of the reporters, scanned the copy, handed the copy to the copy editors and instructed them what heads to place on the stories — heads that would conform with the mental image he had of the not-yet-revamped front page.

Then Len would make his way to

the composing room and instruct the makeup-man, a printer, where to place the stories ... and Page One would be completely revamped and the race with the clock would be won.

Many of Len Feldman's last minute alterations of Page One — performed without benefit of a "dope" sheet, a worked-out pattern — were works of art.

Even Rodin would have been proud.

Len Feldmann spent a great part of his life thanking people for performing the duties for which they were well-paid.

HE WAS FOREVER GIVING REPORTERS mental lifts, especially young reporters. "Nice going last night, kid," Len Feldmann said to me as recently as a couple of months ago. "Fine job. Thank you."

I have always been "kid" to Len Feldmann, despite the slightly disturbing fact that I am 51.

Leonard G. Feldmann is gone, but I will always have fond memories of him. Memories that go back to the days when I was really a kid, and how Len Feldmann encouraged me, told me what a great business I was in.

I can hear him now, telling me that working for a morning newspaper — which requires laboring at night — wasn't all that bad because the labor was fascinating and often satisfying.

"THE HOURS ARE STRANGE AND THEY CAN make the life strange, too," Len Feldmann said to me, "but stick with the business because it's fun and it's exciting and it often makes you feel good.

"Write a story, and in a matter of hours you can step into a bus and spot somebody with the pages turned and his eyes on your story — and in that little time it takes you to walk past him there is a feeling that the whole kind of life you're leading is worthwhile.

"Oh, you're not doing some big thing. You're not a big guy. You're just putting out something that a person can read and maybe get some information from — maybe even enjoy.

"In a couple of seconds, the feeling is gone and you're down at the end of the bus. But what's the difference?

"A lot of people go through their whole lives and never know what it is like to get satisfaction out of a job."

LEONARD G. FELDMANN GOT satisfaction out of his job-and he taught me how to get satisfaction out of mine.

It was an honor and a privilege to work for ... and with ... Len Feldmann — a beautiful, beautiful boss.

Courier-Express — RAY RYAN

Courier-Express sports writer passes away.
Saturday, December 9, 1978
Phil Ranallo: What's New, Harry?

LOSING FRIENDS IS a most distressing human experience. It is part of the price that is paid for living. Nevertheless, sometimes the price seems too exorbitant — like Thursday.

For some of us, Thursday was an extremely expensive day.

Ray Ran died.

Raymond Vincent Ryan started hunting and pecking on his typewriter in the '20s during the "Golden Age" of sports, and the fruit of his labor of love — his excellent prose — graced the sports pages in The Courier-Express for 53 years.

For Ray Ryan, the newspaper business was a beautiful disease. He contracted it at an early age, when he was a kid one month this side of 17 — and was never "cured."

Since he was raised and reared in the newspaper profession more than 50 years ago, when common clichés cropped up in just about every line written on sports, Ray Ryan was a phenomenon, in a way.

To Ray, the World Series was never the "autumnal classic." The big, up-coming game was never "for the whole ball of wax." A home run was never a "circuit clout." Sunsets never "painted a twilight purple," and a baseball was never a "nugget."

Ray's work did not involve the common clichés of sports. Rather, he was very lucid about his writing and dedicated to filling space with good English.

WRITING, RAY RYAN had the rare gift of getting right to the point — in the first sentence of the first paragraph. He took great pains with every story to give a coherent and ac-curate account of the occurrence.

Since he covered Canisius and Little Three basketball for half a century, one thinks of Ray as a basketball writer. He was a student of the game, and he loved it — and wrote about it supremely well.

But the fact is, Ray wrote every-thing well.

And, along the way, he touched all the bases, reported on every sport imaginable — including the six-day bike races when they were the rage.

When harness racing was introduced at Batavia Downs and Buffalo Race-way almost 40 years ago, Ray Ryan was there — and he covered the Ham-burg races nightly for more than 30 years.

Ray, incidentally, was a rare bird when it came to gambling.

He was a guy who saw the light — in a big hurry.

RACETRACKERS WILL find this difficult to believe, but they can take it for gospel. Although Ray was at the track nightly, the last wager he made on a horse was placed in the early '40s.

Ray would explain his "cure" some-thing like this:

"After I'd been around the track a while, a lot of the owners, trainers and drivers got to be my friends. And these friends, in an attempt to repay me for kind words I'd written about them in my column, would tip me on 'sure things' they had entered.

"Well, sometimes I'd have as many as four or five 'sure things' in the same race, and that told me something — especially when some horse other than one of the 'sure things' would win the race.

"I concluded that if these friends of mine who eat and sleep with the horses can't help me, there's certainly no way I can help myself — so I quit."

Ray's experience with the football betting cards also comes to mind.

ONE SATURDAY, SOME 30 years ago, Ray Ryan decided to make his first wager ever on a football card. He picked 10 teams and wagered a dollar on the card. After he'd learned the first nine results, he had nine winners.

His 10th team, Duke if I recall correctly, was playing in a night game. If the Blue Devils won, Ray would hit the card and win something like $150.

Well, Duke lost.

"That's it," Ray squealed, as he read the result on the Western Union ticker machine. "I'll never bet another football card as long as I live."

And he never did.

Ray Ryan also never took an airplane ride in his life, never stayed in a hotel room that was located above the third floor, and never received a traffic citation for speeding.

Why didn't he ever fly in a plane?

"Hey," he'd say, "it bothers me just to look up."

BEHIND THE WHEEL of a car, Ray was no A.J. Foyt.

If you've ever been trapped behind a car cruising along at about 20 mph, and have screamed at the driver and leaned on your horn and gone all but daffy — well, chances are the guy was Ray Ryan.

But Ray was an employer's dream come true. As an employee, he was one in a million.

His Courier-Express attendance record was incredible.

Believe it or not, but save for one occasion about 30 years ago, no member of the C-E sports staff can recall when Ray Ryan didn't show for work — other than two hospital stays when he underwent surgery.

The night he missed 30 years ago was a doubleheader night in the Aud — and the fact that the Canisius Griffs played a basketball game he didn't see and write about caused him pain beyond endurance.

But he made it to work a thousand times — through blizzards and while dragging, physically.

"They need me at the paper," he'd tell his wife, Mary Louise. "I've got to go in, because this blizzard is going to leave them short-handed."

THE COURIER-EXPRESS job was the only regular job Ray ever held in his life. He was that kind of a guy — one job and one woman. Ray was hooked on Mary Louise all his life, and she knew it.

Mary Lou knew it because, through more than 40 years of marriage, Ray was as faithful and dedicated to her as he was to his newspaper.

Theirs was the perfect relationship, probably because Mary Lou was so understanding. She learned, even before her wedding day, not to compete with a big story for her husband's affections.

Now Ray is gone, and this paper will never be quite the same.

Ray Ryan hurt very few people. He did not engage in feuds. He was an ornament to his profession.

I cherished his friendship — and I thank him for being so kind and so generous to a kid copy boy 37 years ago.

Family — TOMMY TROY RANALLO

Phil's first grandson, Tommy Troy Ranallo.
Friday, January 29, 1965
Phil Ranallo: What's New, Harry?

"SAY, HARRY," Sam the Immigrant said, "you haven't mentioned your little grandson in quite awhile. How old is he now — and how's he doing?"

"He's eight months old," Honest Harry replied, "and what an IQ he's got!

"He's a sensational patty-caker. He does it as good as I do.

"When anybody puts on a coat, the kid beams and waves bye-bye.

"SHOW HIM a jar of that baby spinach and he makes like Boris Karloff.

"And the second he does you-know-what, he starts kicking up a storm — and he doesn't stop until somebody changes him."

"What do you do, Harry," Sam said, "when you're the babysitter and the kid starts kicking up a storm?"

"UNTIL THE other day, I was stymied," Harry said, "but then I read something and found out that changing a diaper is a snap."

"You're a better man than I am then," Sam said, "because I know I could never learn."

"Yes, you could," Harry said, "because you've been a baseball fan all your life — and anybody who knows baseball can learn in a minute."

"Really?" Sam said. "Tell me how you learned?"

"I LEARNED," Harry replied, "when I read this piece, Robert Sylvester's column, 'Dream Street,' in the New York Daily News.

"Sylvester quoted the diaper-changing instructions that are contained on the advertising flyer of one of the New York City diaper service companies.

"The instructions are for fathers who have baseball knowledge — or for 'Tomboy' mothers.

"HERE THEY ARE. Sam: 'To change baby place diaper like baseball diamond with you at bat. Fold second base over home plate, put baby on pitcher's mound, then pin first base and third base to home plate.' "

Family — PHIL RANALLO

Phil's second grandson is born.
Thursday, June 29, 1967
Phil Ranallo: What's New, Harry?

"YOUR CHEST IS STICKING OUT, Harry, and you're wearing that extra-proud look," Sam the Immigrant said, "... so let me in on it. Did you connect on a three-horse win parlay, or something?"

"Better than that," Honest Harry replied.

"Yesterday afternoon, at one-thirty — exactly an hour-and-a-half before post-time for the first at Woodbine — it happens.

"My son Tom's wife ... that cute trick of Swedish extraction ... gives birth to her second boy — so Ruby and I have got another little Swedish meatball in the family.

"YESTERDAY, BEFORE WE FIND out, Ruby and I are in the living room, right next to the phone — waiting for Tom's call from Children's Hospital.

"Ruby's sitting there, with her hand on the receiver — and she's not saying a word. She's just waiting, impatiently — and privately squeezing for a girl.

"Then the phone rings and Ruby, in a lightning move, picks it up and says:

" 'What is it, Tom?' "

" 'It's a boy, Ma.' "

" 'That's wonderful, Tom,' " Ruby says, " '... two beautiful boys in a row, I mean — because now you can pass the clothes down.' "

"WHEN RUBY FINALLY HANGS UP the phone, Sam — after maybe 10 minutes — I ask her if Tom tells her what the new baby looks like.

" 'Tom said the baby is very pretty,' " Ruby says to me, " 'cute little nose, blond hair, blue eyes. And Tom especially noticed his ears.'

" 'The baby's ears are nice and small, and very tight to his head, Harry,' " Ruby says, proudly, pushing back her hair with both palms, " 'just like mine.' "

"Then I get the other incidentals, Sam, such as the baby's weight — six pounds and two ounces — which is why I'm taking a shot at 6-2 tonight in the double at Hamburg.

"BY THE WAY, SAM, THIS BABY cost me 50 bucks already, because I blow that size of a bet to Ruby — and she forces me to get the money up the minute Tom calls with the good news.

"If you recall, I told you recently that Ruby — who's sort of a super spy, with extra-sensory perception, which is why I call her 'Mrs. Ninety-Nine' — predicts a long time ago that this baby would be born the last week of June.

"Ruby predicts it, in fact, way back in October — before our daughter-in-law, herself, even suspects that the stork has her name and address, and everything.

"THIS PARTICULAR MORNING, way back in October, Ruby just looks at Perrice, carefully, from across the breakfast table, and when our daughter-in-law leaves, Mrs. Ninety-Nine turns to me and says:

" 'She's going to have a baby, Harry. I can tell by the glow in her eyes.'

"Then Ruby, after studying a calendar for maybe a minute, adds: 'And the baby will be born the last week in June.'

"So I bet Ruby 50 bucks she's wrong ... that the baby won't be born the last week in June.

"My bet, Sam — and it costs me 50 bucks — was that the baby would be born during the Ft. Erie meeting.

"SERIOUSLY, THOUGH, SAM, Ruby, the grandmother, is thrilled. And so is the grandfather. And so are our other four sons, the uncles, and our daughter, the aunt.

"Ruby put it beautiful yesterday afternoon, Sam ... right after the good news.

" 'What a beautiful life we have been blessed with, Harry,' Ruby says to me. 'Our marriage and the fruit of our marriage, five sons and a daughter.'

" 'And now — the fruit of our fruit.' "

Family — SUE RANALLO

Honest Harry and Ruby's only daughter gets married.
Tuesday, September 1, 1970
Phil Ranallo: What's New, Harry?

THE WEDDING CAKE: About 9 o'clock last Saturday morning — the day Honest Harry walked his daughter Sue down the isle — the telephone rang in Harry's home. It was the manager of the bakery from which Harry ordered the wedding cake.

"Oh, my heavens!" Harry said, when the bakery shop manager identified himself. "What happened? Did you drop the cake or something?"

"No, the cake is perfect," the man said. "I'm calling about the money. The cake costs $125."

"Fine," Harry said. "If memory serves, that's the price we agreed on — so just send me the bill and I'll mail you a check."

"I'm afraid that won't do, sir. We'd appreciate it if you'd come over here now and pay for the cake."

"Look, my daughter's being married at five this afternoon, and there are a million things I've got to do, so I can't come. I'll mail you a check when I get the bill."

"THAT WON'T DO, SIR. We simply will not deliver the cake to the reception hall unless you come over here and pay the $125."

"Forget the cake then," Harry said, terminating the conversation by hanging up.

Thirty seconds later, the phone rang again. Harry picked it up.

"This is the bakery shop again," the man said. "Are you coming over and pay for this cake?"

"I believe I made it rather clear about a minute ago that I'm not coming over."

"Then what do you expect me to do with this cake?" the man said in a belligerent tone.

"Well, if you refuse to deliver the cake until I come over and pay for it," Harry said, "I guess there's only one thing you can do with it ... and that won't be easy because it's a pretty big cake."

P.S. — The bakery shop manager did not take Harry's suggestion. He delivered the cake unpaid, proving that everybody gambles a little when forced to.

THE WEDDING PHOTOGRAPHER: Earl Raisen, an artist with a camera, took the wedding pictures ... and Harry is very happy about it because, right off, Raisen saved him at least $100.

Raisen saved Harry that amount of money by corralling him and the wedding party in the Charter House lobby and taking pictures for about 20 minutes, while a couple of hundred guests were upstairs in the reception hall with their tongues hanging out.

Unbeknownst to Harry, the bar could not be opened until he gave the okay. The okay — thanks to Raisen — came 20 minutes late.

During the reception, Sam the Immigrant poked Harry on the shoulder and said: "Do you realize that this Raisen guy — the man who's taking the pictures — is one of the most successful photographers in town? Why, he's even got a television set in his 1970 Cadillac."

"CERTAINLY I REALIZE IT," Harry said. "I wouldn't have him if he wasn't successful because he doesn't need the money, and probably won't get it. Do you think I'm the kind of guy who'd stiff a photographer who needed it?"

Raisen took pictures for about six hours. He must have taken a thousand shots. Every time Harry turned around, Raisen clicked away — including once when Harry was emerging from the men's room.

Raisen also took dozens of pictures of Harry kissing female guests. This annoyed Harry somewhat, so he finally asked Raisen why he was taking all the kissing pictures.

"Your wife Ruby, Raisen said, smiling, may be interested in seeing these pictures in case you refuse to pay."

You're a wise guy, Raisen, Harry said, "so under no circumstances will I mention the Avenue Studio."

TERRY AND JERRY, AND THE TAB: Along about midnight, Terry Kane and Jerry Voskersichian — the two Charter House gentlemen whose catering expertise made it an unforgettable night — turned into the bearers of bad news.

They handed Harry the tab.

Harry, who was 23 sheets to the wind, looked at the tab and instantly became cold sober.

"When am I supposed to pay this?" Harry asked.

"The bill," Terry Kane said, "has to be paid right now, sir, before you leave."

Terry Kane was not kidding.

Which is why this column was written by Honest Harry Monday night — in a guarded room at the Charter House.

Final Roll Call — MARK CORBETT

Phil writes about a young friend who lost his life in the jungles of Vietnam.
Monday, May 29, 1972
Phil Ranallo: What's New, Harry?

THIS MORNING, THE IMAGE OF Mark Corbett Is etched on my mind — Mark Corbett, 21 years old, six feet tall, golden-haired, wholesome, kind, gentle, peace-making, lover of life.

Mark Corbett slept under my roof at least a hundred nights, in the room of one of his pals, one of my sons — but only after he had notified his parents where he was.

He slept under my roof especially on nights that he and Tim had made a stop at one of the young set's jumping joints and had dared to lift a brew or two ... or maybe three.

Mark Corbett would walk into my home on those happy nights, or early mornings, with that impish grin of his creasing his handsome, beardless face, and relate how he and Tim had lived it up — how they had been out on the town.

Mark Corbett, I'm almost sure, never had a fight in his life ... not because he lacked courage, but due to his makeup. He was a non-violent type, a young man who was different than most of us.

BUT MARK CORBETT DID FIGHT, finally, perhaps against his will. He fought less than two weeks in the hell that is Vietnam — and he died in that hell, in December of 1969.

Now, Mark Corbett is a member of the silent minority that today lies under the bare white crosses of a thousand cemeteries in the United States.

Mark Corbett hears no arguments now.

He no longer is commanded by the stale visions of politicians. Fear no longer makes the palms of his hands moist, no longer slithers upon him like a silent monster, groping in the frightening Asian night.

Mark Corbett and the other members of the silent minority, 53,000 strong — most of them boys, with not many seasons behind them — now lie under those bare white crosses.

They are all dead — all gone. The finality of it, on this Memorial Day, brings shivers to the spine — gnaws at the stomach, tears at the heart.

MARK CORBETT AND A LOT OF those other 53,000 who have been sacrificed in that Asian hell never understood the reason for their destiny — their date with early death.

In basic training they told the tales about communism — how communism had to be stopped in Asia before it had a chance to spread, like a cancer, to our shores.

And so Mark Corbett and the rest of them went to that Asian hell.

The blue, dancing eyes of Mark Corbett and the eyes of the rest of those 53,000 — eyes that had winked at pretty girls on the streets of Buffalo and Chicago and Baton Rouge and San Diego — now squinted into the dark void of the Vietnam jungles, almost expecting death.

And death came to Mark Corbett and the rest of the 53,000. They never got a chance to wink at another pretty girl.

They all died and were shipped back to their country, their homes, in rubber bags.

AND THE CLOSED COFFINS WERE met by wailing mothers and fathers and sisters and brothers — especially those whose minds were crossed by the horrifying thought that their loved ones died in vain.

The horrifying thought that Mark Corbett and the rest of the 53,000 were robbed of their youth — by some politicians who worry more about their own careers than the 53,000 careers which have been ended forever.

We will never know what these young men, the flower of our youth, might have been. We will never know which of them might have been a Bert Bacharach and written beautiful music.

We will never know which one of them might have come up with the cancer breakthrough ... or played the running back position for the Buffalo Bills ... or drilled long jump shots for the Braves ... or become mayor and transformed Buffalo into another Toronto ... or written in the style of Red Smith.

Mark Corbett and the rest of the 53,000 are all dead. We will never find out about their lives.

THEY DIED — MOST OF THEM — because a war has dragged on and on and on ... and because men in high places are still serving as cheerleaders for this ghastly war, still preaching that it is a noble and fitting thing for them to have died for their country.

The cheerleaders should be made to live with the ghosts of Mark Corbett and the rest of the 53,000.

Everywhere the cheerleaders go, they should be made to see these 53,000 ghosts — tramping through the eerie Asian night, their faces drawn, their bodies aching with fatigue, the mud of Asia on their boots, trying to get home, trying to get out and put Asia behind them.

This morning, the image of Mark Corbett is etched on my mind. I can see his handsome face, his dancing eyes, his golden hair — that impish grin.

But this beautiful boy is dead. Today, he lies beneath the earth — under a white cross. This is the third Memorial Day that Mark Corbett has been 21.

Final Roll Call — LOU GOLDSTEIN

Well-known Buffalo physical education instructor passes away.
Monday, August 20, 1962
Phil Ranallo: What's New, Harry?

HONEST HARRY is a race tracker who has learned to take losing days in stride. Saturday was different though because Harry lost one of his dearest friends.

Lou Goldstein died.

Lovable Lou Goldstein was a remarkable man who spent most of his 54 years helping people the hard way — by digging into his pockets.

LOU GOLDSTEIN won a Golden Gloves boxing championship when he was 17 and, to all who knew him, he remained a champion the rest of his life.

He was a physical education instructor in the Buffalo public schools for 33 years in the poorer section of the city.

And that's where he wanted to be.

HARRY remembers an afternoon six or seven years ago. A special committee met in the Buffalo Athletic Club to select the recipient of a Brotherhood award.

While the committee members still were working on their tomato juice, someone recommended Lou Goldstein — and the meeting was over.

That's the kind of stickout Lou Goldstein was.

LOU RECEIVED his Brotherhood award on a Saturday night, in Memorial Auditorium, between games of a college basketball doubleheader.

Harry was there and he'll never forget it.

Harry, as he stood and applauded his friend, noticed that tears were welling in the eyes of the tall young man standing next to him.

"I HAD TO be here tonight to see Mr. Goldstein honored," the young man volunteered. "He bought me my first pair of basketball sneakers because my parents couldn't afford to.

"And once when I came to school on a biting cold day with only a sweater, Mr. Goldstein took me into his office and gave me his overcoat and it was new.

"I TOLD HIM I couldn't take the coat," the young man went on, "but he insisted. Mr. Goldstein said to me 'Take it, son, you need it; I can get another one because my credit is good.'"

Lou loved all sports, particularly basketball. In his playing days, he was a fine guard. He had to play guard because he stood only about 5-feet-4.

BUT AT THIS very moment, it's 1 to 20 that Lou is jumping center Up There.

It is not coincidence that a special kind of man who loved people also loved swift racehorses.

Courier EXPRESS

Phil Ranallo   John Galbreath

C-E WRITER HONORED—Phil Ranallo, Courier-Express sports columnist and horse racing writer, was presented the Eclipse Award—highest prize within his realm—Friday night in Los Angeles. It is presented annually by the Thoroughbred Racing Assn. (TRA) for the outstanding article concerning horse racing to be published during a given year. Ranallo was cited for a "What's New, Harry?" column in which he pointed out that in this age of inflationary spirals and cost of living indexes, the $2 bet is the only thing that hasn't skyrocketed. Galbreath, president of the Hialeah (Fla.) race track and master of Darby Dan Farm, was named the TRA man of the year.   (AP)

Eclipse Award presented to Phil in Los Angeles

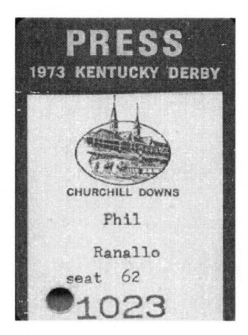

Kentucky Derby press credentials

Buffalo Raceway VIP Card

Page One

Jack West
News Story Under
Pressure of Deadline

Margaret Hammersley
News Series

Steve Waller
Sports Feature Story

Lee Smith
Editorials

Phil Ranallo
Sports Story

Rita Smith
Women's Page Feature Story

Robert Myers
Headlines

American Newspaper Page One Award Winner Phil Ranallo

		Day		O'Donnell		Bemiller		Warlick	Sestak			Dunaway	
Maguire		Barber		Stratton		McDole		Byrd			Tracey		Carlton
Gilchrist		Edgerson			Clarke		Kemp	Dubenion	Shaw			
			Moses		Jacobs				Hudson		Saimes	

The "Bills of the 60s" get together one more memorable time to be honored

'Bills of 60s' Luncheon Is Smash Hit

Bills of the '60s Luncheon

January 3, 1973

Dear Phil:

Congratulations on winning the Eclipse Award.
It is certainly a well deserved honor and all
of us at Rich Products are very happy for you
and Mrs. Ranallo.

Best wishes for a Happy New Year from one of
your loyal readers.

Sincerely,

Robert E. Rich, Jr.

RER,JR/jam

Mr. Phil Ranallo
Courier Express
785 Main Street
Buffalo, New York

Eclipse Award Letter from Robert E. Rich, Jr.

Mr. Ranallo's induction has been graciously underwritten by
Davis-Ulmer Sprinkler Co., Inc. and
Tzetzo Bros., Inc.

- 22 -

Greater Buffalo Sports Hall of Fame Induction Program

BUFFALO COURIER-EXPRESS, Wednesday, October 14, 1996

SPORTS

This Paper Prints more sports results first than all other papers in Western New York combined

Phil Ranallo

What's New, Harry?

"What's with the big goings-on at the Aud -- pardon me, Marine Midland Arena -- tonight?" asked Sam the Immigrant.

"They're inducting Honest Harry into the Greater Buffalo Sports Hall of Fame," replied Dick the Dealer. "Along with a bunch of athletes that Harry helped make famous. Harry should be at the head of the list."

"Darn right," said Sam. "If not for Harry, all people would have known about the stars was how many games they pitched or touchdowns they scored -- not the human-interest stuff the readers really cared about. He ruffled some feathers, too, and always spoke his mind, especially where the Braves were concerned. I doubt John Y. Brown will be in attendance tonight."

"Good riddance -- besides, I hear he's still too busy trying to run the State of Kentucky. Anyway, you get to know the local sports scene pretty well working for the Courier-Express for forty years, and writing a daily column for twenty."

"It's a shame Harry won't be joining any horses in the Hall of Fame," said Sam. "Harry loved the ponies." "Sure could write about them, too. Didn't he win a half-horse trophy one time? Front half, I hope?" Dick chuckled.

Sam didn't laugh. "If you're talking about the prestigious Eclipse Award, given annually to the top racing columnist in North America, that's a serious matter. Harry won it in 1972. Then again, his horse sense was legendary. Remember the time he was the only writer out of 90 covering the Kentucky Derby to pick the top three in order -- Northern Dancer, Hill Rise, and The Scoundrel? 1964, wasn't it?"

"Right, Sam, but it was no big deal to Harry," Dick replied. "He picked the first three Preakness finishers in '64, and the top three in the Derby in '59."

"How's Ruby taking the induction?"

"She's thrilled, Sam. After years of putting up with Harry's weakness for the ponies, she finally gets the recognition she deserves."

"Harry deserves the spotlight too, Dick. He's come a long way from Annunciation High and Canisius College. For crying out loud, the guy never allowed his picture to appear in his column all those years -- too shy, I guess -- and now tonight thousands will see him on TV and at the Arena will get to see his mug. Gives me goosebumps, Dick."

"This is a beautiful arena, isn't it Sam? The young fans in Buffalo are lucky to be able to watch sports in this world-class facility. They have a lot to be thankful for."

"Yeah," said Sam, with a wistful tear in his eye. "But they don't have Honest Harry."

- 23 -

Greater Buffalo Sports Hall of Fame Induction Program

Jack Kemp and Phil Ranallo

Paul Ranallo, right, congratulates Jimmy Ralston at his Ring #44 Boxing Hall
of Fame induction in 2000

HOUSE OF REPRESENTATIVES
WASHINGTON, D. C. 20515

JACK KEMP
THIRTY-EIGHTH DISTRICT
NEW YORK

Phil —

Imagine how honored I was to make "what's new Kerry" again after so many years.

I haven't made the Ranallo column since 1963 when I ran the wrong way (backwards) got tackled & sprained my shoulder. I like this one better.

you're a great friend, thanks again

JK —

Letter from Congressman Jack Kemp

DICK FISCHER ATHLETIC GOODS, Inc.

• 699 MAIN STREET
• BUFFALO, NEW YORK 14203
• PHONE (716) 853-8870

January 4, 1973

Mr. Phil Ranallo, Sports Dept.
c/o Courier Express
795 Main Street
Buffalo, New York 14203

Dear Phil:

At this time I wish I could write words and
paragraphs with the same type of flair that you do,
but there is only one Phil Ranallo.

Congratulations on winning one of the most important coveted awards in newspaper writing. It is
a great compliment to you, and my wife Isabelle,
along with the rest of my family, join me in wishing
you and your family a very healthy and prosperous
New Year.

I sincerely trust that you will be writing columns for many years to come. It looks like the late
Paul Neville was right when he said you are one of
the most outstanding writers in the country and how
he would have loved to have you on his paper.

Good luck, and good health!

Warm personal regards,

Dick Fischer

Dick Fischer

DF:ss

• BUFFALO, N. Y.   • TONAWANDA, N. Y.   • CHEEKTOWAGA, N. Y.   • ROCHESTER, N. Y.   • CLEVELAND, OHIO

Letter from Dick Fischer

SHERIFF OF ERIE COUNTY
10 DELAWARE AVENUE
BUFFALO, N.Y. 14202
⊕
TELEPHONE, 852-6415

B. JOHN TUTUSKA
SHERIFF

May 19, 1967

LEO J. KENNEDY
UNDER SHERIFF

Mr. Phil Ranallo
Sports Department
Buffalo Courier Express
785 Main Street
Buffalo, New York 14203

Dear Phil:

Just a brief note to pass along my congratulations for the recognition that you recently received for your very outstanding sports writing at the Buffalo Newspaper Guild's Annual Page One Ball.

I have always immensely enjoyed your unique "What's New, Harry?" columns and many of the other stories that you have so interestingly written.

Best wishes for continued success in the days that lie ahead. Kindest personal regards, I am

Sincerely yours,

B. JOHN TUTUSKA
SHERIFF

BJT/mh

Letter from Erie County Sheriff John Tutuska

Dear Phil —

Many thanks for the kind words, I'm the 2nd best color man in broadcasting ———

— everyone else is tied for 1st!

Seriously, you were very thoughtful to take time out from your coaching duties to comment favorably on my C.B.S. job. But I'm going to exercise "my" option with the Bills & come back anyway.

all the best, your "literary" fan

J. Kemp

Letter from Jack Kemp

**WESTERN NEW YORK
FOOTBALL CLUB**

HOTEL STATLER HILTON
BUFFALO 2, N.Y. • 856-1567

RALPH C. WILSON, JR.
president

REPLY TO: ONE WOODWARD AVENUE
DETROIT 26, MICHIGAN

November 13, 1963

Mr. Phil Ranallo
Buffalo Courier Express
785 Main Street
Buffalo 40, New York

Dear Phil:

Thanks for the help you have given the Bills so far this
season in your columns. I realize that you are one of
the widely read sports writers in the Western New York
area and appreciate your helping us out.

The team has really struggled to get up off the floor
after another disastrous start, but they are playing extremely hard and, of course, getting a few breaks along
the way.

In any event, I feel now the club will finish with a respectable won and loss record for this year which will
in a small measure reward the fans in Buffalo for their
outstanding support.

Cordially,

WESTERN NEW YORK FOOTBALL CLUB

Ralph C. Wilson, Jr.

RCW:lc

Letter from Ralph C. Wilson, Jr.

RICH PRODUCTS CORPORATION · P.O. BOX 245 · 1145 NIAGARA STREET · BUFFALO, NEW YORK · 14240

TELEPHONE: (716) 883-3211
CABLE: RICHPROD, BUFFALO

July 29, 1976

Mr. Phil Ranallo
Sports Columnist
Buffalo Courier-Express
785 Main Street
Buffalo, New York   14203

Dear Phil:

Seldom have I ever written a letter to a newspaper columnist,
but your column of Tuesday, July 27th on Ed Moses and Mike
Shine was as great a column as I have ever read. It is too
bad that this article cannot be reproduced in a national
magazine.

My youngest son David is an Episcopalian Minister in Washington and I mailed him your article as I thought it might
be excellent material for him to build a sermon around.

Sincerely yours,

Robert E. Rich, Sr.
President

RER/cds

Letter from Robert E. Rich, Sr.

Phil and Dorothy Ranallo

Sports Page from Courier-Express

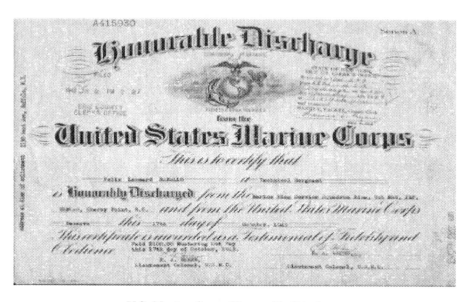

U.S. Marine Corps Honorable Discharge

Promotional advertisement and truck sign for the Courier-Express

Every morning Monday through Saturday on our Sports pages, you'll read the most "quoted" columnist in Western New York.

Phil Ranallo, alias Honest Harry, writes about ANY and ALL subjects . . . the Bills, horse racing, stadiums, and politics.

Nothing escapes this keen observer of local, and even national happenings.

exclusively in the . . .

Courier EXPRESS

Without it . . . You're not with it!

Courier-Express What's New, Harry? Promotional Page

Final Edition of The Courier-Express

Football — BILLS OF THE '60s HONORED

The Bills of the 1960s are honored at the Statler Hilton in Buffalo.
Wednesday, November 11, 1970
Phil Ranallo: What's New, Harry?

MONDAY AFTERNOON, IN THE middle of the luncheon at which the "Bills of the '60s" were honored, the lights in the Terrace Room of the Hotel Statler Hilton dimmed and a fun flick — a film created by Jack Horrigan and Rick Azar — began to roll.

The flick was comprised of Azar interviews with several of the Bills' all-time all-stars, among them Tom Day. Big 88, who spent seven years with the Bills picking up quarterbacks and ball-carriers he had just decked, was asked what he and the other Buffalo players thought of Wilson.

"Wilson is a sweetheart," Day replied, without hesitation. "He's a sweet man — outgoing and natural."

"Your kind words, I'm sure," Azar offered, "will mean a lot to Ralph Wilson."

"Ralph!" Day exclaimed. "Hell, I was talking about Flip — Flip Wilson."

THE NEXT INTERVIEWEE WAS Paul Maguire, the humorist and innkeeper who moonlights as a punter. "My biggest accomplishment, or thrill, as a Buffalo Bill," Paul said, in response to a question put to him, "was teaching Tom Sestak to speak English."

Butch Byrd, the pass defender, told it like it is — or like it was — when asked whether there ever were any racial problems on the club.

"Not really," Byrd said. "On occasion, though, the white players did cry a little about discrimination — but you know how those minority groups are."

Joe O'Donnell, the guard who this season as captain of the offense is an integral part of the pre-game coin toss, admitted he "was helped a lot by a course he took at the University of Michigan — a course in coin recognition."

RON McDOLE AND JIM DUNAWAY appeared on the film together and came across as a comedy team — with McDole deliberately flubbing his lines a half-dozen times before finally getting them half-straight.

At least we think the flubs were deliberate — but if they weren't we certainly can understand why it took John Rauch a year-and-a-half to get his athletes to absorb his complex football style.

When the flick was over, the "Bills of the '60s" were introduced, with each introduction provoking ringing applause from the capacity crowd of more than 600.

Finally, there they were, all of them with the exception of the ailing Pete Gogolak — the Bills' all-time all-stars standing shoulder-to-shoulder on the dais.

THERE THEY WERE, THE CHAMPIONS — Ron McDole ... Jim Dunaway ...Tom Sestak ... Tom Day ... John Tracey ... Harry Jacobs ... Mike Stratton ... Booker Edgerson ... Hagood Clarke ... George Saimes ... Butch Byrd ... Haven Moses ... Stew Barber ... Billy Shaw ... Al Bemiller ... Joe O'Donnell ... Dick Hudson ... Ernie Warlick ... Wray Carlton ... Cookie Gilchrist ... Jack Kemp ... Elbert Dubenion.

It was a moment of wonderful nostalgia.

Some of the all-stars got caught up in the emotion of it all, like Stew Barber, who, after stepping up and ac-

cepting his memento, a beautiful silver
ice bucket bearing the Bills' insignia,
said in a choking voice:

"Until the day I die, I'll remember
my association with these men, these
Buffalo Bills." Barber paused and bit
his lips, in an effort to control himself.
"Especially those two guys — Billy
Shaw and Al Bemiller."

AND LIKE GEORGE SAIMES,
who thanked everybody, then, his
voice quavering and tears welling in
his eyes, remembered the four people
who helped him most — "Lou Saban,
Joe Collier and Richie McCabe ... and
a special thank you to my wife."

The Golden Greek, obviously a man
of deep feeling, was beautiful.

There also were several light moments as Ralph Wilson dealt out the
mementoes.

TOM DAY, INTRODUCED AS the
fellow who often patted Joe Namath
on the derriere, then picked him up,
said: "I liked picking up Namath
because it was the only chance I ever
could get to pick up $400,000."

Ernie Warlick, after accepting his
gifts, looked at Wilson and said, with
only half a smile: "I'll trade these in if
I can just get three games to make me
eligible for my pension."

Wilson had some heartening news
for Warlick.

"Well, Ernie," Wilson said, "I'm a
member of the pension committee and
I think we can work something out."

That a boy, Ralph!

Football — GEORGE BLANDA

The 48-year-old football legend is waived by the Oakland Raiders.
Saturday, August 28, 1976
Phil Ranallo: What's New, Harry?

ON SEPT. 17, 1920, George Halas and his cronies pumped the National Football League's first ball. Seven years later the day — Sept. 17, 1927 — a boy was born in a place called Youngwood, a tiny town in southwestern Pennsylvania.

The proud parents named their new son George Frederick Blanda.

Twenty-two years later, in 1949 — the year Harry Truman began his second tour of duty in the White House while still chuckling at the famous Chicago Tribune headline that read, "Dewey Wins" — George Blanda threw his first pass in NFL competition, with the Chicago Bears.

Halas allowed Blanda to throw a total of 21 passes that first year, and was so impressed with George's play that he figuratively pinched his nose with his thumb and forefinger — and traded Blanda to the Baltimore Colts.

The Colts took one look at Blanda and cut him. Halas then took George back — and you'll never believe this: Halas converted Blanda into a linebacker, and that's the position George played for the Bears for two years — until 1952, when Halas gave him another chance at quarterback.

ONE MIGHT SAY THAT Blanda seized that second opportunity, if one is given to understatement. Because Blanda lasted just short of forever as a quarterback and field-goal man — with the Bears, Houston Oilers and Oakland Raiders.

He earned recognition as professional football's Methuselah and became the first pro football player to perform in four different decades. That's right — four decades! Count 'em— the '40s, '50s, '60s and '70s.

In his 24 seasons as a pro football player — he did not play in 1950 and 1959 — Blanda completed 1,910 passes for 26,909 yards, distance that measures just under 15 miles.

That's a lot of mileage — and Blanda's tank has finally emptied.

FOR GEORGE BLANDA, the guy who played almost forever — the fellow who was born the year Gene Tunney and Dempsey waged their "Battle of the Long Count," the year Babe Ruth hit 60 home runs, the year Lucky Lindy made his solo flight across the Atlantic — "forever" came to an end the other day.

George Blanda — who, believe it or not, played football against Sammy Baugh and behind Sid Luckman and with Bulldog Turner and George McAfee — was waived by the Oakland Raiders.

Blanda's length of service in the pros staggers the imagination. When he first joined the Bears, he was a third-stringer behind two gentlemen who now seem to be part of pro football's stone age — Luckman and Johnny Lujack.

IN 1959, HE WAS CUT by the Bears and was labeled an "over-the-hill" quarterback. But in 1960, he came back — thanks to the formation of the American Football League— and lasted for 16 more seasons.

Astounding!

For me, Blanda's departure from the football scene brought to mind those beautiful days of yore, when the greatest rivalry in the history of sports existed — the rivalry between the American Football League and the

National Football League.

Blanda was an AFL original. He was among the first guys who slipped into AFL jerseys the day the new league was born.

WHEN BLANDA SLIPPED out of his football uniform the other day and walked off into the sunset, it marked the end of a golden era in football — because Blanda was the very last of the AFL originals.

Blanda is one fellow who laments the demise of the American Football League — a guy who as long as he lives will "Remember the AFL."

The AFL, in Blanda's view, was the greatest thing that ever happened to professional football.

Blanda, the last link between the AFL and NFL, makes it clear that the existence of the AFL gave pro football something that's missing in all pro sports today — a special kind of team esprit de corps.

BLANDA'S WORDS, WHICH he has uttered repeatedly the last few years, point out what pro football is today and what it used to be — before the club-owners embraced, stripped the AFL of its identity, and became one big happy family.

"In 1960, the year after my involuntary retirement from the Chicago Bears," says Blanda, "the year when I was 32 years old and 'washed up,' a great thing happened to pro football. The AFL was formed.

"I can still hear the laughter. The entranced NFL owners and their toadies in the NFL sat back and almost split their sides. Or pretended to.

"But after the AFL won two Super Bowls and in general proved its equality, and often its superiority, some of the laughter died down.

"I WENT STRAIGHT TO Houston that first season, 1960, and I played every year in the AFL. Now it's all NFL, but I still think of myself as an AFL player and I always will.

"I only regret that we didn't have a Super Bowl from the very first. But the NFL guys ducked us. They were wise. We'd have held our own — more than held our own."

How's that for esprit de corps?

George Blanda, for me, says it best.

Remember the AFL!

Football — ERNIE DAVIS

The first African-American to win the Heisman Trophy passes away at age 23.

Wednesday, May 22, 1963

Phil Ranallo: What's New, Harry?

"TRULY, SAM," Honest Harry said. "He was the All-American boy. He was the boy millions and millions of fathers have dreamed about.

"He was tall and strong, bull-shouldered and iron-legged, lithe and quick as a panther — and, today, they are going to bury him.

"Today, Sam, they are going to bury Ernie Davis.

"I MARVELED at his football skills many times on television, Sam — and I saw him once in the flesh. I'll never forget that one time.

"I have a reason not to forget.

"It was on a warm night in War Memorial — last June, in the All-America College Bowl game shortly after Ernie had cast his pro football lot with the Browns.

"DAVIS HAD chosen the Browns — and had turned down a lucrative offer from the Bills — because he wished to play in the same backfield with his boyhood idol, Jim Brown.

"When Ernie stepped onto the stadium field that night — and his name was announced — the boos and jeers of twenty-two thousand Bills fans rent the air.

"And the fans never let him up. Throughout the game, they booed Ernie at every opportunity.

"IT'S A STRANGE world, Sam — because that was the last game of Ernie Davis' life.

"Imagine, Sam, Ernie Davis, one of the truly great players of all time, cruelly mistreated by the crowd the last time he carried the football.

"I'll never forget Ernie Davis and that June night at the stadium. How can I? I was one of those selfish Bills fans.

"THIS MORNING, SAM, I couldn't get Ernie Davis out of my mind — so I did something.

"I said a prayer.

"Sam, I have a feeling my prayer was part of a beautiful bouquet to Ernie Davis — a beautiful bouquet of twenty-two thousand prayers."

Football — J.D. HILL

J.D. pledges to take care of the grandmother who raised him.
Sunday, June 13, 1971
Phil Ranallo: What's New, Harry?

THE WOMAN IN THE LIFE of J.D. Hill, the new Buffalo Bill, is "sixtyish" and is on the heavy side, weighing in the neighborhood of 250 pounds. Her name is Claudia Hill, and she is J.D.'s grandmother.

But the All-America wide receiver from Arizona State has always called her mams.

There is a reason. She has mothered him and toiled for him, as a domestic in Stockton, Calif., since J.D. was three years old — since J.D.'s parents were forced to break up the family of 18 children.

"We have a special relationship, my mama and I," says the young man with the sure hands and the very fleet feet who is expected one day to help lead the Bills out of the pro football wilderness.

"It runs deeper than a mother and son relationship. We're friends, real buddies."

J.D. HILL GRINNED, AND when he did, his deep affection for his mama seemed to be etched on his ebony face. "Sometimes I call my mama ugly, but in the most loving way — and sometimes she sits on me to show me who's boss."

Now that J.D. has got his hands on a nice chunk of Ralph Wilson's bread, Claudia Hill is one of the happiest ladies in the land.

But J.D. the tease gave her a most anxious moment before breaking the good news to her a week ago.

Immediately after agreeing to terms with Bills official Pat McGroder, J.D. telephoned mama in Stockton and said:

"Hey, ugly, how are you doing? I've got some bad news for you mama.

"THE BILLS JUST TOLD ME they're not going to sign me. They said they're going to send me to a mental hospital instead."

Mama Hill did not respond.

"Did you hear me mama? They think I'm crazy. Do you think I'm crazy, mama?"

Mrs. Hill replied, "You're my baby, honey, so I can't think you're crazy. What's really the matter, son? Don't they want to give you any money?"

At that point J.D. figured he had been "cruel" long enough.

"Everything's beautiful, mama," he said. "I've signed my contract with the Bills, and I'll be home Monday — to give you a lot of bucks."

Mrs. Hill's shout of glee made J.D.'s eardrum go t-w-a-n-n-g-g-g.

LAST MONDAY J.D. HILL walked into his Stockton home. His mother was seated in her favorite chair, mending a dress, her sewing box was in her lap.

J.D. held the check in his hand for his mother to see. She squinted and said, "move it back a little more, J.D., so I can see it.

J.D. moved the check back about a foot, "Look at all the pretty numbers on it mama. Can you see them?"

Mrs. Hill saw the numbers — because she came out of the chair like a shot, the dress she was mending, the sewing box, the needle and thread, the thimble all sailing through the air.

Then Mrs. Hill put the palms of her hands together as she does when she's in church — and raised her head and looked straight up and said:

"Oh, thank you Jesus."

THAT NIGHT, J.D. TOOK his
mama and his aunt and his cousins
out on the town. "My cousin's name
is Walter Barney," J.D. said, laughing.
"He's the one that everybody used to
say would turn out to be no account
— just like me.

"Anyway, last Monday night we
really lived it up. I went all the way
for the celebration — table wines and
everything, the best cuts of meat, the
works.

When the party was over, J.D. said,
and when he and his mama got home,
they looked at one another on this
memorable night, then wrapped their
arms around one another.

"Now that everything's set, mama,"
J.D. said, "... now that I've got this
good income, you don't have to work
anymore."

CLAUDIA HILL, THE MOST beautiful person J.D. Hill has ever known,
stopped hugging her son. She moved
back a step, put her palms together
again, looked up again and said:

"Oh, thank you Lord."

Football — EDWARD "BUCKETS" HIRSCH & BUDDY YOUNG

Recalling the Rockpile's "Thunderous Football Hit."
Saturday, August 14, 1977
Phil Ranallo: What's New, Harry?

THIS WAS ON A BEAUTIFUL fall day 30 years ago, a day in 1947 on which the old Buffalo Bills were playing the New York Yankees in an All-America Conference football match at the "Old Rockpile" — War Memorial Stadium.

It was the day Edward "Buckets" Hirsch, a fellow with a Kamikaze bent, made the "Thunderous Football Hit" — the day Claude Henry "Buddy" Young, the victim, wound up impersonating a grease spot.

It happened on a kickoff. Buddy Young, the deep man for the receiving Yankees, took the ball in the vicinity of his goal-line and began running back the first kickoff of his professional football life.

Young, a 5-foot 4 1/2 -inch, 155-pounder blessed with world-class speed, streaked up the middle of the field, eluding tacklers, then bolted to his right toward the sideline.

And now, here came the "hit man" — the only Buffalo defender Young had to beat.

Hirsch, running at top speed, had the angle on Young, who had the throttle wide open and was moving so swiftly he was a blur. Then Buckets Hirsch went airborne — hurled his body at Young. And Buckets didn't miss.

C-r-u-n-c-h!

The sound of the frightening collision was heard in the twenty-five cent seats.

"IT WAS A HEAD TO-HEAD crash," Buddy Young said the other day, as he sipped a bottle of beer in the Turf Club at the Fort Erie Jockey Club. "We banged helmets — and my helmet was split open.

"The terrific hit, by Buckets, sent me flying and I slammed against the players' bench. Now, you won't believe this, but it's true. When I began to gather myself up, I happened to look down at my feet and both my shoelaces were broken.

"That's right — Hirsch hit me with such a shot that the impact busted my shoelaces.

"Elmer Hirsch was one tough son of a gun on the football field. I know he's a police officer here, with the Amherst Police Dept. Next time you see Buckets, say hello for me.

"Tell him I'll always remember that shot he gave me. It was a helluva hit. I remember the hit, and can feel it, every time I come to Buffalo — or think of Buffalo."

BUDDY YOUNG IS LIVING proof that they don't pay off in this world according to size — even in the violent world of pro football. Despite his physical dimensions, Buddy was a top-quality pro halfback for nine years.

And, prior to turning pro, he made it as one of the all-time great college halfbacks at Illinois.

"I always regarded my small size as a plus for me," Young said. "My size — plus the things I'd hear people say about guys my size — gave me added incentive to succeed.

"A lot of the people who talked to me, before I went to Illinois, had what I call the 'they say' syndrome. What I'd hear from them would be something like this:

" 'You know, Buddy, they say that track sprinters and small people — like you — simply can't make it in big-time college football, or professional football.'

"When I'd hear that, I'd say to myself: 'Who the hell are they?' "

IN 1944, BUDDY YOUNG showed the "they say" folks a thing or two by enrolling at Illinois and becoming the first legitimate world-class sprinter to make All-America in football. And he made All-America as a freshman at Illinois.

Young did it by breaking Red Grange's single-season touchdown record at Illinois. Buddy, the little freshman, scored 13 touchdowns that year — and most of the touchdowns came on spectacular long runs.

And what a sprinter Buddy was!

In 1944, while representing Illinois in a track meet in Cleveland, Young set a world record for the 45-yard dash with a clocking of 4.5 seconds.

Young spent the next year, in 1945, in military service. In 1946, with the war over, he returned to college and led the Illinois football team into the Rose Bowl.

THEN, AFTER HIS sophomore season, Young quit college and turned pro for a legitimate reason. He wanted to earn some money so he could support his mother and sisters and brothers.

Buddy wanted to help because he remembered how it was for the Young's on the South Side of Chicago — since he was one of nine children from a fatherless family on welfare.

Young's star glittered in the pros for nine years, five of which he spent in New York.

Pro football, in Young's view, hasn't changed much in the 30 years that have passed since he was part of the show.

"Football," he said, "is still running with the ball and blocking, and tackling.

"But there is one major difference," he added, smiling. "The players today make much more money."

For the last eleven years Young has served as a special assistant to Pete Rozelle, commissioner of the National Football League. He has been described as a troubleshooter for the NFL players.

YOUNG TOILS AROUND the year lining up off-season job opportunities for the players, as well as for the underprivileged teenagers who have been graduated from high school in the top 10 percent of their class, and have been accepted to college.

In the Buffalo area, Young works with John Skorupan of the Bills in lining up the jobs.

Friday, Buddy Young took a day off from work and visited the Ft. Erie race track as a guest of Harvey Johnson, one of his Yankee teammates in the '40s.

And if you don't think Young can still run, you should have seen him sprint from the cashier's window after his horse, Mr. Sonny, bounced home a winner in the fourth race.

Young, by the way, had a reason to run.

Mr. Sonny's win price was $168.90.

Football — JACK HORRIGAN

Buffalo Bills PR director passes; considered one of the greatest columns of Phil's career.
Monday, June 4, 1973
Phil Ranallo: What's New, Harry?

AS THE YEARS GO fleeting by and a man grows older and his yesterday's stretch back a long way, he becomes much more aware of the inevitable — the final roll call.

One by one they go, the special people.

Nevertheless, a man is never prepared for the shock of thumbing through a newspaper and stopping at a certain page and finding a special friend gazing at him.

This happened again Sunday morning.

John Patrick (Lefty) Horrigan gazed at me from that newspaper page — Jack Horrigan, one of the most courageous men I have ever known.

Horrigan hand-wrestled Death for seven long years, in a manner I have seen it struggled against by only one other man in my lifetime — the late William S. (Bill) Coughlin, the longtime baseball writer for The Courier-Express.

IT IS A MEASURE of courage that Jack Horrigan fought Death, year after year, and that he won great victories over it, year after year.

To taste the fear of Death, as he did, and to choke it down for 2,500 days and make a fine career, as he did, was a continuing — and extraordinary — act of bravery.

It is incongruous, I know — since Jack Horrigan is dead — but for some reason or other I feel he achieved a victory over Death ... perhaps because he cheated it for so long.

His great struggle brings to mind John Donne's sonnet, the one that starts, "Death be not proud," and ends; "And Death shall be no more; Death, thou shalt die."

JACK HORRIGAN'S opponent, Death, sought him out in the form of cancer. He first met it in 1966, when his case was diagnosed and doctors informed him they didn't expect him to live out the year.

But Jack Horrigan wasn't going to die that fast and leave his adoring wife, Liz, and all those wonderful children — those nine children.

Not Jack Horrigan. So the battle was on.

Jack had the kind of will-power, and faith, that could keep Death up a tree — and he somehow managed to keep it up there for seven years.

Long enough to live and be at the side of one of his sons, Jeremiah, during a trying period in Jerry's life — when the young man's convictions and actions against the war in Southeast Asia landed his name on Page One.

JACK HORRIGAN, the battler, made Page One, too, with one of the most beautiful and touching declarations I have ever heard uttered by a father: "I will remain at Jerry's side; he is my son ... and I love him."

In his short life of 47 years, Jack touched more than his share of the bases — as a sailor in World War II, wire service reporter for United Press, Buffalo Evening News sportswriter, Buffalo hockey Bisons publicity director, American Football League public relations director, and Bills public relations director.

As he touched each of these bases, he made a mark.

But he made his greatest mark in life as a husband and a father. This was a man of principles and ideals. He had all the virtues in abundance.

IN THE LITTLE world of thoroughbred racing, which is a lot like the big world but more pleasant, the quality most honored is something called class.

Class is difficult to define, but racing people recognize and respect it in a horse or in a man.

John Patrick Horrigan — the man Liz Horrigan called "Lefty" — was all class.

He was a man of great faith, an ornament to his parish.

He will be buried Wednesday, but his style lives on in all men of high moral value.

When Jack Horrigan breathed his last breath Saturday, God was there — "Waiting for Lefty."

Football — ROBERT JAMES

Bills great is discovered by Elbert Dubenion.
Tuesday, September 16, 1969
Phil Ranallo: What's New, Harry?

"THE SURPRISE PACKAGE ON this Bills football team, Sam," Honest Harry said, "is the ferocious and fearless kid from Fisk University, Robert James, who Sunday won his way into the hearts of 46,165 Bills rooters by proving he is commander of the club's 'Suicide Corps.'

"James is such a surprise that his name does not appear in the 1969 Bills press-book. No pro club tapped him in the draft. He was discovered long after the draft by Elbert Dubenion, the once-wonderful pass receiver who now toils as a talent scout for the Bills.

"Last June, Dubenion, on a swing through the south, stopped at Nashville and took a look at the 1968 Fisk football movies. The star of the movies was Robert James, a linebacker in college. One thing worried Duby — did the kid possess the speed to be a pro?

"DUBENION CONTACTED JAMES and found out.

" 'The boy showed me he had plenty of speed,' Dubenion said yesterday. 'I clocked him at 40 yards three times, and each time he ran it a tenth of a second faster.'

"Then Duby grinned.

" 'I should have let him run it a few more times,' Duby said, 'Maybe he'd have broken the world record.'

"Dubenion got James' signature on a Bills' contract that same day — in the last week of June, the day after the 1969 Bills press book already had rolled at the printers.

"When you watch Robert James in action, Sam, you'd never dream he was a product of a school in which the girls outnumber the boys by 2-to-1 — 600 to 309.

"I DON'T KNOW WHAT THE curriculum is at Fisk, but I wouldn't be astonished to learn that the Nashville school conducts a course in mayhem — and that mayhem is Robert James' major.

"The 'Suicide Corps,' of course, is that group of specialists who reportedly feast on raw meat and are sent into the game to participate in plays on which the Bills surrender the football on kickoffs and punts.

"Members of the 'Suicide Corps,' they say, are never fed the day before, or the day of, a game – for a reason.

"They are kept hungry so they will have great desire to bag and devour their prey — the enemy who happens to gather in a kickoff or a punt.

"They are labeled the 'Suicide Corps' because they are expected to 'give up their lives,' if necessary, in their attempts to get – and eat — the man with the ball.

"ROBERT JAMES IS THE FIRST member of a Bills 'Suicide Corps'- since the celebrated wild man, Henry Rivera, who while attempting to commit suicide may kill the man with the ball and wind up being charged with murder.

"Sunday, against the Jets, Robert James didn't literally kill any of the world champions. But James did satisfy his voracious appetite.

"James 'ate' Jet after Jet after Jet.

"The fierce fledgling footballer from Fisk 'ate' so much that coach John Rauch, if he expects James to be hungry for the Oilers next Sunday, had better keep the kid away from the dinner table all week.

"Against the Jets, Robert James

had an amazing 'eating' percentage of .714.

"SUNDAY, THE BILLS KICKED off and punted a total of nine times — four kickoffs, five punts. On two punts, the Jets allowed the ball to roll dead. Thus, Jet kickoff and punt receivers were fair game seven times — and on five of those occasions James 'ate' the Jet with the ball. So James was 5 for 7 — a percentage of .714.

"One of Robert's 'meals' was a fantastic soup to nuts job. It came on a punt. As the 177-pound James tore down the field, a Jet blocker hit him amidships.

"James kept his feet, knocked the blocker to the ground, pivoted, darted about 10 yards to his right, and devoured the Jet with the ball — Mike Battle.

"Off the football field, James does not appear to be a fellow who feasts on athletic violence. He is shy and usually speaks only when spoken to — and he wears horn-rimmed glasses.

"In action, he wears contact lenses.

"WHEN I LEARNED THIS, I ASKED Jack Horrigan how James manages not to lose the lenses when he meets foe on one of his patented head-on crunches.

" 'I don't know,' Horrigan said. 'Maybe he shuts his eyes an instant before impact.'

"Robert James is a deeply religious young man, Sam. Before meals, he bows his head and blesses himself.

"The kid, you might say, is a holy terror.

"It's my guess that Elbert Dubenion's discovery — Robert James — will soon become the 'people's choice' ... even with O.J. in our midst.

"Duby is understandably proud."

Football — RON JAWORSKI

The "Polish Rifle" is truly one in a million.
Wednesday, February 9, 1977
Phil Ranallo: What's New, Harry?

WELL, THEY'VE NAMED Bruce Jenner, the Olympic decathlon champion, winner of the James E. Sullivan Memorial Trophy — labeled him "the outstanding amateur athlete in the United States in 1976."

And I disagree.

If the Amateur Athletic Union had sent me a ballot, I would have cast my vote for Ron Jaworski, the young fellow from Lackawanna who plays quarterback for the Los Angeles Rams — whenever Pat Haden and James Harris don't.

I think Jaworski got robbed by the AAU.

What's that? You say Ron Jaworski wasn't eligible for the Sullivan award ... that he isn't an amateur, that he gets paid.

Listen, friend, last season Jaworski made less money, as a Ram quarterback, than most of the "name" amateurs got paid for doing whatever their "thing" is — football, basketball, tennis, track and field, soccer, lawn bowling.

Jaworski's Ram paycheck was $29,700, which in the world of sports these days is nickels and dimes. I mean, most college quarterbacks would refuse to throw a spiral for that kind of chicken feed.

But, back to the Sullivan award ...

I can't figure out, for the life of me, how the AAU could declare Jaworski ineligible. Why, I'm willing to wager a week's pay that in 1976 — the year the award is for — Jenner made more money than Jaworski.

ALTHOUGH JENNER HAS stated that "reports of instant riches after my decathlon victory were simply built up by the media," I believe it's safe to say that Bruce did not exactly go hungry when he took off his track suit.

Right after the Olympics last summer, Jenner signed a neat contract with the American Broadcasting Co., as a sports commentator for one thing.

And you know what those television network sports commentators get paid. There probably isn't one of them who makes less than $29,700.

Let me interject here that I'm not intimating the network sports guys are overpaid — even Paul Maguire, the super critic.

WHAT INTRIGUES ME about Ron Jaworski, and why I feel he should have been eligible for the Sullivan award, is this:

Jaworski played football in 1976 for peanuts, for $29,700, at his own insistence.

Jaworski, before the 1976 NFL season began, was offered a tremendous raise in pay by Carroll Rosenbloom, owner of the Rams, and Ron turned the raise down!

Last summer, Jaworski, whose $29,700-a-year contract had expired after the 1975 season, was called into Rosenbloom's office — and the Ram owner offered Ron a $700,000 five-year contract.

That's $140,000 a year, quite a jump from the $29,700 Jaworski was making.

JAWORSKI TOLD ROSEN-BLOOM he'd sign the contract only if it was included in the fine print that he was the Rams' starting quarterback.

Rosenbloom said no and Jaworski refused to sign.

So Jaworski played out his option in 1976, settled for $29,700, minus 10 percent —turned his back on $140,000!

In my view, Jaworski, by refusing a $110,300 increase in pay, retained his amateur status.

The "Polish Rifle" is one in a million, perhaps the most extraordinary athlete in the history of sports.

Jaworski wants to play football more than he wants money!

Amazing!

NOW, TAKE BRUCE JENNER. After the Olympic Games last summer, did Jenner keep throwing the javelin and discus, keep high jumping, keep pole vaulting, keep running the hurdles and the mile?

No, he didn't.

Shortly after leaving the long-jump pit, Jenner proved he was no amateur.

Bruce chatted with the ABC people, made that sports commentator deal, and flew out to Hollywood and talked with the film moguls, who lined up a screen test that could make Jenner the next Tarzan, or something.

What Jenner did was start to make big money.

Jenner made poor Ron Jaworski look like a coin-collector.

BUT WHEN IT COMES TIME to select the Sullivan award winner, as it did the other day, Jenner is declared the winner and Jaworski isn't even eligible.

I don't understand.

Jaworski turned down $140,000 and took $29,700. How could a guy possibly do more than Jaworski did to prove, in the eyes of the AAU, that he's an amateur?

Now, I'll admit that "The Polish Rifle," by doing what he did, certainly failed to convince people that he is a smart quarterback.

But he certainly convinced everybody that he's an amateur.

He should have won the Sullivan award.

Also, the Dunlop award, come to think of it.

Football — JACK KEMP

Kemp, president of the AFL Players Association, negotiates players'
contract with ease.
Friday, July 12, 1968
Phil Ranallo: What's New, Harry?

"WHO IS JACK KEMP?"
That question was asked the other day —with tongue in cheek, of course — by John Gordy, the Detroit Lions guard who is president of the National Football League Players Association.

Gordy made his unkind and un-called-for query when Kemp, president of the American Football League Players Association, announced the AFL players "would not support the NFL strike, had no thought of strik-ing, and deplored such action."

Wednesday, John Gordy — along with millions of pro football fans — found out who Jack Kemp really is. They learned that Kemp is much more than a quarterback for the Bills.

JACK KEMP, THEY LEARNED, is the extraordinary, 32-year-old gen-tleman-businessman-athlete who sat down with the AFL club owners and negotiated a two-year contract that satisfied all concerned — players and owners.

They learned that the American Football League, although still per-haps a year or two away from reaching parity with the NFL on the field of football, is eons ahead of the NFL in the field of management-player rela-tions — thanks to Jack Kemp.

Class, they say, will tell — and it has told with Kemp. He negotiated with the owners peacefully and quietly. He gave a little and took a little — and won a fine contract for the players he represents.

KEMP'S APPROACH WAS THE direct opposite of that employed by Gordy, who has done considerable raving and ranting. Gordy's noise has alienated the NFL club owners and is chiefly responsible for the NFL im-passe.

The NFL strike was called because of the failure of Gordy and the own-ers to agree on a single phase of the pension plan — an item that wouldn't affect the players until almost the year 2000.

To base a strike on such a minor item is ridiculous. The owners have refused to yield for a sound reason, however. If they back off now, they know that in the future they must meet all player demands to avoid strikes.

Gordy and the association's attorney, the ambitious Daniel Schulman, have painted all the players and all the own-ers into an embarrassing corner.

WEDNESDAY, WHEN THE AFL owners and players reached agree-ment, Kemp attributed consummation of the contract to a lack of publicity.

"We've been quiet purposely," Kemp explained, "When you make definite and extravagant public statements, you lose your flexibility."

In other words, Kemp and the AFL owners worked out their differences — had their family quarrel — in private, behind locked doors.

Gordy and the NFL owners on the other hand, are street-fighting. Their family quarrel is public — and a fam-ily squabble is difficult to settle while the neighbors are watching.

BACK TO KEMP, THOUGH. Jack Kemp, the man, is so remarkable that his AFL playing colleagues three years ago elected him their president ... de-spite the fact he is a political scientist who leans to the right.

Kemp backed Barry Goldwater in 1964, lined up with Ronald Reagan in

1966, and currently is in Richard Nixon's corner — and Goldwater, Reagan and Nixon are hardly the types you'd expect to find as presidents of unions.

Kemp, the union leader, stated his position — as president the AFL players — a couple of months ago.

"We went to the National Labor Relations Board for certification," Kemp stated, "only to protect ourselves from outside unions which were making overtures.

"WE ARE NOT A HARD-LINE organization. We are trying to negotiate with the owners in an atmosphere of amity and mutual cooperation.

"Still, in a $75-million business, the players deserve ... yes, demand ... that they be represented in areas of common interest such as salaries, pensions and general working agreements.

"But I can assure you that the AFL Players Association does not take the egalitarian, orthodox, socialistic approach to negotiations.

"We are more interested in progress than publicity."

JACK KEMP AND THE AFL players made progress Wednesday — with not much more than a peep from anyone.

So —

"Who is Jack Kemp?"

It's this corner's guess that Jack Kemp is a man the National Football League, at the moment, needs desperately.

Football — JACK KEMP RETIRES

Football star enters political arena.
Wednesday, March 25, 1970
Phil Ranallo: What's New, Harry?

TWO BUFFALO BILLS COACHES — Joe Collier and John Rauch — dedicated themselves to finding a man to replace him ... and failed. A battalion of quarterbacks, both fledglings and veterans, gave it their all in attempts to win his job ... and failed.

Almost Sunday after Sunday, a stadium full of "experts" abused him and ridiculed him and maligned him, in all-out efforts to get him to flea from the park ... and failed.

Neither those two coaches, nor that battalion of rival quarterbacks, nor those thousands of grandstand quarterbacks — nor the critical sports writers — could make this man run up the white flag.

He was the indomitable quarterback — the quarterback who would not die.

THE BILLS PERFORMANCE GRAPH, during the man's eight-year presence, resembled an inverted "V." The Bills were not too much when the man arrived in 1962 — and they are not too much today, as he departs.

In between, though, there were the glory years ... and anyone who elects to point a finger at the Buffalo Bill most responsible for those years of achievement and triumph must point at this man — Jack Kemp.

Abuse and ridicule often become monkeys on the backs of professional athletes. They can't live with it. Ted Williams, for example, expectorated, Roger Maris shouted and pouted. Jack Kemp took it all, unfair and unkind as it was, like a man — without so much as a whimper.

FOR SOME STRANGE AND unexplainable reason, Kemp — even in the years of glory — was treated as if he were the villain with the black top hat and handlebar mustache demanding the rent-money from the fair maiden.

A warm night in late August of 1967 comes to memory — the night the Bills played the Philadelphia Eagles in an exhibition game.

In the middle of the fourth quarter, Kemp trotted into the game in relief of the injured Tom Flores, and a giant segment of the War Memorial Stadium crowd of 41,488 gave Jack a shameful and merciless — and totally undeserved — greeting.

It was a demonstration which would have cut the heart out of a lesser man, shattered him emotionally, rendered him totally useless.

It did not do these things to Kemp.

ON THE FIRST PLAY, KEMP — with the boos and the hoots and the cries of derision still ringing in his ears — fired the ball 50 yards in the air ... to Elbert Dubenion. The play was good for 64 yards and a touchdown.

After the game, Kemp, asked to comment on the treatment the fans had given him, said:

"It hurt a little ... but I understand. It's the nature of the game of football."

That was the gentleman's way of putting it — Jack Kemp's way.

Jack Kemp, on the football field, was the complete professional; a man who did his job to the best of his ability; a man who understood the fickleness of the pro football fan.

JACK KEMP IS A MAN I admire.

He is a man of intelligence and high values — values that go far beyond his next paycheck, his next skiing adventure.

He is a man with considerable awareness of the world in which we live.

He is a man who played the violent game of football and battled fiercely to win, but always left the brutality behind when he stepped off the field.

Being a sports writer who often was critical of him, I will always be grateful for that.

I wish Jack Kemp good luck in his new venture — his venture into the political arena.

Football — VINCE LOMBARDI

Packers coach steps down after they defeat Oakland Raiders in
Super Bowl II.

Saturday, February 3, 1968

Phil Ranallo: What's New, Harry?

VINCENT T. LOMBARDI, the extraordinary man who scaled and planted his flag on professional football's highest mountain, has taken that "long, hard look" at himself and has stepped aside — stepped off the football field.

It was, perhaps, the last thing he wanted to do.

Plotting the Sunday afternoon wars ... pacing the sidelines ... calling the shots from football's front-line trenches ... violently tugging at his trousers in the heat of combat ... have been Lombardi's life.

But he has given up this life, voluntarily and at a time when he has stated ... and most certainly believes in his heart ... that "The history of the Packers is not in its past, but in its future."

WHY HAS LOMBARDI stepped aside?

Was the role of wearing two hats at Green Bay — as head coach and general manager — getting to be too much for him?

Hardly. Nothing is too much for men of Lombardi's fiber and makeup and mold.

Then why?

It could be that Lombardi stepped off the football field because he is a man of deep feeling and deep emotion ... a man of complete dedication — a dedication that was transmitting to too many people the wrong picture of the real Vince Lombardi.

IT IS POSSIBLE THAT Lombardi, after taking that "long, hard look," actually liked what he saw — but disliked ... and probably was hurt deeply ... by what he suspected other people

saw.

Lombardi's insatiable appetite for victory ... his declaration that "victory isn't the only thing; it is everything" ... his habit of calling a spade a spade — little by little began transmitting that wrong picture.

A large segment of the masses colored Lombardi ruthless, discompassionate, arrogant, disrespectful of the conquered — as he was colored a year ago when, in all sincerity, he made the bold and bald statement that the best in the AFL did not measure up to the best in the NFL.

THE FACT THAT THE public's picture of him disturbed Lombardi became evident this season — particularly after his club's Super Bowl victory — when he turned diplomat, politician ... and refused to say almost anything.

Lombardi, in that post-game interview on Super Sunday, was the epitome of sweetness and gentility. He did not resemble Vince Lombardi, the football coach who wants to win more than anything else.

Once, a long time ago, Lombardi said: "Football is a hard and tough game — and you must be hard and tough to win."

On Super Sunday, he was soft and tender.

THE GUESS HERE IS that Vincent T. Lombardi, after taking that "long, hard look" at himself, was intimidated by what he suspected a large segment of the masses saw — so, Thursday, he stepped aside.

His decision to step aside leaves a giant hole in pro football. No man in the history of the game has made such an impact on the "Violent World" — not even Paul Brown, the one-time miracle worker at Cleveland.

It is also the guess here that Lombardi will not be comfortable seated behind a desk in the general manager's office — and, in a year or two or three, will find another mountain to scale.

HE MAY FIND THAT mountain in New York — as coach of the Giants or the Jets. Lombardi is the kind of man who can't help but relish the challenge of scaling another mountain.

But he won't accept the challenge until he has proved his recent statement, his statement that "The history of the Packers is not in its past, but in its future."

Let the Packers win a couple more titles, under their new boss, Phil Bengtson, and Lombardi will feel free to search for that new mountain.

If this all comes to pass, Lombardi will find that new mountain and will be back where he belongs — on the football field.

Football — NFL - AFL MERGER

Phil believes the NFL - AFL merger is a bad move by owners.
Wednesday, March 18, 1970
Phil Ranallo: What's New, Harry?

"WHEN A GUY MAKES A MIS-TAKE, Sam, he usually tries to correct it, if afforded the opportunity to do so," Honest Harry said, "unless, that is, he's extraordinarily light-headed, due to absence of the substance that's supposed to fill the space between his ears — gray matter.

"Now, I certainly don't want to charge with being light-headed those 26 poor souls — or, in this particular case, those 26 rich souls — who happen to own the 26 teams In the National Football League.

"But what can I do? I've got no alternative.

"At the moment, those 26 light-headed rich souls are laughing and living it up in Hawaii, frolicking on the beaches of Waikiki.

"To paraphrase what that television announcer says in that anti-cigarette smoking commercial: 'Why are these 26 owners laughing?'

"THESE 26 OWNERS — RALPH WILSON and Wellington Mara, Lamar Hunt and Art Modell, and the rest of them, along with their wizard, Pete Rozelle — have made a monumental mistake.

"They have killed a rivalry that was unmatched in the long history of all sports — the red-blooded rivalry that existed between the NFL and the now-out-of-business AFL.

"It was a rivalry that bred millions of new pro football fans — including women and little girls.

"Thanks to the rivalry, customers flocked to the parks as never before, enabling the owners to fill their treasure chests to overflowing.

"Thanks to the rivalry, the television networks became pawns in the hands of the owners, enabling the wizard, Pete Rozelle, and his AFL counterpart to come up with those incredibly lucrative teevee contracts.

"THE OWNERS' BLUNDER FIRST BECAME evident 15 months ago, when the Jets astounded the Colts in the Super Bowl. Fans by the millions suddenly realized that the days of this matchless rivalry were numbered.

"Full impact on the enormity of the mistake hit home last Super Sunday, when the Chiefs clobbered the Vikings, and everybody knew that something extra-special had come to an end — because the AFL died with that great victory.

"It would be quite a task to locate a pro football fan — either pro-NFL or pro-AFL — who would not admit that stripping the AFL of its identity will cost the sport a good chunk of flavor and appeal.

"THOUSANDS OF VOICES HAVE BEEN raised — starting with the voice of Angelo Coniglio of Amherst, a champion of the AFL and a man of common sense — in a common plea to the 26 owners to correct their mistake and retain the identity of the AFL for the good of the game.

"But the 26 owners — most of whom think of the fans last — are too busy to hear the plea.

"The owners are too busy alienating the fans. They are too busy treating the fans as if the fans were their personal suckers by constantly raising ticket prices and by making exhibition games part of their season-ticket package.

"A pro football fan — in the opinion of most of the 26 owners — is a guy or gal who is lucky he or she has a ticket.

"THE 26 OWNERS REFUSE TO TUNE in on the fans' wavelength, refuse to listen to the fans' plea that they would prefer two leagues with separate identities.

"Instead, the 26 owners — Ralph Wilson and Wellington Mara, Lamar Hunt and Art Modell, and the wizard, Pete Rozelle — play in 'their' Waikiki sandbox and wrestle with giant problems such the shape of the ball, et cetera.

"The death of the great NFL-AFL rivalry isn't so much as mourned by the owners.

"They act as if there is a law that professional football has to be the No. 1 sport forever.

"So they do nothing for the fans — except abuse them on occasion.

"In my opinion, Sam, the 26 National Football League owners — Ralph Wilson and Wellington Mara and the rest of them — are a bunch of ding-a-lings."

Football — GERRY PHILBIN AND BILL MAZER

Philbin recalls his college days at UB.
Saturday, June 28, 1969
Phil Ranallo: What's New, Harry?

GERRY PHILBIN, ONE OF JOE NAMATH'S teammates, could be in serious trouble as soon as word gets back to Pete Rozelle. Philbin, the University of Buffalo's gift to the New York Jets, spent a good chunk of Friday afternoon in Dennis Brinkworth's Saratoga.

The Saratoga is a Delaware Ave. pub with a horse-racing motif ... and Philbin, throughout his stay in the Saratoga, was surrounded by "unsavory characters" — sports writers and sportscasters.

Philbin was in town to speak at a testimonial dinner, in the Statler Hilton, for an intimate friend — Kevin Brinkworth, the handsome, young attorney with whom Gerry played football with at UB.

Brinkworth is aspiring to political office in November, as a councilman-at-large.

"I just hope I don't jinx Kevin," Philbin said, grinning. "All my visits to Buffalo the last five years, as a Jet, have been in vain. The Bills have beaten us every time."

THE JETS ALL-LEAGUE DEFENSIVE end, after the newsmen had picked his brain on the sports story of the year — the Joe Namath story — got to reminiscing about his days at UB.

"Until my senior year at UB," Philbin said, "I didn't think I had a chance to make it as a pro. I just didn't think I had the ability. Maybe it was because of my size. I weighed only 195 then.

"I remember standing in War Memorial Stadium, near the tunnel, Sunday after Sunday, and watching the Bills jog on and off the field. I'd see Cookie Gilchrist and I'd marvel at his size.

"And Gilchrist's a back! I'd say to myself. He's one of the smaller ones.

"So I thought I had no chance.

"But one man changed my thinking — Bill Mazer.

"Bill Mazer provided me with incentive. He sold me on myself as a football player. He was like a father to me.

"DURING MY LAST TWO YEARS AT UB, a day never went by that Bill didn't talk to me — either on the football field, or in the dressing room, or on the telephone.

"One night, in my junior year, right after we'd completed the football season, Mazer picked me up in his car and drove me to Ken Stoller's health club, which was on Genesee St. then.

"I started lifting weights that night, under Stoller's guidance. And an amazing thing happened after working with the weights for four months. I put on 35 pounds — got up to 230.

"When I reported for spring practice in April, a lot of guys — after looking at my new build — laughed. They figured I wouldn't be able to get out of my own way because of the added weight.

"But I amazed them, as well as myself. I was actually faster ... and much stronger. You know what happened then. The rest of the UB players stampeded to Ken Stoller's place.

"I GUESS I HAD A PRETTY GOOD senior season, because when it was over a member of the Bills staff approached me and offered me a thousand dollars to sign.

"The thousand sounded terrific, but I decided to wait until I consulted Mazer.

"When I told Bill about it, he advised me not to sign. He told me I'd get a lot more if I waited — and it was good advice.

I waited and was drafted by the Jets — and got a lot more than a thousand.

"I'll always be indebted to Bill Mazer. I've got to be. There's a chance I wouldn't be a pro today if Bill Mazer hadn't been there to encourage me and to keep driving me — and to take me to Ken Stoller's place.

"Why, Bill Mazer even kept me in clothes when I was at UB. He used to give me all his old sports jackets — sports jackets that were just like new."

THE TALK WANDERED BACK TO the Joe Namath story. "I talked to Namath the other day," Philbin said, "and I'm optimistic he'll be there July 12th, when we open camp."

A big grin creased Philbin's face.

"I've got a special interest in Namath," he said. "I own some shares in his new business — Broadway Joe's, the short-order restaurant chain he's opening. So he's got to play to protect my Investment."

Philbin, incidentally, is in the restaurant business himself. His Long Island supper club — "The Goal Post" — had its grand opening June 4, the night before Namath announced his retirement.

Philbin laughed again.

"When the Namath story broke, I got a peculiar feeling," he said, "because I'd invited Pete Roselle to my grand opening."

Football — JOHNNY RODGERS

Outstanding college football player can't avoid off-field issues.
Sunday, November 26, 1972
Phil Ranallo: What's New, Harry?

WHEN A FOOTBALL PLAYER BECOMES a celebrity, he plays the game in a goldfish bowl — and he also lives in one. Anything he does, on or off the field, receives a considerable amount of attention.

No one knows this better than Johnny Rodgers, Nebraska's marvelous all-purpose back.

Rodgers, at the moment, is whirling around in the eye of a hurricane of controversy — a hurricane generated by his off-the-field wrong-doings and by the pontificating of moralists, whose objective is to deny him the Heisman Trophy.

The Heisman Trophy is the award that is presented annually to the "outstanding college football player" in the land.

Rodgers stands head-and-shoulders above the field ... despite his lackluster Thanksgiving Day performance against Oklahoma, a game in which he seemed to be carrying the weight of the world on his back — which, in a way, he is.

RODGERS IS A YOUNG MAN WHO HAS made mistakes ... and he has been paying the price for more than two years. His mistakes, his scrapes with the law, have polarized conservative moralistic Nebraskans.

A segment of the Nebraska press has dedicated itself to picturing Rodgers as sort of a Baby-Face Nelson in football togs.

Rodgers' trouble started when he was an 18-year-old freshman at Nebraska — when few people beyond the city limits of Lincoln knew who he was.

Rogers committed a crime. He and two other youths held up a gas sta-tion, a robbery that netted $90. A year later, they were caught and Rodgers admitted his guilt.

He was put on probation for two years, a penalty that denied the privilege of driving a car.

SIX MONTHS LATER, HE WAS AT A party with a teammate, Rich Glover, the Cornhuskers' All-America middle guard. Glover's girl wanted to go back home for some reason, and Rodgers drove her.

He ran a red light and was nabbed by the police.

While awaiting trial for driving with a suspended license, Rodgers was riding with a friend who was speeding 90 mph. The police stopped the car, thought they smelled marijuana — and Rodgers was held on suspicion of possessing the weed.

It was a bum rap, and the possession charge was dropped for lack of a shred of evidence.

Then Rodgers' trial came up on the probation violation offense and the running of the red light — and he was dealt a 30-day sentence.

RODGERS APPEALED AND HAS not yet served the sentence. If his appeal is denied, the hope here is that Johnny Rodgers will serve his 30 days in a cell with something to fondle — the Heisman Trophy.

Rodgers is sorry for his sins. He has tried to make amends by spending a large share of his spare time visiting schools and hospitals and telling boys to stay on the straight and narrow.

Bob Devaney, the Nebraska coach, has been Rodgers' No. I defender — a role that has put him in a bad light in the eyes of thousands of Cornhusker loyalists.

Pressure was brought to bear on Devaney to throw Rodgers off the team after each of the three incidents — the gas-station heist, the red-light running and the bad marijuana rap.

But Devaney wouldn't budge. He remained in Rodgers' corner.

"THE GAS STATION THING HAPPENED before Johnny joined the varsity," Devaney says, adding that he has paid that debt with two years of probation. "And I didn't think I should help ruin a kid's life by throwing him off the team for driving with a suspended license ... or for riding, as a passenger, in a speeding car."

Devaney also thinks that Rodgers deserves the Heisman Trophy because he is the "best college football player in the country."

The moralists, though, including New York columnists Dick Young and Gene Ward, don't agree. They regard Rodgers as ineligible for the award and apparently want the Heisman given to the best football player in the land who has never done anything wrong ... or at least never been caught.

Football — ED RUTKOWSKI

"The Gallant Warrior" would play any position necessary.
Wednesday, August 27, 1969
Phil Ranallo: What's New, Harry?

TIME RUNS OUT ON EVERY-ONE. Monday morning, unfortunately, time ran out on a spirited athlete who may have been the most remarkable Buffalo Bill in the 10 year history of the club — Eddie Rutkowski.

For six years — almost from the moment he signed with the Bills in 1963 — the sword of Damocles hung over Rutkowski's head.

For six years he was in imminent danger of being cut.

Somehow, though — for six years — Eddie Rutkowski managed to escape with his professional football life.

Monday he did not escape. The sword fell dead-center.

EDDIE RUTKOWSKI IS A PER-FECT example of what a person can accomplish if he has the desire and the courage, the determination and the dedication, the esprit de corps and the burning ambition to succeed.

Young boys and young men on the verge of giving up and throwing in the towel should research Eddie Rutkowski's pro football career.

In 1963, when he was graduated from Notre Dame, Rutkowski was among the unwanted. Both the NFL and AFL passed him up in the draft.

The Bills finally signed him as a free agent. Rutkowski got his tryout with the Bills and made the club.

HIS SPOT ON THE SQUAD, HOWEVER, was never secure. Year after year, when cutdown time approached, the Bills coaches would always look Rutkowski's way first — with cleavers in hand.

They'd swing the cleavers and they'd miss, and Rutkowski would be a Bill for another year.

Four or five years ago, when Lou Saban was swinging the cleaver, Rutkowski appeared to be doomed.

Saban, just prior to an exhibition game, announced publically that Rutkowski was getting his last chance in this particular game.

"IF EDDIE DOESN'T SHOW ME something," Saban said, " ... if he doesn't prove to me that he belongs, I am going to cut him because I'll have no choice."

You know the rest.

Rutkowski showed Saban considerably more than something.

Rutkowski, with do-or-die pressure on him, made two or three sensational catches of passes flung by Daryle Lamonica, who obviously had compassion for his one-time Notre Dame teammate.

Also, Eddie made a nifty runback with a punt or kickoff.

RUTKOWSKI'S PERFORMANCE WAS the high spot of game, from the Bills' viewpoint — and Eddie's job was saved.

Saban, if he had cut Rutkowski after that ball game, would have been run out of town.

For six years, Eddie Rutkowski was a football "general practitioner." He had no specialty.

For six years he was the end — also the flanker back, running back, safety man, punt-return man, kickoff-return man and quarterback.

When the Bills were very good, from 1964 through 1966 and when they were very bad, especially last year, Eddie Rutkowski did everything for this club but hurt it.

LAST YEAR, WHEN THE BILLS were at their worst, Rutkowskl was at his best. When the Bills quarterback corps was decimated, he stepped into the breach and did an adequate job.

John Rauch will never forget Rutkowski.

Eddie is the guy who came within an eyelash — one yard — of pulling the rug from beneath the powerful Oakland Raiders late last season when the Raiders were led by Rauch.

The Bills voted Rutkowski the most valuable player of the 1968 club. I'll remember him as the most courageous.

IF EDDIE RUTKOWSKI IS THROUGH as a professional football player, there is no need for alarm. He is certain to be a rousing success at whatever he chooses to do.

He can't help but be a success. The strains of the Notre Dame victory march have never stopped ringing in his ears.

Eddie Rutkowski is a political science major. If he chooses politics, he could be mayor of this town one day.

Football — GALE SAYERS

The doors of the Hall of Fame open for Gale Sayers.
Tuesday, January 18, 1977
Phil Ranallo: What's New, Harry?

ON A NOVEMBER DAY in 1968, they carried Gale Sayers off on a stretcher in Wrigley Field. His knee was wrecked, bent 90 degrees sideways. Several of his teammates became nauseous when they looked.

The great running back of the Chicago Bears had suffered what the physicians called a "terrible triad" — two torn ligaments and a ruptured cartilage on his right knee.

The medical men told Sayers he would never play again.

But Sayers, the most spectacular running back in the history of professional football — until O.J. Simpson came along —put the lie to the medics' dour declaration.

Gale Sayers came back, and the torturous route he took coming back is a profile in courage.

Shortly after he underwent surgery on the battered knee, they handed Sayers a pair of crutches, but he refused to use them. Instead, he flung himself into an almost around-the-clock therapy program.

For the five weeks his leg was in the cast, Sayers repeatedly flexed the muscles in his knee — at the cost of excruciating pain — to reduce atrophy.

When the cast was removed, he began exercising three times a day, an hour at a crack — on a stationary bike. He lifted weights daily, with emphasis on the leg press. He even bought his own whirlpool.

LATER, HE STARTED running outdoors. For two months, he ran and ran and ran, but always straight ahead — never cutting or shifting his weight. Then one day, six months after the doctors had told him his career was over, Gale put himself to the test.

Sayers, with a football nestled in the crook of his right arm, ran and cut to his left. No pain. Then he cut to his right. No pain.

Then he ran straight ahead at full speed, slammed on the brakes by planting his weight on his right leg, and pushed off to his left. No pain.

It was the happiest day of Sayers' life.

The knee was sound. He was running a la Gale Sayers again, with the cutting and darting and fancy maneuvers that made his style a thing of beauty on the football field.

SAYERS CAME BACK IN that 1969 season and, with a Chicago club that lost 13 of 14 games, won the NFL rushing title with 1,032 yards — and cemented his position as the finest all-purpose back in NFL history.

His five-year "stats," after the 1969 season, were astonishing:

— Rushed 4,866 yards in 935 carries for an average of 5.1 yards,

— Caught 111 passes for 1,313 yards, an average of 11.7 yards.

— Returned 91 kickoffs for 2,781 yards, an average of 30.6 yards.

— Returned 28 punts for 391 yards, an average of 14 yards.

— Completed four passes for 111 yards.

— Scored 56 touchdowns, 39 on rushes, 9 on pass receptions, 6 on kick-off returns, and 2 on punt returns.

— Totaled 9,462 yards for the five years, a season average of 1,892.

UNFORTUNATELY, THAT 1969 season was Sayers' last hurrah. He injured the other knee in a 1970 pre-season game and was never the same again. He appeared briefly in two games in 1970, and two in 1971, then quit.

Although Sayers' comeback was limited to one fleeting season, it was most worthwhile because of the beautiful black-white relationship it cemented between his teammate, Brian Piccolo.

The relationship may have made the world a more understanding place.

AND WHO'LL EVER FORGET Sayers' speech, the one he made at the Chicago team banquet a month before Piccolo died of cancer — after Gale had received an award as "Football's Most Courageous Player."

Sayers said he didn't merit it.

"This award is mine tonight, but it is Brian Piccolo's tomorrow — because I am going to give it to him. I love Brian Piccolo and I'd like all of you to love him, too.

"Tonight, when you hit your knees, please ask God to love him"

Tears streaked down Sayers' cheeks.

All of this comes to mind this morning because Monday the doors of the Football Hall of Fame opened and a special guy walked in — Gale Sayers.

Football — SUPER BOWL III
(Baltimore Colts vs. New York Jets)

This game is regarded as one of the greatest upsets in American sports history.

Monday, January 13, 1969

Phil Ranallo: What's New, Harry?

"THE BUBBLE HAS BEEN BURST, SAM," Honest Harry said. "Broadway Joe Namath, the matchless one, and the magnificent New York Jets gouged a giant hole in the NFL bubble on Super Sunday — and the ear-splitting explosion has been heard around the football world.

"In 60 beautiful football minutes, Broadway Joe, the best quarterback God ever created, and fellows named Matt Snell and George Sauer, Johnny Sample and Randy Beverly, Jim Turner and Jim Hudson, Gerry Philbin and Dave Herman exposed the big, bad, brash NFL bruisers as mere mortals.

"It was learned, when this unforgettable football day was done, that the Baltimore Colts, champions of the entire NFL, put their pants on just like the guys and gals who live in my neighborhood — one hairy leg, or lovely gam, at a time.

"Everybody dresses that way — but the Jets.

"THE REMARKABLE NAMATH AND HIS Jet set performed a miracle in the Orange Bowl — the miracle of cramming footballs down the throats of the Colts, a thousand other NFL coaches and players, and perhaps 50 million heretofore arrogant NFL loyalists.

"It is heart-warming to study the final score, 16-7, and realize that the NFL rooters who put their money where their big mouths were and confidently gave away the 18-1/2 points fell only 28 points short of cashing their bets.

"These NFL people lost their money. But the day wasn't a complete loss for them because they won a considerable amount of humility.

"Let these now-humble NFL people find solace, if they can, with the thought that they will get a shot at revenge in the next Super Bowl, in a mere 365 days.

"It could be worse. It could be leap year.

"IF YOU THINK THE GAME'S OUTCOME was embarrassing for these people, think of most of the poor, pitiful AFL football writers — the ones who abandoned the AFL ship and jumped aboard the Baltimore barge.

"The Jets and the AFL win the battle, but most of the AFL writers 'die' with their boots off. For these typewriter-pounders, being garbed in hairshirts for a year is a small price to pay for treason.

"Namath, if you recall, mentioned these turncoats in his post-season remarks. 'I hope,' the great one said, 'that they eat their pads and pencils.'

"The Courier-Express football writer, by the way — Jim Peters — did not abandon ship, and did not yield to the brainwashing that took place in Miami during the buildup to the game.

"Peters listened to the right guy — Joe Namath.

"THE THING STARTED OUT AS IF the Colts were going to run the Jets right out of the ball park. On the Colt's first play from scrimmage, Earl Morrall threw one of those dinky drop-off passes to John Mackey, and Mackey thundered 19 yards to the Colt 46.

"This was followed by four straight rushes — two each by Tom Matte and Jerry Hill — and, suddenly, Baltimore had a first down on the Jet 31.

"After those five overpowering plays, there weren't many people willing to give a nickel for the Jets' chances.

"Then, though, on the next play, came the game's turning point. Hill took a handoff from Morrall, but Philbin busted through and slammed Hill for a three-yard loss.

"It was the turning point because, for some strange reason, Morrall decided to rip up the Colt game plan. He went to the air and stayed there most of the day — thank heavens!

"THE JETS WON THE BALL GAME early in the second quarter, the fourth time they had the ball. Joe Namath's passing and Matt Snell's running propelled the Jets for 80 yards and a touchdown — a touchdown that ripped the cloak of invincibility from the Colts.

"That touchdown made the Colts doubt themselves. They began to remember what Namath had been saying all week. They began to believe in Joe.

"At the game's end, the Colts were converts.

"So life in the AFL, from this day, on will be beautiful.

"Jim Turner, the Jets' wonderful field-goal man, put it perfectly, Sam. Turner wrapped it all up in one beautiful sentence.

"Turner, with beads of perspiration streaking his cheeks — and with an infectious victory smile on his bright face — said 'I'd like to say to everybody in America — welcome to the American Football League.' "

Football — ERNIE WARLICK

Buffalo Bills football star is cut just three games shy of a pro football pension.
Monday, August 22, 1966
Phil Ranallo: What's New, Harry?

"I'VE BEEN A SPORTS NUT ALL my life, Sam," Honest Harry remarked Saturday night as he and his sidekick watched the Bills maul the Houston Oilers. "But I've got to admit I'm not quite the nut I used to be — because pro sports has gotten too cold, too cruel.

"Take big Ernie Warlick there, for example — a guy who in four years of dedication to the Buffalo Bills won a spot in the heart of every single person who ever passed through the War Memorial Stadium turnstiles.

"There's Ernie Warlick tonight, on television — in civilian clothes, helping Rick Azar do the commentary. And why is he there? He's there because the all-business Bills elected to cut him — three games short of the number he needed to become eligible for a pension.

"IMAGINE THAT, SAM? For four years, Ernie Warlick sweats and bleeds for the Bills — and makes a very important contribution to the team — and when he's three games short of his goal, they cut him down like he was a diseased Dutch elm or something.

"I certainly understand that a pro football team's objective is victory ... and that in pro sports there is very little room for sentiment ... and that if a fellow can't quite cut the mustard he has to go.

"But Ernie Warlick's case is different. Here is a truly remarkable human being. Warlick claims he's 34 — but everybody knows he's closer to 40, particularly his wife and his 20-year-old son.

"HE PLAYED PRO FOOTBALL at his age because he is made of some-thing special — because he elected to tax his huge, aging body to the limits to better his family's lot in life. And these last couple of years, he had to keep hanging in there because it was so close — the pension, I mean.

"You know, Sam, more and more I begin to understand why Lou Saban gave it all up and went to Maryland. Lou is a man with a giant heart — and when be left he sort of gave the impression pro football was getting too hard-hearted.

"I have the feeling that it would have crushed Lou Saban if they had made him draw a big X through Ernie Warlick's name. Maybe Lou left because he didn't want to have to do something like that.

"THAT DAY LAST WEEK — that day Warlick was chopped — Ernie took it like a man. He did not utter one unkind word about the people who chopped him — and the newspapermen kept saying that Ernie Warlick went out like a champion.

"Strong men — such as Ernie Warlick — cry in private."

Football — RALPH WILSON

Honest Harry calls Buffalo Bills owner/founder a
"man of integrity."
Sunday, November 12, 1972

Phil Ranallo: What's New, Harry?

IN THE 13-YEAR EXISTENCE OF the Buffalo Bills, this observer has attempted to play it right down the middle with Ralph Wilson. The owner of the Buffalo Bills has been praised and defended whenever praise or defense seemed in order.

Wilson has been criticized and rocked by this corner, to a degree matched by no one, whenever his deeds seemed to merit criticism or rocking — on Wilson's practice of tying tickets to exhibitions to the sale of season tickets for regular league games, for example.

It is necessary, therefore, to defend Wilson on the "Name the Stadium" question, the problem that was resolved last Tuesday when the County Legislature voted Ralph Wilson to name the Bills new playpen in Orchard Park "Rich Stadium."

Since Ralph Wilson is one of the soundest businessmen I have ever met, he astounded me a couple of weeks back when he offered to pay the county $1.5 million over a 25-year period if the county would name the new facility "Buffalo Bills Stadium."

SOUND BUSINESSMEN DO NOT GIVE AWAY $1.5 million, and Ralph Wilson was offering to do just that — give away $1.5 million.

There was no way Wilson could have benefited — by as much as a dime — from the name "Buffalo Bills Stadium." Unless one questions Wilson's integrity.

The name, "Buffalo Bills Stadium," would have made Wilson proud, naturally, but that would have been his only benefit.

It boggles the mind that anyone would be carried away enough by community spirit — or "be dumb enough," to use Wilson's own words — to surrender $1.5 million without anticipation of some kind of monetary gain.

But Wilson was "dumb enough" for this reason:

He was of the opinion that the name, "Buffalo Bills Stadium," was more identifiable with Buffalo — the heart of this community — than any other name.

Wilson was willing to pay $1.5 million to get the legislature to do what they should have done in the first place without remuneration — give the stadium a name with "Buffalo" in it.

AT FIRST WILSON LEANED toward the name, "Erie County Stadium," as did County Executive Edward V. Regan. Both Wilson and Regan agreed that "Erie County Stadium" would best give the county identification — rather than a commercial name.

Later Wilson changed his mind when it was suggested by this corner, in an Oct. 22 article, that if the objective was to give the community national identification and enhance its image, this could be best done by labeling the facility "Buffalo Bowl" ... or "Buffalo Stadium" ... or "Bills Stadium."

Wilson bought the idea and, a week later, made his $1.5 million offer to the county if the facility were named "Buffalo Bills Stadium."

Ralph was community spirited enough, "dumb" enough to surrender $1.5 million as a token of his appreciation to the community and its people — for their allegiance to his football team for 13 years.

THERE WAS ONE PROVISO IN HIS offer — that he have the right to change or sell the name at a future date, subject to approval by the county. This demand raised the eyebrows of the legislators and the community's anti-Wilson forces.

"If the name 'Buffalo Bills Stadium' is selected, I have no intention of ever changing it," Wilson explained. "But if I ever sold the club, the new owner might want to change the name of the team and therefore, change the name of the stadium."

The legislators refused to consider Wilson's offer and chose "Rich Stadium."

The legislature's action — along with its rejection of Wilson — is being applauded in many quarters.

This corner is not applauding, however, because it refuses to applaud mistakes.

RALPH WILSON CAME OUT OF the "Name the Stadium" debate with a slightly discolored eye — a tarnished image. This is unfortunate. It is also extremely unfair. Ralph Wilson is a man of integrity.

I believe him when he says he would never sell or change the name. He would not stoop to the business of being a stadium name broker.

Tuesday, when the legislators turned their backs on Wilson, they did Ralph a big favor — a $1.5 million favor.

Tuesday Ralph Wilson made a cool $1.5 million — probably more than even J. Paul Getty has ever made in a single day.

I've said this before and I am saying it again because it merits repeating. Ralph Wilson, the man the legislators snubbed, is the man who has done more for this community — from a sports viewpoint — than anyone else.

RALPH WILSON, THE GENTLE-MAN from Detroit, is the man who had the courage to take a big gamble — a two or three million dollar gamble — and bring pro football to Buffalo in 1960.

Wilson's football team was the catalyst in Buffalo's transformation into a big league sports city.

Without Wilson, the pro sports teams of Buffalo — the Bills, the Braves, the Sabres — might never have been.

Naming the 80,000-seat facility in Orchard Park "Buffalo Bills Stadium" — and accepting Wilson's $1.5 million donation — would have been a noble gesture.

"Buffalo Bills Stadium" would have served as a monument to the team and the man who shuffled into Buffalo in 1960, put some sports spice into our lives and put Buffalo on the pro sports map.

Friends — MORT O'SULLIVAN

Athlete and friend devotes his life to helping others.
Tuesday, May 25, 1971
Phil Ranallo: What's New, Harry?

MORT O'SULLIVAN IS CON-STRUCTED along the lines of a Sherman tank. He is six-by-six and could pass as the anchorman of Ireland's tug-o-war team. His large, florid, scrubbed face seems to have the words "Erin go bragh" etched on it.

In his hey-day in the late '40s, when he was dribbling basketballs for Canisius College, nobody ever fooled with Mort ... because fooling with Mort was almost a guarantee of a hurried trip, on a stretcher, to a hospital's emergency room.

Yet, at the moment, O'Sullivan is trembling.

He is shuddering at the thought that he may be compelled to make a speech Wednesday night, when he will be honored by his army of friends at the annual Bishop Fallon High School sports dinner in the Hearthstone Manor.

"I don't know what I'm going to do," O'Sullivan says, in all sincerity. "I doubt I'll be able to stand the embarrassment. I'd do anything to get out of it. Why would they do something like this to me?"

MORE DESERVING MEN HAVE BEEN given testimonials, no doubt, but offhand we can't think of one. Mort O'Sullivan has spent his life surrounded by kids — nine of his own and hundreds of others fortunate enough to have fallen under his wing at Fallon High, where he has served as basketball coach the last 19 years.

He is a Father Flanagan in layman's garb. A boy in trouble is a boy who gets O'Sullivan's undivided attention. He has come to the assistance of young felons — and has guided more than one of them back to the straight and narrow.

He leaves no stone unturned in his efforts to get his young athletes enrolled in colleges — on athletic scholarships — and when he lands one for a poor boy, Mort whistles while he works ... as a security guard on the midnight to 8 a.m. trick at Bell.

O'Sullivan, incidentally, has toiled those ghastly hours all of his married life, but for a reason — so he can be free to do his labor of love as Fallon basketball coach, a position whose remuneration amounts to not much more than nickels and dimes.

"YOU DON'T FOOL KIDS," John McCarthy, head scout of the Buffalo Braves, said the other day. "They're all nuts about Mort, he has a way with kids, he relates to them, gets across to them. I know. Mort has worked with me the last two years at my summer basketball camp.

"Mort's the most humble man I've ever known. Everybody's nuts about him, not only kids.

"One night last week, we were discussing the upcoming O'Sullivan party and a friend of mine asked my wife, Dorothy, how well she knows Mort — and Dorothy, who has been in Mort's company only three or four times, said: 'I know Mort well enough to love him.' "

Then McCarthy spoke of O'Sullivan's relationship with his children, all of whom address their dad as "Mort."

"You have to hear it to appreciate it," McCarthy said. "Mort has a special ring to it when it comes from the lips of his children — a ring of deep respect and affection."

JOE NILAND, WHO RECRUITED O'Sullivan and coached him at Canisius College, said Mort probably was the most popular basketball player in the school's history — with his teammates and with the Memorial Auditorium fans.

"If there ever was a 'people's choice,' " Niland explained, "it had to be Mort O'Sullivan, and this was extraordinary because Mort was a substitute in his last three years as a Canisius player.

"In the late stages of a game, the fans would chant 'We want Mort' ... 'We want Mort' — and when I'd put him in, the place would explode; the fans would raise the roof.

"He was quite a basketball player, too. He had a great freshman season — freshmen were allowed to play on the varsity in those days. Why, he started as a freshman, in the backcourt with my brother, Tom, and that was a terrific Canisius team, if you recall. We had guys like Leroy Chollot, Hank O'Keeffe, Bob MacKinnon and Torn Muller.

"Mort was a fabulous dribbler. MacKinnon remarked the other day that Mort was the first guy in this area to dribble the ball behind his back — and Bobby's right.

"BUT MORT INJURED A KNEE late in his freshman year and it cost him his speed. He never fully recovered from the injury, but he stuck it out for three more full seasons and always was ready when I needed a man to freeze the ball.

"And what a tough guy! He was absolutely the toughest kid I ever coached — fantastic with the dukes. He could put out the lights on a guy with one shot — with either hand. But he never looked for trouble," Niland grinned.

"One day In the gym, one of the guys — a fellow who was six inches taller than O'Sullivan and built like Li'l Abner, got brave and gave Mort a terrific shot with an elbow.

"Well, when Li'l Abner saw the fire in O'Sullivan's eyes as Mort started toward him, all the bravery melted away and he turned and ran for his life. He ran right out of the gym."

A few years ago, there popped up in Canada a racehorse whose appellation fit Mort O'Sullivan to a tee. The horse's name was Good Old Mort — and the steed developed into the best racehorse in Canada, which figured.

Good Old Mort O'Sullivan — the best, truly a beautiful man.

Friends — PANARO'S LOUNGE
Police raid well-known Buffalo restaurant.
Monday, May 22, 1967
Phil Ranallo: What's New, Harry?

"THE NAME OF THIS PLACE is Panaro's Lounge," the man said, puffing on an expensive cigar and studying his inquisitive visitor, "but a lot of people don't call it that any more. A lot of people now refer to it as 'That Restaurant.'

"And it isn't fair," said Mike (Snowball) Panaro, manager of the West Side restaurant which two weeks ago gained notoriety when federal, state and local police raided a stag party and arrested numerous patrons, among them several alleged members of the Cosa Nostra.

"I've managed this restaurant for 20 years, and for 20 years I've concentrated on running a clean, respectable restaurant — a place where you'd be proud to bring your wife for dinner ... a place where you'd be served quality food and be treated as ladies and gentlemen.

"And now this happens.

"I'M HEARTSICK," said Mike (Snowball) Panaro, who acquired his nickname a half-century ago — when he was a young boy, in his pre-teens — when his constant companion was the family dog, a spitz named "Snowball."

"Two days after this thing happened," Mike Panaro went on, "it was early in the afternoon and I had just got out of my car and was walking toward the restaurant. I saw this group of young teenagers — kids of high school age, in front of the place.

"One of the kids was standing right in front of the door — right under the sign that says 'Panaro's Lounge' — and the kid had a violin case in his hands. And then he opened the case and pulled out a toy machine gun — and as he did, another kid standing near the curb, with a camera, took his picture.

"I ASKED THE KIDS WHAT they were doing, and the kid with the toy machine gun said they were taking the picture so they could show it to the other kids in school and have some fun.

"The kid with the violin case said — with this real smart grin on his face — that he was going to tell the kids in school that they had better watch out because he was the new Al Capone's right-hand man.

"When I heard the kid say that," Mike Panaro said, "I was stunned — and I couldn't even scold him. I couldn't scold him because I felt too much like crying.

"THEN, JUST THE OTHER NIGHT, there were these four ladies in the restaurant, seated at a table and having dinner — four ladies who, to my knowledge, had never been in the place before. And all through dinner they giggled.

"Then, after the four ladies had been there an hour or so, one of them called me over to the table and asked me if I was the manager — and when I said I was, she asked me if I knew what time the mobsters were coming in."

Then Mike (Snowball) Panaro took a drag on his big cigar, removed it from his mouth, inspected the one-inch ash, and said:

"The backbone of the business in this place is private parties — stags and banquets, shows and political parties, testimonial dinners ... things like that.

"WE HAD 16 PARTIES IN March,

17 in April and 8 so far this month —
and we had a stack of parties booked
for the rest of this month, and for
June and July. But since the raid, it's
been nothing but cancellation after
cancellation.

"The raid has ruined us.

"You know that sign — the one that
reads 'Sorry, We're Closed … Private
Party' — the one the police and the
papers made so much about after the
raid?

"Well that sign is 15 years old and
I've hung it on the door a thousand
times, every time we've had a party
that has added up to 100 people or
more.

"IN MARCH AND APRIL and so
far this month, I have hung that sign
on the door 20 times.

"The party that ruined us — the
one two weeks ago — was booked on
March 27, and the man who booked
it guaranteed us 150 people, which
meant he had to pay for 150 meals, regardless of how fewer than 150 showed
up.

"Well, the night of the party —
Monday, May 8th — more than 215
showed up. And that's 50 more than
we can handle on the main floor — so
the rest of them had to be set up in
the banquet room we've got downstairs.

"We use the downstairs banquet
room for small parties — or for over-
flows.

"AND WHEN WE BOOK A party,
we don't know who's coming. They can
be garbage men, or business men, or
anybody. All we know is that a certain
number of people are coming — and
that we are going to have to feed them.

"So, when they started to walk in
for this May 8 party — the one they
raided — I noticed that some of them
were questionable. But what was I

supposed to do? Was I supposed to
throw them out?

"I don't have the right to throw
them out.

"A lot of people have the impression
that when the raid took place, all the
people who were arrested were in the
downstairs banquet room, holding a
Cosa Nostra meeting, or something.

"THAT IS NOT TRUE and the police know it — I mean, the police knew
it after they made the raid.

"Because when the police stormed
in, the ones they arrested were scat-
tered all over the place — three or
four at the bar, a couple at this table
upstairs, another couple at that table
upstairs, a half-dozen or so just standing and talking upstairs.

"Just a few were downstairs.

"And the ones who were downstairs
— the ones who were arrested, I mean
— when they heard the commotion,
tried to hide in one of my storerooms.
How do I know why they tried to
hide? I was upstairs.

"ALL I KNOW," MIKE PANARO
said, "is that this thing that happened
has ruined this place — and I'm heartsick. I'm heartsick because this place
means a great deal to us — particularly to my brother, Pat.

"I'll get along, regardless, because I
can work. But my brother Pat — who
happens to own this place — can't
work.

"Five years ago, Pat was in an auto
accident — and the accident paralyzed
him, totally. He can't move a muscle.
Somebody even has to feed him. He's
in a nursing home.

"SINCE THE ACCIDENT, Pat's ex-
penses have been pretty heavy — for
doctors and nurses, and for the nursing
home — and every dime has come out
of this restaurant.

"So now, Pat's in trouble — and I'm heartsick."

Golf — ROBERTO De VICENZO

*The greatest of all rule mishaps occurs at golf's 1968
Masters Tournament.*
Monday, April 15, 1968
Phil Ranallo: What's New, Harry?

"SATURDAY AFTER SATUR-
DAY, Sam," Honest Harry remarked,
"millions of golf buffs in this country
watch — via canned television — a
program that is called 'The Wonderful
World of Golf.'

"Yesterday afternoon, these same
millions — plus millions of other
sports fans who thrill to 'live' championship competition — watched what
certainly must be called 'The Ridiculous World of Golf.'

"On the 17th hole of yesterday's final round of the Masters Tournament
– one of the most prestigious golf tests
– Roberto De Vicenzo rolled in a putt
for a birdie three.

"WHEN THE PUTT DROPPED,
hundreds and hundreds of people who
rimmed the 17th green cheered, for
the clutch birdie had lifted De Vicenzo
into a first-place tie with Bob Goalby.

"De Vicenzo, an Argentinian with a
kind face and a bald head, tipped his
cap, courteously. Then Roberto's playing partner Tommy Aaron, marked De
Vicenzo's card — and inadvertently
marked down a 'four' instead of a
'three.'

"A few minutes later, when the round
was over — and when everybody
thought that De Vicenzo and Goalby
would meet today in an 18-hole playoff for the title — disaster struck the
Argentinian.

"THE TOURNAMENT OFFI-
CIALS carefully checked the players'
cards and discovered the error on De
Vicenzo's card — the card Roberto
had verified while caught up in the
emotions of it all. The officials then
solemnly rendered their decision.

"They placed De Vicenzo's second

because one of the rules of golf states
that the player is responsible for his
own score.

"It did not matter that perhaps 25
million people — plus a regiment of
tourney officials — saw De Vicenzo
make that three on 17.

"What mattered was that Aaron had
made a mistake and put down a 'four,'
and that the ecstatic De Vicenzo had
verified it.

"WHEN THE CHANGE was an-
nounced, De Vicenzo's world was
shattered on his 45th birthday, and the
hearts of millions of sports fans bled
for him at least a little.

"De Vicenzo took the bitter blow
with incredible graciousness. There
was not even a trace of indignation on
his kind face, just a trace of embarrassment.

" 'I do stupid thing,' he said. 'When
I feenish and look at card, I do not see
numbers because I am in daze. I feel
sorry ... but I congratulate my friend,
Bob Goalby.'

"ROBERTO DE VICENZO, SAM,
is the world's most magnanimous 'loser.' He is a matchless sport. The manner in which he conducted himself,
when he learned he had 'lost,' made
him a winner from coast to coast.

"It's strange, Sam, but it's true.

"Everything sad these days seems
to happen in the State of Georgia, the
'unpeachy' state which a couple No-
vembers ago elected to its highest office a former restaurateur who won the
governorship with his 'act of heroism'
... his refusal to serve the black man.

"About 10 days ago, in Atlanta, millions and millions of us watched via
television, the climax of that immense

American tragedy — the funeral of
the great black man who fell victim to
the bullet of the senseless assassin.

"YESTERDAY, IN ANOTHER
Georgia city, Augusta, millions and
millions watched a small tragedy — a
sports tragedy — the placing second
of Roberto De Vicenzo who fell victim
to a senseless rule of the game of golf.

"It must be said, though, in all
fairness to the governor of Georgia,
that he did not write the unfair and
senseless rule that proved so costly to
De Vicenzo.

"The senseless rule is the work of
the governors of golf — the 'masterminds' who make up the United States
Golf Assn. and the Royal and Ancient
Golf Club of St. Andrews, Scotland.

"The 'masterminds' — after what
happened at Augusta yesterday —
should call an emergency meeting ...
and do some rule rewriting."

Hockey — BUFFALO SABRES

Several Buffalo Sabres players go to the Ft. Erie racetrack to have some fun.

Monday, April 16, 1973
Phil Ranallo: What's New, Harry?

THE BUFFALO SABRES, those good, good skates who last week set the community on its ear with their gritty performance against the Montreal Canadians, are still the toast of Western New York and Southern Ontario.

This was evident Sunday afternoon, at the Fort Erie Jockey Club, where track management wined and dined the Sabres in the Turf Club, the posh facility inhabited by a strange breed — people who can actually afford to bet on racehorses.

Fort Erie officials had their hands filled when word got out that the Sabres were on the premises.

A swarm of "kids," all autograph seekers who ranged in age from 6 to 66, made a valiant effort to invade the Turf Club and get an in-the-flesh look at their heroes, but to no avail.

The "kids" had to wait till the dust cleared, after the last race, when the Sabres exited from the Turf Club and headed for the parking lot.

SIX SABRES — Tim Horton, Mike Robitaille, Rick Martin, Norm Gratton, Tracy Pratt and Craig Ramsey — were on hand to challenge the bangtails and dine on thick cuts of roast prime rib.

Two members of the Sabres brass also showed up and took their shots at the ponies — Seymour H. Knox III, keeper of the keys to "Fort Knox," also known as Memorial Auditorium, and Dave Foreman.

Knox took only a little shot. When the day was five races old, Seymour had made only one wager — a place bet on Lil Whirler in the first race. Seymour cashed his wager on Lil Whirler, which finished right where he

bet him — second — then turned his back on the betting windows.

"I'm saving my winnings," Knox said. "I'll take the money to the bank in the morning."

ROBITAILLE, THE hard-working defenseman, was most elated to be a guest of Fort Erie management — because it saved him the price of admission. Mike, you see, would have been at the track anyway. He is hooked on thoroughbred racing.

"I got involved last year when a friend down the street introduced me to the sport." Robitaille said as he peeked over the top of his racing form.

"My barber, who owns a couple of horses, also helped get me interested in the game. So credit my friends with getting me into this."

Robitaille said he visited Fort Erie every day last year and plans to be a regular again this season.

What does Mrs. Robitaille think of Mike's involvement in horse racing?

"I'VE GOT AN exceptional wife. She doesn't keep me too tied down." Robitaille smiled the smile of a fellow who is boss in his family. "I'm tied down all during the hockey season. If I had a wife who tied me down in the off-season, I think it would be too much."

Seated across the table from Robitaille was Craig Ramsey.

"I don't bet the horses," Ramsey said. Then Craig pointed to the boss, who was seated beside him — his wife, Susan.

"Susan does the betting for me. She makes the big money."

Mrs. Ramsey confessed that her luck had not been too good on this day.

"I've only won a little money today," she said in a tone that made her listeners wonder if she realized there are people who actually lose at the track.

RICK MARTIN MADE two bets, lost them both and wasn't too happy with the tipsters who had approached him and relayed their "good things" to him. "The best tip I had today came from a guy who told me to plant my corn early."

As Martin was speaking, Harry Carmichael, a St. Catharines, Ont., gentleman who owns a horse that was competing in the featured Jacques Cartier Stakes, walked up to Dave Foreman.

"Im a loyal supporter of the Sabres," Carmichael said to Foreman. "They're a fine, game club ... and they've given me great pleasure this season."

Then Carmichael handed Foreman a $50 win ticket on his horse, a colt named Delaying Tactics.

"TAKE THIS TICKET, Dave, and if my horse wins, cash it and divide the money among the hockey players."

Carmichael's gesture moved the Sabres – to the point where they were tempted to sing, "For He's a Jolly Good Fellow."

When the race was over, the Sabres were wishing that Carmichael owned a faster horse.

Delaying Tactics finished fourth.

Hockey — BUFFALO SABRES RESPOND TO PHIL'S COLUMN

Sabres VP David Forman invites Phil and Ruby to a Sabres game on behalf of the Knox family.
Tuesday, February 27, 1973
Phil Ranallo: What's New, Harry?

THIS WAS SUNDAY morning. The phone jingled. The caller was David G. Forman, the Buffalo Hockey Sabres administrative vice president who only minutes before had read Honest Harry's disclosure that the Sabres had "pulled a Ralph Wilson" and jacked up the Sabre ticket prices for next season.

Forman was not irate. But it was clear his day had not been brightened by Harry's inference that the Knox brothers, Seymour and Northrup — thanks to the 50 cents to $1.50 hike in ducat prices — would spend the 1973-74 NHL campaign laughing all the way to the bank.

Forman, after giving part of the Sabres' side of the case — "the $10 million initial investment, the high cost of operating the club," et cetera — said something that put Harry in mild shock.

"How would you and your wife," Forman said, "like to be my guests at the Pittsburgh game tonight?".

Harry didn't respond immediately. He feared a trap.

A FEW SECONDS LATER, however — right after Ruby, who had been getting an earful on the kitchen extension, rushed over to her son, poked him in the ribs and gave him the "yes" sign with a nod of her head — Harry told Forman he'd be delighted to accept the invitation.

In mid-afternoon, Harry's second thoughts began to get the best of him. He said to Ruby that perhaps it would be wise to phone Forman back and beg off.

"Why?" Ruby asked.

"I can see Forman now," Harry said, "grabbing me by the lapels and shaking me furiously the instant I get within arms' length of him."

"I don't care what Mr. Forman does to you," Ruby said. "We're going. You're not going to cost me the chance to rub elbows with members of the society.

The Seymour Knoxes and the Northrup Knoxes and the Paul Schoellkopfs sit right near the Formans. We're going."

So the engagement was kept.

FOR THE MOMENTOUS occasion, Ruby selected her finest, the best of her wardrobe — a $19.98 wine-colored pants suit, $9.50 fashion boots that were a steal at the last "pup" sale, a string of pearls made of high-quality paste, and a bracelet with 27 charms dangling from it.

Since it was Sunday, Harry chose his Sunday suit, the garment whose pants seat is almost not shiny, scuffed black shoes, argyle socks, a clean shirt and his favorite tie — the inch-wide one he's been wearing since Carry Back won the 1961 Kentucky Derby.

When Harry and Ruby arrived at the arena, Forman met them, gave Harry a small glare, then escorted them to their seats, beauties in the third row of the "golds," between the team's benches and smack dab on the red line.

During a break in the action, in the middle of the first period, somebody yelled to Harry, "How do you like your seats?"

HARRY TURNED TO HIS right

and noticed it was Seymour Knox. "The seats are great," Harry replied, "especially tonight since we're the guests of Dave Forman and you — and the price is right."

At the end of the first period, Forman escorted Harry and Ruby to the Sabre directors' room, a luxurious joint in the arena where refreshments are served.

Forman did the honors and handed his guests something other than sarsaparilla.

Harry, fearing the worst — a "mickey" — did not indulge immediately. When Forman turned his head away a minute, Harry handed his drink to Ruby — and Ruby did her duty.

She sipped Harry's drink, gave it her okay and handed it hack to Harry.

A bit later, Forman noticed Harry's inch-wide tie and smiled. He visited his office, returned with a tie with the Sabre emblem on it and told Harry to put it on "for luck."

Harry obliged since it was a new tie.

THEN IT WAS BACK to the game. In the middle of the second period, Harry heard a sound one does not often hear at a hockey game — the ringing of a telephone. He turned toward the sound and saw Seymour Knox pick up the receiver.

It was Northrup Knox on the line, calling from Florida. Seymour, over the phone, then proceeded to give his brother a slap shot by slap shot description of the action on the ice.

For Ruby, it was an unforgettable evening. She had a ball all night, chatting with the Formans and the Knoxes and the Schoellkopfs and the Dean Jewetts — and making those between-period and post-game visits to the plush directors' room.

When the night was done and Harry and Ruby began their walk out of the arena, Ruby said, "I hope the Knoxes

raise the ticket prices again soon — because I'd like to do this again."

Hockey — TIM HORTON

Buffalo Sabres star killed in car crash.
Sunday, February 24, 1974
Phil Ranallo: What's New, Harry?

NOW YOU WILL NOT swell the rout.
Of lads that wore their honors out,
Runners whom renown outran
And the name died before the man.
— Alfred Edward Housman

HAD A.E. HOUSMAN KNOWN Miles Gilbert Horton — and the tragedy that was to befall this special Sabre — he would have had Tim Horton in mind when he penned that poem 60 years ago.

Tim Horton had not worn out his honors when he met sudden death. His name was still in bright lights and in the headlines on the sports pages.

Tim Horton was still the leader of the Buffalo Sabres — on the ice and in the dressing room.

Tim Horton was still the Sabre player who had the greatest influence — all for the good — on his young teammates.

The young Sabres always leaned on Tim Horton.

And Tim Horton's shoulder was always there — until Thursday.

TIM HORTON WAS 44 YEARS old when he died — an extraordinarily high age for a hockey player. But he was such a hockey player, such a man, that wonderful things began to happen the moment Punch Imlach plucked him from the Penguins and he laced on his Sabre skates.

I do not regard as coincidence the arrival of Tim Horton on the Buffalo hockey scene and the transformation of the Sabres from a ragtag hockey unit into a competitive, representative NHL team.

He was a true-born major-leaguer who had "quaffed champagne" from

four Stanley Cups — as a Toronto Maple Leaf — and he oozed class.

His stature as a major-leaguer and his class rubbed off on the "kids" ... on Perreault, Martin, Schoenfeld, Robert and the rest of them ... and enabled the Sabres to work that small miracle last season by making the playoffs.

TIM HORTON WAS NOT AN electrifying hockey player ... except to astute hockey observers who could fully appreciate the big little things he did so perfectly.

Yet, there was something electric about him.

Perhaps this electricity was generated by how well he played this violent game at age 44.

All hockey addicts — little kids who play in the peewee leagues and dream of one day making it to the majors; the 15,858 fans who watch the Sabres game after game — marveled at Tim Horton.

Now, that special charge of Tim Horton electricity has been short-circuited — by death.

And there is a blackout of mourning.

To the Sabres — and to the Sabre fans — Tim Horton was a symbol of pride and determination and achievement.

WE MOURN A REMARKABLE athlete. He was remarkable because, at 44, he was still a plus on the ice ... and because his appearance — he was lean and taut and strong — made him look 10 years younger.

He was a man who could endure pain — the pain of hockey with a 44-year-old body and the pain of injury.

He played the last game of his great

career in deep pain — from a puck he had stopped with his jaw in practice.

Then, after that last game, against the Maple Leafs, he went out into the night and died — before he barely had time to get his skates off.

One of the masses mourning the death of Tim Horton is Ray Cullen, a former National Leaguer who was one of Tim's intimate friends.

"TIM WAS DIFFERENT THAN most pro athletes," Cullen, a St. Catharines, Ont., automobile dealer said. "Most athletes, when they are nearing the end of their athletic careers, wonder what they're going to do when they get out in the world.

"Not Tim.

"Tim played the game he loved for 25 years – the fiercely competitive game of hockey — and made it big. And when he put the skates away, he wasn't going to have to wonder.

"Tim already had made it big in the business world, which is also fiercely competitive, with his highly successful chain of donut shops. The rest of his life was all set.

"Now ... this tragedy."

Monday afternoon they will bury Tim Horton.

It seems incredible.

This is small consolation to his family, I know, but the gates of Hockey's Hall of Fame are ready to be swung open.

Hockey — GORDIE HOWE

Phil talks about Howe's greatness and durability at 51 years of age.
Wednesday, October 17, 1979
Phil Ranallo: What's New, Harry?

GORDIE HOWE is unreal! I mean, how does Howe do it? Gordie Howe is so ancient; he's a flesh-and-blood hockey antique. This remarkable and indestructible Methuselah on skates who'll glide into the Aud tonight is so old that he's Willie Stargell's senior by 13 years.

Howe, for heaven's sake, is even older — by two years — than Earl-Weaver!

Gordie is so old that his hair turned to silver long, long ago — along about the time he celebrated his silver anniversary in the National Hockey League.

He's so old that Lloyd's of London would be willing to lay him odds of 20-to-1 that he couldn't blow out all the candles on his next birthday cake on one try.

Now, there's no way you're going to believe this, but I give my word of honor — it's true.

When this fellow, Gordie Howe, first saw the light of day, Calvin Coolidge was in the White House, Babe Ruth had just completed his 60-homer season, Shirley Temple had yet to be born and the stock market had yet to crash.

HOWE'S HOCKEY days, they say, date back to shortly after he got his first slap from the doctor who delivered him on a blustery March day in 1928, in a tiny town called Floral, in Saskatchewan.

His legions of adulators insist that Gordie was born on skates. That's not the truth, but it's close.

The truth is — according to eye witnesses in Saskatchewan — baby Gordie Howe, after going through the crawling stage, did not learn to walk, but learned to skate.

Then one of the folks in Floral had the presence of mind to give little Gordie a hockey stick — and that, friends, was it.

Gordie Howe has been drilling holes in goaltenders ever since.

HOWE SCORED HIS FIRST National Hockey League goal 33 years ago, when gasoline went for 20 cents a gallon, way back in 1946 — long before the birth of any of the Buffalo Sabres Gordie will play against tonight.

Don Luce, the oldest Buffalo Sabre, was born two years after Howe turned on his first red light.

Why, when Gordie slammed home his first NHL goal, Scotty Bowman was a 13-year-old in knickers, and Chuck Knox had just turned 14!

Howe, who'll be 52 on March 31, has spent most of his life on skates. In his lifetime, he's been on more ice than Canadian Club or any rye, bourbon, scotch or gin you care to mention.

Whenever he visits the zoo, the polar bears smile at him.

HOWE IS THE MOST durable hockey player who ever lived. If all the bones Gordie has had broken in his hockey career could be collected and placed on view, they'd resemble the remains of a dozen people, minimum.

If all the catgut that's been used to close the gashes Gordie had ripped in his hide was made available to Spaulding or Wilson, there'd be enough to string at least a thousand tennis rackets.

The one-time pride of the Detroit Red Wings — and the current pride of the Hartford Whalers — is so tough that once, about 15 years ago, he was on the operating table at 2 in the afternoon and on the ice at 8 that night.

They say if Howe happened to die, there'd be nothing to worry about because Gordie would suit up right after the funeral.

GORDIE HOWE is the greatest all-around hockey player who ever lived. There are some hockey buffs who claim this isn't true, that the greatest is that Canadian, Guy Lafleur.

But their claim is invalid. In fact, it's utter nonsense. After all, Lafleur has hardly lived. He's only 28.

In the interest of fairness, the Lafleur people should hold their judgment in abeyance until the proper time — along about the year 2003 when Lafleur is 52.

Although Howe has been part of this world since Gene Tunney was the heavyweight champ, Gordie still plays a full shift in game after game.

He has slowed down a bit, naturally — but he still possesses a pretty good burst. And, 33 years after he banged home his first NHL goal, he's still scoring.

HIS STATISTICS are dazzling. Gordie holds the all-time record for NHL games played (1,690) and NHL goals scored (788). He's also the league's all-time point champion with 1,811.

Toss in Howe's World Hockey Assn. "stats" and his major league totals for games played and points scored both exceed 2,300.

And he's still looking ahead!

When will he retire?

"Hey, look," Howe says. "I'm nothing special. I'll just retire at 65 like everybody else.

"As my old friend, Al Kaline, always said: 'When you're walking to the ballpark and hoping to hear the game's been postponed, even if the sun is shining, you know you're near the end of your career.'

"I haven't reached that point yet."

GORDIE HOWE is the most revered player in all of hockey. This was learned, first hand, by what a Canadian customer did nine years ago, during the Sabres' first season, on Howe's first visit to the Aud.

The Canadian, while entering the Aud, was asked what he thought of Gordie Howe.

He didn't reply.

He merely took off his hat and placed it gently over his heart.

Tonight, the extraordinary Howe visits the Aud again.

It's a game that shouldn't be missed.

A guy like Gordie Howe will never pass this way again.

Hockey — PUNCH IMLACH

The "kid" teaches the Toronto Maple Leafs president a lesson.
Saturday, November 21, 1970
Phil Ranallo: What's New, Harry?

A YEAR-AND-A-HALF AGO, C. Stafford Smythe, the acrimonious president of the Toronto Maple Leafs, fired Punch Imlach as coach because, as Smythe put it, Punch was too old for the game.

Wednesday night, "Old Man" Imlach returned to the scene of Smythe's "crime"—Maple Leaf Gardens — and transformed the joint into a fountain of youth as he directed his Buffalo Sabres to a 7-2 goring of the Leafs.

Stafford Smythe's mouth, at last report, was still agape.

Thursday morning, "Kid" Imlach stood in the center of Nichols School's Dann Memorial Rink, as his Sabres drilled — and Punch looked as satisfied as if he had Smythe stuffed into one of his hip pockets.

AFTER A WHILE, IMLACH skated over to the boards, where three or four visitors were standing ... and one of the visitors, Dick Fischer, immediately filled the Sabre coach's ear with something Punch surely must have been dying to hear.

"The uniforms looked great on television; the bison on the jerseys was really sharp, just perfect," Fischer said, referring to the Sabres' road uniforms, which, of course, Dick sold to the club.

Then, somehow, the talk got around to the Sabres' great victory.

Imlach was asked, kiddingly, how old how he felt after the game — after the humiliation of Smythe and the Leafs was glorious history.

IMLACH'S FACE WRINKLED into a big grin. "Well, I was a little tired, to be honest with you ... from getting up and down on that bench so often and rooting whenever our guys got a goal."

Stafford Smythe's name was mentioned — as well as the fact that when the Sabres had built their lead to 4-2, Smythe had split the Gardens, left the premises, perhaps because he cannot stand the sight of blood, at least when the blood is his.

"I guess as far as Smythe was concerned," Imlach said, "nothing worse could have happened to him."

Punch smiled again. "They tell me Smythe's got a meeting set for this morning — with Leaf management."

THE MANNER IN WHICH THE Toronto fans treated Imlach — first with a standing ovation and later with chants of "We want Punch" — Smythe had to suspect he was in the wrong building ... or the wrong city.

And the Toronto fans rooted for the Sabres all the way, raising the roof each time Buffalo scored a goal.

It was, perhaps, a first in sports, sort of a phenomenon — a visiting team playing a home game on the road.

Imlach admitted he didn't know what to expect when he entered the arena and started to make his way to the Sabre bench, a few seconds before the first face-off.

"I guess I figured there'd be the usual things — some boos, some cheers. I certainly didn't expect a standing ovation.

"I'm pleased that they thought enough of me to do that."

THE TORONTO GAME MEANT so much to Imlach that for the first time in his life he sweated through a countdown. He explained that Tuesday as he was about to leave the Sabre office with John Anderson, his aide-de-camp, he glanced at his watch and said:

"It's 6 o'clock, John — exactly 24 hours till we walk into the dressing room in the Gardens.

"Later, while we were having a beer, I noticed it was 8 o'clock and told John that in exactly 24 hours they'd be dropping the puck."

Then Imlach, who is as recognizable to Canadians as Casey Stengel is to Americans, related his Queen E experience.

"I drove up early Wednesday afternoon, well ahead of the team bus. On the way, at least a couple dozen guys who passed me on the Queen E glanced over and smiled — and gave me the thumbs-up sign.

"One fellow held up his game-tickets."

IMLACH WAS ASKED THE DATE of the Sabre next go with the Maple Leafs. "December 13th, here — and they'll be waiting for us. They were waiting for Wednesday's game, mind you, but now they're really waiting.

"After that, we play them on consecutive nights — December 20th here.

"I can't tell you how much I'm hoping it'll be a very Merry Christmas."

Hockey — RICK MARTIN

Sabres rookie about to break the rookie scoring record held by teammate Gilbert Perreault.

Friday, February 18, 1972

Phil Ranallo: What's New, Harry

THE SABRES 90-MINUTE DRILL in the Nichols rink had just ended. Rick Martin, the winger with the powerful shot that is being heard around the hockey world, glided along the ice, gracefully, toward the seating area at center rink.

Martin stepped off the ice, went clomp, clomp, clomp up the wooden stairs, settled himself on the seating timber of the top row, inhaled deeply a few times, then bent over and started unlacing his skates.

Martin's every move was under the scrutiny of two young gals, both easy on the eyes, who were seated two rows in front of Rick, and perhaps eight or ten feet to his right.

As Martin unlaced, the two dolls gazed at him — admiringly, swooningly.

Rick Martin never noticed.

COULD IT BE THAT RICK MARTIN has nothing on his mind but his next goal — Goal Number 39 — the one that will make him the National Hockey League's No. 1 rookie goal-scorer of all time?

"Not really," Martin said toweling his sweating, handsome face.

"I'm aware of it — I know I'm only one goal away — but I'm not going to let it dominate my play. If it comes it comes.

"I don't want to be known as a fellow who plays hockey to score records.

"I want to be known as a fellow who plays to the best of his ability. I want to pass and play my position properly and win, not just score.

THOSE WORDS, IN PRINT, READ like a stereotyped dissertation memorized by someone who has the

world in the palms of his hands and is attempting to convince someone that success has not gone to his head.

They have a different ring, however, when uttered by the 20-year-old Martin.

Martin is sincere.

The young Sabre star credits the teammate whose record he is on the brink of shattering – Gil Perreault — with more than a fair share of his rookie net-filling achievement.

"Perreault", Martin said, "is the fellow who sets me up."

So there is no animosity between the two Sabre stars.

"JUST THE OTHER DAY," Martin pointed out to accent the relationship he has with Perreault, "Gil said to me: 'Look, Rick; don't worry about the next goal — you'll get it.'

"Then Perreault said he was glad for me. He told me that if his rookie record was going to be broken, it might as well be broken by one of his friends — me."

Martin was asked how his family was reacting to his NHL exploits — his parents and his two older sisters and two younger brothers.

"I guess they're proud — and excited."

Martin laughed.

"My two brothers — they're 10 and 12 — think that having a brother playing in the NHL is the greatest thing that ever happened.

"THEY'VE GOT A PRETTY GOOD reason to think that way, too. Every time I see them, they ask me for stuff — hockey sticks, pads, pants, jerseys, skates — and they get it."

As Martin continued to discuss his

family, it was learned there is no way that Rick can miss ramming home Goal No. 39 one of these nights.

If Martin runs into a slump — gets shut out for a few games — all he has to do to break out of it and slam home No. 39 is make arrangements for his parents, Alfred and Rollande, to come watch him play.

Father Alfred and Mother Rollande are Rick's good-luck charms. When they are in the arena Martin is absolute murder.

"SINCE I'VE BEEN IN THE NHL, my parents have seen me play three times, twice in Montreal, which is our hometown, and once here in Buffalo, the night we played Oakland about a month ago.

"And I scored in all three games. In Montreal, I got one goal in one game and two in the other, and I got the hat-trick in the game they saw against Oakland."

Martin said his parents would not be in Memorial Auditorium tonight when the Sabres meet the Pittsburgh Penguins.

If Ma and Pa Martin change their minds though, and make a surprise visit to the arena, there's no question.

Rick Martin is sure to make hockey history.

Hockey — STAN MIKITA

Hockey legend invented the curved stick, called it "The Mikita Curve."
Monday, April 21, 1980
Phil Ranallo: What's New, Harry?

WHEN STAN MIKITA put away his skates and called it a career last week — after 22 years in the National Hockey League — the hockey world showered him with glowing verbal bouquets.

They called Mikita "Mr. Chicago Black Hawk," labeled him one of the game's all-time greats, and pronounced him "instant Hall of Fame material."

Fine and dandy. All the tributes were deserved.

Nevertheless, in the tribute department, Stan Mikita was short-changed — did not receive all the credit due him.

I mean, to my recollection, not even one person bothered to mention that Mikita, during his tour of duty in the NHL, also made his mark as one of sports' all-time great inventors.

For the last 20 years, all hockey players — with the exception of goaltenders — have owed Stan Mikita a debt of gratitude.

The game's heaviest hitters — the guys who fire pucks as if the disk are coming out of small cannons — are especially indebted to "Mr. Chicago Black Hawk."

Why?

Because Mikita's the guy, who, with his inventiveness, came up with the "Mikita Curve" — the curved stick blade which enables hockey players to put a little more ring into their shots.

STAN MIKITA BECAME hockey's "Thomas Alva Edison" by accident, and the great accident occurred roughly 20 years ago, to the best of Stan's memory, during his second or third season with the Black Hawks.

"We were practicing one day and my stick broke," Mikita said. "The break made the blade cup a little — formed a kind of 'V' in the hitting surface.

"I was about to skate off and throw the stick away. But the puck came to me. So I took a shot with the cupped blade, from about 30 feet in front of the net — just a wrist shot — and the puck seemed to really take off.

"And I scored on the play. Normally, you're not supposed to score from out there. But this shot beat the goalie because it had a little extra zing to it."

BEFORE THE PRACTICE session ended, Mikita took a few more shots with the bent stick and became convinced the shots had much greater velocity than usual and the puck was easier to control.

When the practice ended, Mikita got his brainstorm.

"After I showered," he said, "I got a new stick and decided I had to find a way to bend the blade a little bit.

"First, I soaked the stick in boiling water. Then I stuck the blade under a door in the dressing room, propped the handle of the stick on a chair and left it there overnight."

Thus, the first hockey stick whose blade bore the shape of a crescent moon — the now famous "Mikita Curve" was produced.

"THE NEXT MORNING, when I returned for practice," Mikita said, "I taped up the stick and used it. A couple of days later Bobby Hull started experimenting with a curved stick, too.

"The other guys on our club laughed at Bobby and me for using the sticks. But they didn't laugh for long.

"When Bobby, with the curved stick,

starting pounding some powerful shots into the net — and when I started experiencing a little more success on my shooting — they all switched to the new sticks.

"And the guys on the other clubs in the league soon caught on, too. Before the season was over, almost all the players were using curved sticks."

The "Mikita Curve" is still in style. It's used by virtually all who play in the NHL.

THE "MIKITA CURVE" certainly paid dividends for Stanley Mikita. In his 22 seasons with the Black Hawks, Mikita scored 541 goals, a mark topped by only five players — Gordie Howe, Phil Esposito, Bobby Hull, John Bucyk and Maurice Richard.

Mikita is No. 2, behind Howe, in all-time assists with 926. And he's third in all-time total points with 1,467.

Not bad for a guy who stands 5-feet-9 and weighs less than 170 pounds!

But the little guy, in his heyday, could skate like the wind and stick-handle the puck through a New York subway train, artistry which earned Mikita, a native of Czechoslovakia, the sobriquet, "The Uncheckable Czech."

Despite his size, Mikita, in his early NHL years, was a terror on skates — one of the roughest, toughest fellows ever to play the game.

AND HE HAD SOMEWHAT of a mean streak, which he acquired in his formative years in St. Catharines, Ont., where he grew up after being brought from Czechoslovakia at age eight.

Young Mikita got to love hockey immediately because the game afforded him the opportunity to "fix" certain kids in St. Catharines who got their kicks by taunting Stan for his terrible English.

Mikita "fixed" them with savage body checks. After a few seasons in the NHL, Mikita rid himself of the mean streak, stopped taking a lot of penalties and became a "good, good boy" — good enough to twice win the Lady Byng Trophy, the NHL's sportsmanship award.

How did he manage to change his ways?

"I like to think I matured a little."

TOUCHING ON THE subject of violence in hockey, Mikita said there has always been violence in the game, but that the violence of a few years ago was of a different type.

The violence back then came in the form of hard body-checking," Mikita said. "But now it comes in the form of high-sticking and fighting.

"Years ago, the players took the body much better. Now, instead of good body checking, there's a lot of high-sticking – mainly, I think, because the kids are never taught how to body check.

"Why, in the series we're watching right now — between the Black Hawks and the Sabres — we haven't seen a good body check yet."

Hockey — MIRACLE ON ICE

An unbelievable upset at the Winter Olympics.
Sunday, February 24, 1980
Phil Ranallo: What's New, Harry?

THE POOR RUSSIANS may never get over it.

Nothing, absolutely nothing, can ever be a more crushing blow to their national pride than what those remarkable U.S.A. icemen have done to Russia's athletic pride and joy — the "invincible" Soviet hockey team.

The U.S.A.'s disassembling of "The Big Red Machine" was astounding.

Every bit as astounding, say, as Slippery Rock whipping the Pittsburgh Steelers ... or Sammy's Deli defeating the Pittsburgh Pirates or the 97-pound weakling beating up the neighborhood bully ... or the mouse bringing the elephant to his knees.

What the boys from Massachusetts and Minnesota — the amazing "Boys of Winter" — did to the Russians Friday evening could lead to the Soviet skaters getting some bad news when they return to the homeland.

If Leonid I. Brezhnev happened to watch the Russians' performance on the Lake Placid ice, there's a chance that, within a fortnight, the poor guys will be toiling at the front, in Afghanistan — armed only with hockey sticks

ENTERING THESE Olympic Games, the Russians had established themselves as equal to the NHL level of competetion, on the strength of the number they'd done in the not-too distant past on several NHL teams and the NHL All-Stars.

There seemed no way that the young kids from the U.S.A. could cope with the likes of Valeri Kharlamov, the right winger who'd terrorized NHL defensemen with his bursts from nowhere; Boris Mikhailov, the gifted and emotional captain; Vladimir Petrov, the swift-skating center; Vladislav

Tretiak, the acrobatic goalie, etc.

The Russians were such overwhelming favorites Friday night that some sportswriters, in their pre-game columns, made like quislings, ran up the white flag of surrender, gave the U.S.A. no chance and predicted a runaway Russian victory.

Those sportswriters, at this moment, of course, are doing the logical thing. They're devouring those pre-game columns, garnished with a dab of thoroughly soured Russian dressing.

AGAINST THE U.S.A., the Russians looked like a different team. I mean, where were those famous Russian rushes up and down the ice? And all that magical, pin-point passing? And that skating speed that couldn't be matched?

The Russians in no way resembled the team which humiliated the NHL All-Stars a year ago because the plucky U.S.A. kids would not let them.

The Soviet forwards need full control of the puck coming out of their home zone to do those things.

But they rarely had full control Friday night. The young and tireless Americans kept them bottled up with tremendous defensive play and full rink checking.

As the game wore on, it seemed the Russian defensemen, made to struggle for every inch of the ice by the pestiferous U.S. kids, were happy just to clear the puck.

IN THIS UNFORGETTABLE hockey match, the good guys — the Americans — were the ones making the dizzying passes, skating around defensemen and maintaining control of the puck at all costs.

Superb physical conditioning, excellent teamwork, first-rate coaching, a matchless esprit de corps — and great goaltending — were the cornerstones of the U.S.A. victory.

The Russians outshot the U.S.A. by a lopsided 39-16, but had the door slammed in their faces 36 times by the handsome Bostonian, Jim Craig.

Craig made numerous outstanding saves. Let it be known, however, that the Russians did a lot of their firing long before they could see the whites of Craig's eyes — took many of their shots from way downtown.

The Russians, in a word, panicked, especially in the third period when they resorted almost exclusively to shots from distant ranges.

IN THE NINTH minute of the third period, with the Russians in front by 3-2 — and with the world waiting for the roof to cave in on the courageous Americans — it happened.

Mark Johnson pulled the trigger and beat Russian goalie Vladimir Myshkin to tie the score at 3-3.

Now, the U.S. kids were within reach of realizing their "impossible dream."

A minute-and-a-half later, the American captain, a fellow named Mike Eruzione, fired the puck past Myshkin and into the net, and, for the U.S. kids, their "impossible dream" had come true.

Amazing!

For being given the opportunity of seeing this great hockey match, live and in color, a few hundred thousand Western New Yorkers will be forever grateful to the Canadian Broadcasting Co.

THE AMERICAN network, ABC, failed to show the game live, since faceoff was at 5 p.m. and ABC refused to disrupt its regular programing, claiming hockey is not much of an attraction to American audiences.

ABC telecast the match during its regular Olympic programming, starting at 8:30.

Anyway, after the end of the second period of the re-run, Jim McKay, ABC's Olympic anchorman, said the third period would soon begin, and then informed his listeners that, although the game was long over, he was not giving the final score.

"Some viewers would rather not know," McKay said, "so I'm not going in spoil it for them."

Then, maybe 10 minutes later, when Ch. 7 broke in with one of its "updates" — to plug its 11 o'clock news show — Irv Weinstein, the guy who seems hooked on Irv Weinstein, spoiled it for them.

Weinstein stated that one of the top items at 11 would be the U.S. hockey team's great victory over the Russians.

Thanks, Irv.

Hockey — GILBERT PERREAULT

The best team player and the most unselfish player in the National Hockey League.

Saturday, April 7, 1979

Phil Ranallo: What's New, Harry?

FOR QUITE A SPELL now, some of the "experts" have been getting their kicks by flinging mud at Gil Perreault.

You've heard the knocks against the guy. They go something like this:

— Perreault is the most over-paid player in the NHL.

— He gives his best, plays the game all-out, only when the mood strikes him.

— He is not overly courageous, does not like the rough stuff.

Well, they're all bum raps.

If Perreault happens to command the highest salary in the National Hockey League, it's understandable. He's as good a hockey player as there is in the NHL.

Gil Perreault, from this vantage point, is the NHL's most exciting man on skates.

He's the swiftest skater in the game.

He's the most talented passer in the business.

And he's also hockey's most unselfish player.

If Perreault has a flaw, it's his unselfishness. The guy actually over-passes the puck, repeatedly turns down shots — high-percentage shots — in an effort to feed teammates.

IMAGINE THAT!

In this sports era, in which so many of the athletes seem to be playing mainly for No. 1 — in which the general philosophy appears to be, "Hooray for me and the heck with you" — Gil Perreault concentrates on passing the puck!

Perreault is a great team player.

He simply will not shoot the puck unless he sees the whites of the goaltender's eyes — and even then he sometimes passes off.

Gil is one of the very few performers in the NHL who plays the game of hockey as if he were part Russian — or as if he had been coached by the Russians.

The Russians' style is Perreault's style.

You always look for the open man — and you always pass the puck unless you've got a point-blank shot.

GIL PERREAULT is a fellow who could double his goal production if his priorities matched those of so many of today's athletes — if he were statistics-mad and placed his goal-scoring above the welfare of his team.

Gil's career record, for his nine years as a Sabre, accents his unselfishness — 300 goals and 460 assists.

That's right!

Thursday night, in that match with the Boston Bruins, Gil reached a career milestone — netted his 300th NHL goal — and, to the best of my knowledge, nobody bothered to mention it.

That 300th goal wasn't mentioned, wasn't noticed, for the simple reason that, regardless of what Perreault accomplishes, it's expected.

I MEAN, NONE OF the wondrous things Perreault does on ice is a surprise. Why, he's supposed to do those kind of things, isn't he? After all, he's Gil Perreault, isn't he? He should have gotten that 300th goal long ago, right?

Well, if Perreault happened to be a guy who worried most about No. 1, worried most about Gil Perreault, those career totals of his would be reversed.

He'd have 460 goals and 300 assists,

instead of vice versa.

Perreault's career assist total, by the way, may be the most legitimate assist figure among players performing in the NHL today.

Not too many of Gil's 460 assists are the phony kind, the kind the official scorers credit to guys who happen to inadvertently touch the puck preceding a goal.

The majority of Perreault's assists are true assists — amassed by laying deft passes on the sticks of teammates.

A PERFECT EXAMPLE of the Perreault method was in evidence Thursday night, in the match with the dazed Bruins.

In fact, there were three perfect examples.

I'm referring, of course, to the three show-stopping passes Perreault dealt off for easy scores — twice to Danny Gare and once to Jacques Richard.

No, sir; in the "true assists" department, nobody in the NHL is Perreault's equal.

Gil Perreault is better than anyone in the NHL at setting up teammates for good shots, and for opening goals.

Yes, sir; the way Perreault skates in close on those plays, draws the defense to him, then passes to the open teammate, you'd swear he was a $325,000-a-year hockey player.

It's time he started getting his due.

So, let's hear it for Gil Perreault, the best team player — and the most unselfish player — in the National Hockey League.

Holidays — FATHER'S DAY

Enjoying a special day made just for dads.
Monday, June 16, 1975
Phil Ranallo: What's New, Harry?

SUNDAY WAS FATHER'S DAY. In Honest Harry's castle, this was easy to tell — because Ruby and the six children made their annual sacrifice. They permitted Harry to be first in the bathroom.

And, while Harry shaved and showered, no one lodged a claim of foul — no one rapped on the bathroom door impatiently and squealed, "For heaven's sake, Dad!"

As Harry lathered up and hummed "That Old Gang of Mine," he thought about the day — Father's Day — and what a father really is.

• A father is a guy who, when washing or showering, always uses the tiny piece of soap that has been abandoned by his children, in favor of a nice, new cake of soap.

• A father is also the fellow who, when brushing his teeth, works out of the other tube of toothpaste, the near-empty one his kids refuse to squeeze any longer.

• A FATHER IS THE poor chap whose arrival at home in the evenings is often awaited by his children, unhappily, because their misdeeds earlier in the day prompted their mother to warn them, "Wait till your father gets home!"

• A father is a guy who for five years waged a battle with his sons against long hair, and lost the battle, and now is allowing his own sideburns to thicken and lengthen.

• A father is a fellow who, since the Beatles era, could not understand his kids' taste in music, but who last week sneaked downtown to the record shop and purchased a Rolling Stones album.

• A father is a guy who no longer is able to impress his children by telling them he lived through the Depression and started with nothing, because he knows — as well as his kids do — that they're all back where he started.

• A FATHER IS A fellow who, if his daughter is grown up and married, will be forever grateful, for the simple reason that he no longer has to wait up all night until she comes home from a date with the good-for-nothing he knew was up to no good.

Sunday, when Harry finished shaving and showering, he returned to the bedroom and ran into another Father's Day treat. He was able to dress immediately, without interruption, because Ruby had ironed a white shirt in advance.

Then Harry went downstairs and bumped into another Father's Day special.

There, on the breakfast room table, was The Courier-Express, completely intact, including the sports section.

Alongside the newspaper were two more surprises — a tall glass of orange juice and a piping-hot cup of coffee.

JUICE AND COFFEE, on a normal morning — any morning other than on Father's Day — are "you get them yourself, Harry; I'm feeding the kids" items.

And while Harry sipped his juice and scanned the race results and entries, Ruby remained silent — never once said that she thought he should at least forget about horses on Sunday.

After breakfast, Harry, surrounded by his children, began to unwrap his presents.

"I know I do a lot of beefing," he said, "about having a car that's twice as old as Secretariat, and about never having anything but petty cash in my jeans, and so on.

"So please forgive me.

"Today — Father's Day — I realize how good God has been to me; how fortunate I am to have six children.

"AND SIX GOOD children you are. Because — look — six presents."

The two gifts Harry appreciated most were from his two oldest sons — the latest edition of the American Racing Manual and an 8-by-10 autographed picture of Angel Cordero Jr.

Later in the day, Harry was given complete control of the television set. He was allowed to watch Pele do his thing for the Cosmos — without argument from Ruby or any of the kids.

And for the rest of the day, it went like that. Everybody bent over backwards for Harry.

Which is why Harry felt so good this morning when things returned to normal and he wound up eighth in the bathroom.

Holidays — INDEPENDENCE DAY

Phil's take on the American flag comes from his life experiences and from his experience as a former U.S. Marine who served in World War II.

Sunday, July 4, 1971

Phil Ranallo: What's New, Harry?

THE AMERICAN FLAG, on this Independence Day, is not serving as a substitute for a length of rope in a tug of war contest with super-patriots tugging away at one end and peaceniks yanking away at the other.

It is a good sign, an indication that we have come a long way in a year and a half.

Starting with the Moratorium in October of 1969 and extending through last Independence Day and the long hot summer and frightening fall of 1970, a lot of people in this country — most of whom had good intentions — went slightly bananas over the flag.

The problem, of course, was that the whole American flag "thing" had become a referendum on the war – a development that was as strange and silly as a debate about the length of a man's hair.

THE FUROR OVER THE FLAG got its roots when some peaceniks burned it at anti-war demonstrations — and when the Reader's Digest started giving away flag decals for automobiles — and when someone else designed decals for cars which incorporated the peace symbol with the flag.

Cars would roll to a stop at a red light — one car adorned with the Digest decal, the other with the dove-flag decal — and the drivers would glare at one another, regard each other as the enemy of this country.

Then there was the man on Long Island, a veteran of World War II who flew his flag upside down to signify his feeling that the United States was in a distressed condition due to it's involvement in Vietnam.

They took him away in handcuffs.

THERE ALSO WAS THE happening in New York City, on Moratorium Day, when Mayor John Lindsay ordered the flag flown at half-mast on municipal buildings in respect for the Vietnam dead, and a councilman went scrambling up on the roof of City Hall and raised the flag to full mast, as if it were Mount Suribachi.

Then there was "Honor America Day" in Washington last Independence Day — an idea dreamed up by Hobart Lewis of Reader's Digest, one of President Nixon's most fervent supporters.

Despite the dazzling fireworks display and the parade of stars and the gay music, there was something joyless about "Honor America Day."

Bob Hope and other John Wayne types seemed to be saying that if we would only get together and go to church and wave the flag a little more, then everything would be all right.

THEIR WORDS SOUNDED VERY shallow to Americans who were of the opinion that America was not honoring the promises it made on the first Independence Day 195 years ago. They were not outrageous promises, but they still have not been kept.

Today there is no "Honor America Day" celebration in Washington.

That is a good sign, an indication that the flag no longer is being used as a symbol of partisan support — which, to many, is as much a desecration of the flag as when one burns it.

We must be on the right track.

On this Independence Day nobody is

wrapping himself in the flag, or worshiping the flag, or burning the flag, or struggling over who owns the flag.

TODAY THERE IS NOT the despair that existed last Independence Day, even though the tragic war has not come to an end.

Today, there seems to be a reason for at least a small celebration.

Maybe that landmark decision last week — when the Justices of the Supreme Court stood up and were counted — has something to do with it.

They voted for freedom – a legitimate reason for waving, or flying, the flag.

Holidays — MEMORIAL DAY

I consider this one of the most moving Memorial Day columns I have ever read. Williamsville native John A. Anderson, United States Army Specialist-4, is remembered. This column is reason enough for me to complete my father's book. I hope you enjoy it as well.

Friday, May 31, 1968

Phil Ranallo: What's New, Harry?

IT WAS MEMORIAL DAY — the day to remember and, in early morning, the sky was a dull gray and the air was cool. The young boy got out of bed, washed his hands and face, brushed his teeth, combed his hair and dressed.

He did not go down for breakfast.

Instead, the young boy climbed the stairs to the third floor and made his way to a corner of a room — to his mother's cedar chest, which once held the linens and the sheets and the pillowcases and the things that brides-to-be collect.

The cedar chest no longer holds such things. It now holds things much more precious — things such as the babies' first pairs of shoes, old photo albums, Confirmation certificates, elementary and high school diplomas — and a special American flag.

THE YOUNG BOY PICKED UP the American flag — the precious flag that five years ago covered the coffin of his grandfather, a sailor in World War I.

The young boy removed the flag from its plastic protective bag, unfolded it carefully, placed it on a bed and smoothed out the wrinkles — with gentle movements of the palms of his hands.

Then the young boy hunted for — and found — the eight-foot flagstaff. He affixed the flag to the pole.

He stepped down the stairs and walked out to the front upper porch — and positioned the base of the pole in its metal holder on a corner post of the porch railing.

The boy stood there for a minute, watched the flag flutter in the gentle, cool breeze, then went down for breakfast.

AT THE BREAKFAST TABLE, the young boy joined his father, who was sipping coffee and giving unusual attention to a particular page in The Courier-Express — Page 46.

The story of this Memorial Day — and what it means — was told on Page 46.

Page 46 was stark reality.

The story on Page 46 was told in 67 pictures — head-and-shoulder pictures of the 67 Western New Yorkers — soldiers, sailors and Marines — who have paid the terrible price in the hell that is Vietnam.

The young faces of some of these fallen warriors were creased in warm and beautiful smiles. The faces of others were sober.

ALL BUT ONE OF THESE 67 warriors now rest under cold and damp earth — "Lying so silent by night and by day, sleeping the years of their manhood away."

The other young warrior — Specialist-4 John A. Anderson, United States Army, 415 McKinley Rd., Williamsville — will be buried this morning.

Once, all 67 of these fallen warriors, who now are no more, were just like the young boy who performed the flag duty yesterday.

They played and they laughed and they swung baseball bats and they

kicked footballs and they wrestled
and they raided the cookie jar and
they cried and they loved — and were
loved.

NOW, THEY MAKE UP THE
TRAGIC story that is told on Page 46.
Now, they are no more. Now, they are
only treasured memories.

Thursday morning — Memorial Day
morning — Page 46 was stained by
a million tears — tears shed by the
mothers and fathers and sisters and
brothers and wives and others who
knew and loved the 67 fallen warriors.

Page 46 is the Memorial Day story.

Page 46 one day will turn yellow,
from age, and then a light brown —
but, for those involved, it will remain
forever a tear-stained treasure.

Holidays — MOTHER'S DAY

Phil thinks about the past and the present.
Monday, May 15, 1967
Phil Ranallo: What's New, Harry?

SUNDAY CAME UP BRIGHT and beautiful — so bright and so beautiful that it was obvious somebody had planned it that way.

For it was Mother's Day.

Honest Harry, Sunday morning, at Mass spent the entire hour living in the wonderful past — the wonderful days of his boyhood.

They will always be wonderful, unforgettable days — because mother was there — mother, the great lady with the matchless apron strings.

SHE WAS THE LADY WHO first told him he was now a young man — and proved it by buying him his first pair of long pants.

Knickers would be no more.

She was the lady who hundreds and hundreds of times — when he was guilty of minor misdeeds — threatened to blow the whistle on him when Pa got home from work. But she never did.

She was the lady who took him to his first Bison baseball game — and kept taking him to the park at least once or twice a week, for years and years.

SHE WAS THE LADY WHO always bought him a box of popcorn, along about the third inning, and shared it with him — and never failed to stand and cheer when Ollie Carnegie got the meat part of his bat on a fastball.

She was the lady who taught him to drive a car.

She was the lady who insisted that he give college a try.

These were the wonderful, unforgettable moments of his boyhood that flashed through Harry's mind Sunday morning, at Mass.

AND AS THEY FLASHED through his mind, Harry said the rosary in honor of that great lady — a special rosary, whose beads are made of pressed flowers from a spray that graced his mother's coffin five years ago.

Then, when Mass was done, Harry went home — with his memories. And at home, he noticed that, for him, the present is as beautiful as the past.

He noticed it at the dinner table, when every so often his sons and his daughter looked their mother's way — admiringly.

"HOW LUCKY CAN A MAN get?" thought Harry as he, too, looked at Ruby — admiringly.

"In my life," he thought, "there have been two matchless ladies, back-to-back."

Holidays — MOTHER'S DAY II

My soldier brother (John Ranallo) is in the United States Army on this date.

Monday, May 13, 1968

Phil Ranallo: What's New, Harry?

ABOUT 5,000 MILES SEPARAT-ED the mother and one of her sons — her soldier son she had not seen in more than 20 months — since that day in early September of 1966, when he hugged her and kissed her and went away.

On this Mother's Day, the young man, a sergeant in the United States Army, was standing in a telephone line at a U.S. Army base in Fulda, a little West Germany town that nestles in the mountains, 60 miles from Frankfurt.

Night had fallen in Fulda and the sergeant already had missed dinner. He had passed up dinner for a reason. A visit to the mess hall would have cost him his place in the telephone line — and perhaps all hope of getting his call in.

THE MOTHER WAS IN HER home, surrounded by her other five children and her two grandchildren. This was her day and she was happy — but her day was not yet complete. The sergeant in Germany — her son, John — was on her mind.

The mother, possessed of a sixth sense — as all mothers are — stationed herself in a lounge chair, beside the telephone. She read the Sunday paper and sipped coffee and waited and waited.

Finally, it happened. The telephone rang. The mother picked up the receiver and before she said hello, she knew — because of a mother's wonderful sixth sense — that her wish had come true.

"HELLO," THE MOTHER said.

"Hello, Ma. It's me, John," the sergeant said. "Happy Mother's Day, Ma. I miss you and I love you and I can't wait until I see you again."

The mother and the son spoke for 11 minutes — except eight very brief interruptions, when the sergeant had words with his father and his sister, his four brothers and his sister-in-law, and his 4-year-old nephew, who is his God child.

Then the mother and the son said goodbye — and the mother placed the receiver back on the phone.

"My John sounds big and strong and beautiful," the mother said. "I can also tell by the way he sounds that he is a soldier — a sergeant."

THEN THE PROUD MOTHER had a long and happy cry. She was surrounded by her family — and she had spoken to her soldier son, John.

Mother's Day was complete.

Horse Racing — BLACK STALLION MOVIE CREW

When a Hollywood movie crew films some racing scenes for the Black Stallion movie at Ft. Erie Race Track, some funny things go on.
Tuesday, August 9, 1977
Phil Ranallo: What's New, Harry?

YOU CANT TRUST THOSE fellows from Hollywood.

Yes, sir, the guys in the movie industry will do anything, stoop to any level, if they think it'll help make their flick a box office hit. It's suspected that they may even go so far as to apply a giant syringe, loaded with "go" juice, to the hip of a poor racehorse.

So, racing fans, remember this:

If you happen to visit a motion picture theater next spring and take in that racetrack movie, "Black Stallion" — the flick whose racing scenes were shot recently at the Fort Erie Jockey Club — the "two-mile classic" that highlights the film may be a "boat race."

Another thing — if you know your Fort Erie horses and are proficient at horse identification ... and are able to identify the thoroughbred in the "two-mile classic" whose real name is "Ore Ismorr" ... lean over to the dude sitting next to you in the theater and try to make a big bet on that horse.

What I'm saying is, it has come to light that some kind of hanky-panky may have gone on in Fort Erie's "back room" — in the barn area — before "Ore Ismorr," which runs in the "two-mile classic" under an alias, stepped out on the track and did his thing in front of the movie cameras.

I mean, it has been revealed, by the Fort Erie Jockey Club stewards, that somebody got to the horse, "Ore Ismorr," recently with a needle.

NOW, WHETHER SOMEBODY got to "Ore Ismorr" before, or after, he ran in the "two-mile classic" in the movie, "Black Stallion," nobody knows. All that's known, for sure, is what the Fort Erie stewards have disclosed, and it is this:

On Monday, Aug. 1, at Fort Erie, "Ore Ismorr" ran in a real horse race the sixth at the border track. And "Ore Ismorr" won the race by three-quarters of a length, paid $10.50 — then later flunked his urine test.

"Ore Ismorr" ran in that Fort Erie race — and probably in the movie's "two-mile classic" — while under the influence of procaine, a drug that is definitely a no-no around the racetrack,

Whodunit? Who slipped the stuff to "Ore Ismorr" — nobody knows.

But the finger of accusation is being pointed in all directions — especially in the direction of the fellow from Hollywood.

FOR EXAMPLE, THE executive producer of "Black Stallion" is Francis Ford Coppola, the renowned movie man who directed "The Godfather" — and landed an Oscar for the superb job he did in the flick about the underworld dons and their henchmen.

Well, a lot of people are almost willing to swear that the syringe job on "Ore Ismorr" was done by one of Marlon Brando's boys.

There are droves of other folks though, who suspect that the guilty party is Mickey Rooney, who plays the role of a horse trainer in the "Black Stallion."

Personally, I don't think Mickey Rooney or any of Marlon Brando's boys stuck it to "Ore Ismorr."

I happened to see Rooney on Sunday at Fort Erie where he spent the day betting with both fists — and Mickey looked completely innocent to me.

THE FELLOW WHO'S No. 1 on my list of suspects, to tell you the truth, is Francis Ford Coppola — and if I refreshen your memory, I'm sure you'll understand why I'm wondering about Mr. Coppola.

About two weeks ago when Courier-Express sports writer Mike Jankowski visited Fort Erie to chat with Mr. Coppola about the movie, "Black Stallion," Jankowski found the film man located under one of the track's park benches — and Mr. Coppola remained under the bench throughout the interview.

Now, why would a guy do that? Right?

I've got to conclude that anybody who hides under a park bench, while he's being interviewed, has something to hide.

NOW, ALLOW ME TO get serious for a moment — since it is an extremely serious matter when it is discovered that a racehorse has performed with an illegal medication in his system.

The horse, "Ore Ismorr," is trained by Frank H. Merrill Jr., who owns the 5-year-old gelding in partnership with Beverly Bronfman. Both Merrill and Miss Bronfman have impeccable racetrack credentials.

For 30 years, Frank Merrill has been one of the most successful — and most respected — trainers in Canada.

The Fort Erie stewards have announced that, as a result of evidence gathered during the course of their investigation, the case involving the positive test of "Ore Ismorr" has been referred to the Ontario Racing Commission "for any action the Commission deems necessary."

UNTIL THE COMMISSION makes a final judgment in the case, the stewards said, Frank Merrill will be permitted to continue his business of training racehorses on the Fort Erie Jockey Club grounds.

Oh yes, the Fort Erie stewards also stated that the horse, "Ore Ismorr," "is hereby declared unplaced" — considered to have been an also-ran in the race — "for all purposes except pari-mutuel wagering, which in no way shall be affected."

In other words, racing fans, if you blew some money on the race in which the horse was drugged, and now are thinking of making an attempt to get it back through legal action — don't bother.

For you the race stands "official."

Horse Racing — DANCER'S IMAGE

Derby winner Dancer's Image is disqualified.
Wednesday, May 8, 1968
Phil Ranallo: What's New, Harry?

LAST SATURDAY AFTERNOON, when Dancer's Image made his magnificent charge through the long Churchill Downs stretch to win the Kentucky Derby, Lou Cavalaris Jr.'s cup of joy spilled over. The big man held the thoroughbred racing world in the palms of his strong hands.

Sweat and toil and 18-hour days on the racetrack had at last paid off for the 46-year-old racehorse trainer, who just a decade ago had been a mere peasant in the sport of kings, working almost exclusively with patched-up, gimpy-legged $1,500 platers and barely scratching out a living.

In just 10 years, Lou Cavalaris had accomplished an almost impossible mission.

The burly fellow with the pink cheeks and the iron-gray hair had come all the way — from the racing game's nadir to its zenith; from rubbing liniment on the legs of a glue-factory candidate to rubbing liniment on the legs of a dream colt, a 2½ million-dollar chunk of horseflesh, a Derby winner.

THE VICTORY OF DANCER'S IMAGE seemed to be a just reward for Lou Cavalaris — a reward for the heartache and the agony he had endured for months and months, following the humane destruction of Cool Reception, the colt which fractured a leg while finishing second to Damascus in the Belmont Stakes last June.

So there was Cavalaris, last Saturday afternoon in the thoroughbred trainer's promised land — the winner's circle at Churchill Downs, with the wonderful colt, Dancer's Image, beside him and with the racing world in the palms of his strong hands.

Then, Tuesday morning, the world that Cavalaris had held and fondled for less than 72 hours blew up in his pink-cheeked face — like a hydrogen bomb. The Churchill Downs stewards called in Cavalaris and told him the incredibly tragic news.

THE STEWARDS REVEALED THAT traces of a medicinal agent called phenylbutazone, the generic name for butazolydin, had been discovered in a urinalysis of Dancer's Image — and that Dancer's Image had been disqualified and that Forward Pass had been declared the Derby winner.

Cavalaris hasn't been heard from since he left the stewards' room at 11:45 a.m. Tuesday.

Several telephone calls were made to the Brown Suburban Hotel in Louisville — the hotel in which Cavalaris established headquarters during his Derby stay in the Kentucky city.

"Mr. Cavalaris is in his room and has informed us he does not want to be disturbed — for any reason," the hotel switchboard operator told this reporter on the first call, at 1:15 p.m.

ANOTHER CALL WAS MADE AT 3 p.m. This time, a Cavalaris associate said: "Lou's in shock. I don't think he'll ever get over this. He's been in his room for three hours, just sitting in a chair with his face buried in his hands — and crying."

At 4:30 p.m., a third call was made. Edgar Lee, the hotel manager, said: "Just a few minutes ago, I went to Mr. Cavalaris' room and he was gone — and so was his luggage. He didn't check out. He just left. I'm going to forward his room bill to Mr. Fuller."

A Toronto turf writer said late Tuesday night that Cavalaris most likely was on his way home. "Lou and his wife are very close," the writer said. "He wants to talk to her first — just as he did when the Cool Reception thing happened last year."

TUESDAY WAS A "DARK" DAY at the Fort Erie Jockey Club — unusually "dark." It was "dark" because there is no racing at the track on Tuesdays, and it was "dark" because all of Cavalaris' friends — trainers, owners, jockeys, grooms, hot walkers — were in deep shock after hearing the news.

"Having a urine test come up positive," trainer Yonnie Starr said, "is a trainer's horror. The trainer lives in fear that something like this will happen to him. What's happened to Cavalaris is a tragedy — and it can happen to any trainer."

Dr. Neal Mendelson, one of the continent's most respected veterinarians, said: "I have known Lou Cavalaris for 15 years and I know that he is at the top of the list of ethical trainers.

"The rules regarding usage of this medicinal agent, phenylbutazone, should be reviewed — in the best interests of the horse racing industry."

DR. MENDELSON, WHO, ALONG with Dr. Don Fishman, has performed numerous equine "miracles" on the operating table at the Valecrest Surgical Center in Burlington, Ont., stated that "phenylbutazone does not in any manner stimulate or depress any of the vital functions of a horse — rate of heart beat, nervous system, et cetera."

A trainer who, for obvious reasons, elected to remain anonymous said: "The people who run racing are out of their minds. This stuff is used on athletes in all sports — football, hockey, baseball, track. Why not on horses?

"For a trainer to have this stuff in his armament and not be able to use it freely is ludicrous. The rule, in Ontario, states you can use it on a horse 48 hours before a race. You can follow the rule and, with certain horses, it'll still show up in the test. And if it shows up, you're dead — even though you followed the rule. It doesn't make sense."

CAVALARIS, OF COURSE, SOON will be exonerated — probably next Monday, the day of his next hearing. But he has been destroyed. The stigma of it all will be everlasting.

There are small people who forever will point accusing fingers at him and whisper such evil racetrack words as "drugger," "doper" and "fixer."

It isn't fair.

Besides, it cost Lou Cavalaris the realization of his dream — the saddling of a Kentucky Derby winner and, perhaps, a Triple Crown champion.

Horse Racing — FAT TONY
THE BOOKMAKER

Betting on horse races that have already been run.
Thursday, January 28, 1960
Phil Ranallo: What's New, Harry?

HONEST HARRY, that fellow who is an integral part of off-track betting, and a few of his fearless, parlay-playing friends were discussing the enemy — the bookmakers.

Harry and the boys, keeping pace with the times, were taking a poll. They were trying to settle on the right man for their "Bookie of the Decade" award.

When Honest Harry got the floor, he nominated Fat Tony, claiming that that large lump of a man was the bookie who left the most indelible mark of the "Frantic Fifties."

Harry had his reasons, too. But first, a little background.

Harry has bet horses all his life. He has bet them before and after post-time — when he didn't know which horse had won, and when he did.

Naive natives — those who think a quarter-pole is a fellow who is three-quarters something else — perhaps doubt it is possible to bet a horse after the race is over.

They're so wrong.

IN THE MID FIFTIES, clobbering bookies with bets on nags which already had been saliva-tested and cooled out, was almost as simple as picking an argument at the breakfast table.

The conniving bettors tools were a Wilmington, Del., phone number, a financial deposit at the Wilmington site, an Armstrong sheet and, of course, a bookmaker.

WILMINGTON, amazingly — and illegally — received and sold to clients instantaneous results from all tracks. If, for example, a six-furlong race went at 4:15, Wilmington would give you the winner at 4:16 1/2. One result cost $15.

Bookies regarded the Armstrong sheet as the last word in post-times. If the Armstrong listed post for the seventh at Rockingham at 4:15, you had no difficulty belting that race at 4:10 or earlier.

Those in on the Wilmington deal, like Honest Harry, reaped a harvest with the bookies — particularly during the fall of the year when tracks frequently move their post-times ahead due to bad weather, thin crowds, earlier darkness, etc.

Harry, after making the Wilmington deposit, needed only patience and a few bucks for phone tolls. He'd work it this way: He'd call Wilmington daily — say at 4 on the dot — and ask what post time was in the seventh at Rockingham.

Every once in a while, things were ideal. Actual post time was perhaps 4:04 as against 4:15 in the Armstrong. Under those conditions, he'd buy the race from Wilmington and immediately call his bookie.

THE UNSUSPECTING bookie would take Harry's bet without a question — until he got blistered four or five times, that is. Then he'd shut Harry off. Harry simply would hunt up another bookmaker — another victim.

ONE DAY, a friend told Harry that a certain bookmaker, Fat Tony, was too smart to be past-posted. Tony, the friend said, would give a client only a "time" bet on anything close to post-time.

A "time" bet works this way: The bettor calls the bookie, say at 4:14.

The book says he'll accept only a time bet If the bettor agrees, then the bet counts only if the race goes off at 4:14 or later. If the race goes before 4:14, it's no bet.

Harry bet his friend he could past-post Tony.

For a solid week, Harry bought the seventh at Rockingham from Wilmington, then called Tony and bet $100 to win on a horse he knew had been a loser in the race. Each time Tony gave Harry a time bet.

In other words, Harry made six $100 bets on six losers — and it didn't cost him a dime because of the time-bet angle.

This disturbed Tony, since he figured that was $600 he could have collected.

Harry, knowing Tony was ripe, instructed his friend to tell the bookie about the Wilmington deal. "Just tell him," Harry said, "that it may help him sometime when he needs a result real quick."

TWO DAYS LATER, Harry bought the seventh at Rockingham. The winner was a mare named Betty Button. Harry immediately called Tony.

"Tony," Harry says, "I'd like to bet $100 to win on Giant Killer in the seventh at Rocky."

Tony, who in the previous minute had been doing a little long-distance telephoning himself, says: "You're on, Harry."

"You're not giving me a time bet, Tony?" Harry asks.

"No," Tony says, "No time bet."

"Fine," Harry says. "And by the way, Tony, in the same race give me $200 to win on Betty Button."

Fat Tony quietly fainted.

Betty Button paid $29.80. The next day, Tony gave Harry $2,680, the winnings of a $200 bet, minus the $100 lost on Giant Killer.

Who says there's no honor among thieves? Fat Tony, incidentally, won the "Bookie of the Decade" award in a breeze.

Horse Racing — THE FIX

Several jockeys allegedly used an electronic device to shock their horses into running faster.

Wednesday, May 30, 1979

Phil Ranallo: What's New, Harry?

A RACETRACKER I happen to know — a long-time Fort Erie patron — has informed me he owes an apology to Gary Gibson, the jockey who Monday was dealt a five-year suspension by the Ontario Racing Commission.

Gibson, after riding a horse named Jay's Rick in Sunday's fourth at Fort Erie, was nabbed in possession of an electrical device, commonly referred to as a "joint" or "buzzer" around the racetrack.

A "joint" is a battery-operated shock device, small enough to fit in the palm of a hand, that's used to electrify a horse, make him run faster than he wants to run and faster than the sharpest handicappers think he can.

"I'm at the Fort Sunday," the racetracker said to me. "And I make a nice bet on Gibson's mount in the fourth race, Jay's Rick, who, as you know, runs slower than a mule and finishes up the racetrack, second-last.

"Well, after the race, when Gibson's dismounting in front of the stands, I make his eardrums twang. I tell him, among other things, that he does a great job of pulling the horse I bet my money on.

"NOW, THOUGH, I FEEL guilty about what I did — and I'd like to apologize to Gibson. After all, since he went so far as to use a 'joint' on his horse, I now know that Gary Gibson was giving me a 100 percent, honest effort."

The racetracker's view, of course, was a distorted one. Nevertheless, it was possible to get the picture, especially when the racetracker said:

"Look, at least Gibson was trying to win the race. I'd like to see them go after the jocks who pull horses."

The Gary Gibson incident brings to mind the jockey Robert Pion case, at Fort Erie in May of 1968.

One morning that May, the stewards, while reviewing the films of the previous day's races, noticed that jockey Pion, during the stretch run, scratched the neck of his mount several times.

Then, 50 yards before the finish line, Pion's hand opened and an object dropped to the track.

I saw the films of the race — and the camera work was perfect.

THE FORT ERIE stewards then called in Pion and ran the film for him — in slow motion. Slowly, on the film, Pion's hand opened and an object dropped out of the hand and fell to the track.

A steward, who had followed the fall of the object on the film with a pointer for Pion's benefit, then asked the jockey what the object was.

"What object?" Pion said in a surprised tone.

The steward ran the film again — forward and then backward — and again with the pointer, followed the fall of the object from Pion's hand to the ground, then the rise of the object from the ground Back into Pion's hand.

"What is that object?" the steward repeated.

"I don't know what you're talking about, sir", Pion replied, "I don't see anything."

Pion got off with 30 days.

The Pion horse, incidentally, won the race — at 6-to-1.

THEN THERE WAS THE "saga" of the all-time champion of "joints"

— Slick Jim, a jockey who did his cheating at Midwestern tracks, where stewards had spent years trying to nab him with the goods.

One day, the story goes, a snitch informed the stewards of Jim's modus operandi.

When Slick would pull his horse up after a victory, the stewards were told, he'd fling the "joint" — with an almost unnoticeable flip of the wrist — toward the outside rail on the backstretch, where a colleague would pick it up.

So the stewards set a trap for Slick.

One day, as Slick crossed the line a winner on a 25-to-1 shot, the stewards had a patrol judge rush to the side of the colleague on the backstretch.

Naturally, when Slick was pulling up the horse on the backstretch this day, he spotted the patrol judge next to his colleague, and did the smart thing. He hung on to the "joint."

THE PATROL JUDGE then mounted an outrider's horse and accompanied Slick as he returned to the area in front of the stands — to the clerk of scales, where the riders weigh out.

There, the stewards greeted Slick and invited him into their chambers for a little chat.

The stewards, never taking their eyes off Slick, escorted him into their private men's room. Then they ordered him to start undressing, reasoning that they'd find the "joint" secreted in some part of his clothing.

Well, Slick went all the way, stripped down to his birthday suit — yet no "joint" was found.

Slick had outfoxed the stewards again — especially one particular steward.

Later that night, this particular steward, while undressing for bed, reached into one of his coat pockets, felt a foreign object and said to himself, "Hey, what's this?"

HE PULLED THE OBJECT out of his pocket and — that's right — it was a "joint." Slick Jim had deftly unloaded it in the steward's pocket as he was being escorted to the steward's chambers.

The steward never reported the discovery, of course, because his embarrassment would have been too great.

Slick Jim made the disclosure himself — but only to intimates — and had the audacity to pen an anonymous letter to the steward suggesting that he sew his pockets closed for the good of racing.

Horse Racing — FORGED TICKETS

Aqueduct and Belmont Park tracks discover forged winning tickets.
Wednesday, March 11, 1978
Phil Ranallo: What's New, Harry?

BEATING THE RACES is an almost impossible trick. But not for one rare bird who — since coming up with a "key to the game" a year or so ago — has enjoyed numerous field days at Aqueduct and Belmont Park.

This bird is so rare that he gets to the payoff windows, with stunning regularity, without ever listening to inside information or stable whisper, without ever glimpsing tout sheets — and without ever using a Racing Form.

The only thing this fellow uses, to beat the races, is counterfeit pari-mutuel tickets.

Although New York Racing Association officials claim he has not struck since last November, they admit that the rare bird — labeled "The Phantom Forger" by New York race writers — has ripped off New York tracks for "roughly $25,000."

There are some track sources that scoff at that figure however, and estimate that the guy's "take" is closer to $75,000.

Whatever the amount, NYRA officials and gumshoes are red-faced, now that the rare bird's deeds have been leaked to the press —since they regard this kind of publicity as embarrassing to the tracks.

The guy operates strictly with $50 and $100 tickets. He removes the horse's number on a losing ticket, replaces it with the winning number, then cashes it the next day.

"THIS GUY IS AN artist, the best we've ever seen," said Clem Imperato, systems manager for Automatic Totalisators, which operates the tote machines and computers at Aqueduct.

"We're not sure how he does it, but we suspect that after he erases the losing number, he uses a printing press of some kind to impose the right number.

"One day he tried to cash a $100 ticket on a horse on which the payoff was over $2,000, so the mutuel clerk — following procedure — picked up the phone to call me to okay the payout.

"At the sight of the phone check, the man ran away. We knew then, of course, that the ticket was a dud. But the thing is, we examined the ticket for 10 minutes and could find nothing wrong with it.

"Only later, after more examination, did we find out the ticket was false."

The Achilles heel in the rare bird's modus operandi is his inability to do the counterfeit job fast enough to cash the tickets the same day.

It's much more difficult to cash a phony ticket the next day, since only the cream of the pari-mutuel clerks cash previous days' tickets.

WHICH BRINGS TO MIND the famous French forgers of a dozen years ago — the most talented group of pari-mutuel ticket alterers in the long history of racing.

Over a two-year span, these guys cashed a half-million dollars worth of phony tickets at racetracks in Gay Paree before being nabbed.

This ring of forgers included a super chemist, who may have been the most knowledgeable ink specialist since the days of the quill.

Every ticket the super chemist altered was a work of art, a Mona Lisa on pasteboard ... so perfect that no track cashier ever hesitated to cash it — despite the fact that every cashier in France was on the lookout for the doctored tickets.

The master forgers concentrated their efforts on the jumele-betting races, France's version of the American exacta races.

The forgers were exceptionally fond of the jumele for the important reason that jumele payoffs are usually fat and juicy, often running as high as 1,000-to-1 since the fields in French races are usually double the size of those in U.S. races.

The French forgers operated this way:

THE ON-TRACK MEMBER of the ring would buy a legitimate ticket or two on the jumele. Then shortly after the horses crossed the finish line, and the 1-2 finishers in the race were posted on the toteboard, he'd leave the track and join his forgers.

The forgers did their off-track work in a panel truck, which would be stationed in a different location every day — a mile or two from the track.

Then, in the truck, the super chemist would go to work. He'd mix his special concoction, use it to remove the numbers on the ticket, then print on the ticket the winning jumele numbers.

Then one of the forgers would hurry back to the track — and cash.

The forgers never cashed more than two tickets a day — making it impossible for track pari-mutuel employees to discover until the end of the racing day that more winning tickets had been cashed than had been sold.

It took a terrible stroke of luck to do the forgers in.

ON THE DAY THEY WERE nabbed, the on-track member of the gang did everything letter perfect. He bought one legitimate jumele ticket, waited until the numbers of the in-the-money horses were posted on the board, then left the track and delivered the ticket to the super chemist.

The super chemist altered the ticket — perfectly.

Then the other guy returned to the track, nonchalantly walked up to a cashier, handed him the altered ticket — and the cashier immediately called the cops.

The cashier and the French cops merited no medals for nabbing the forgers, however.

Unbeknownst to the forger who tried to cash, no ticket had been sold on the first two finishers in the race — since no bettor with the correct first horse had coupled that horse with the second horse.

Therefore, according to the rules of racing, holders of tickets on the first and third horses were declared the jumele winners.

The doctored pasteboard was the forgers' ticket to jail.

Horse Racing — AVELINO GOMEZ

Jockey killed in a spectacular spill at Woodbine Racetrack in Ontario, Canada.

Monday, June 23, 1980

Phil Ranallo: What's New, Harry?

RIDING RACEHORSES is a most dangerous occupation.

The jockey roulette wheel — the wheel of death — is constantly spinning. And every time a jockey puts a leg up, he does so with the knowledge that this may be the time his number will come up.

Saturday afternoon, at Woodbine, jockey Avelino Gomez's number came up.

His chest crushed in a sickening spill during the running of the $112,535 Canadian Oaks, Avelino Gomez died four hours later — on the operating table at Etobicoke General Hospital.

Avelino Gomez, whose riding wizardry earned him numerous sobriquets — "El Perfecto" ... "The Cuban Hawk" ... "The Cuban Cannonball" — was the most colorful figure ever to grace the thoroughbred racing scene in Canada.

And, in the view of this observer, "El Perfecto" was also the best rider — better than Sandy Hawley, better than Jeff Fell. In fact, Gomez, in his prime, was as good as the best anywhere — if not better.

Riding a racehorse, in a way, is like playing the piano. It's all in the touch. To be a champion race-rider, you've got to have the touch of a concert pianist.

The only communication between the horse and the jockey is through the fingers and hands — through the reins.

IT'S ALL IN THE touch.

And Avelino Gomez had a golden touch that enabled him to attain the goal of riding more than 4,000 winners in his career — a milestone reached by only six other jockeys in the 400-year history of horseracing.

Although he delighted in entertaining the customers with his antics in the saddle, before and after races, Gomez was one of the most fierce competitors ever to get astride a racehorse — a man with burning pride and an endless hunger for victory.

In his heyday, Gomez, with his showmanship, actually lured people to the racetrack.

And, when things were going right for him, as they so often did, Avelino, out of sheer exuberance, would leave the fans laughing and cheering — by catapulting himself vertically from the saddle.

ON THE RACETRACK, Gomez gave no quarter and asked no quarter. And he would fight at the drop of a riding cap, even though he was every bit as bad a fighter as he was good a rider.

His numerous fights with fellow rider Hugo Dittfach — all of which Avelino lost – are legend in Canada. Hugo and Avelino fought in the jockeys' quarters, in the walking ring, in the winner's circle — yet always remained friends.

Gomez was a fellow who delighted in rubbing it in — as evidenced by the photograph of the finish of a stakes race at Arlington Park in 1962.

In those days, Gomez was doing much of his riding in the States — and most of his fussing and feuding with the tempestuous Manuel Ycaza.

THE PHOTOGRAPH, taken from the infield, shows Gomez's mount, Porvenir II, hitting the finish line a head in front of Oink, a horse ridden by Ycaza.

Gomez, whose horse is on the outside, has his head turned to the left, and he's looking Ycaza straight in the eye — with a giant grin on his face and with his tongue stuck way out.

Gomez was the top percentage rider in racing history. In his 36-year racetrack career, the 52-year-old "El Perfecto" won with 24 percent of his mounts — scoring roughly 4,100 victories in 17,000 rides.

And his horses earned $11.6 million in purse money.

BORN IN THE SHADOW of Havana's Oriental Park, Gomez worked as a bellhop in a Havana hotel before drifting to the racetrack as an exercise boy. Later, he went to Mexico City, where he got up on his first mount in 1944, at age 16.

In 1950, Gomez came to the States for the first time and rode briefly that year in Ohio and Florida.

The next summer he rode at top tracks in Chicago, piloting Curandero to victory in the $100,000 Washington Park Handicap, and winning other stakes with Bernwood and Andy B.W.

The Korean War was on at the time, and when Gomez returned to his native Cuba ahead of a draft call for the U.S. Army, his status as a resident alien was lifted.

Thereafter, he was allowed to ride in the U.S. only when he was riding for Canadian horse owners.

SO, ALTHOUGH GOMEZ was a sporting legend in Canada — where he rode for the last years — he never received the widespread acclaim in America that his abilities so richly deserved.

The lack of national recognition, however, did not disturb Gomez.

"What I could have achieved as a jockey, if I'd ridden in the States all those years — that doesn't bother me," Gomez often said "And I don't blame anyone for it.

"I broke the law in the U.S. It was a bad thing to do. I accept the consequences."

Gomez leaves a wife, Patricia, a native of Buffalo, and three children — Avelino Jr., 19, Jacqueline, 18, and Matthew, 17.

Mickey Gomez, Avelino's brother, said Sunday night that Mrs. Gomez is planning to have her husband buried in Buffalo.

THE FATE THAT BEFELL Avelino Gomez should serve as a reminder that every time a jockey gathers the reins on a thoroughbred he is taking his life in his hands.

The jockey knows this, and it is a fact of racing life that should be remembered more often by horse-players who risk only their money and do not refrain from black-guarding the jockey who is putting his life on the line.

Saturday, at Woodbine, the people who wagered on Gomez's mount in the Canadian Oaks lost their money — and Avelino Gomez lost his life.

Horse Racing — NORTHERN DANCER IS DERBY WINNER

Northern Dancer is the first Canadian horse to win the Kentucky Derby.

Sunday, May 3, 1964

By PHIL RANALLO

LOUISVILLE — Maybe a good little horse can't beat a good big horse — but Northern Dancer, the mighty mite from Canada, proved Saturday that a great little one can.

The Dancer, the Dominion's most celebrated product since Canadian Club, dazzled Hill Rise and 10 other Yankee rivals with his sensational hoof work as he snatched thoroughbred racing's No. 1 prize — the Kentucky Derby.

With stone-faced Bill Hartack cuddled on his strong back, the hickory-tough Dancer won the 90th edition of the Churchill Downs classic like a true champion.

He displayed a giant heart by fighting off a desperate late bid by Hill Rise, the colt which had been billed as the "Wonder of the West" — and he ran the fastest mile-and-a-quarter in Derby history.

With 100,000 pairs of eyes riveted on his glistening mahogany hide, the magnificent Dancer charged under the wire a neck before Hill Rise. It was another 3-1/4 lengths back to the third horse, The Scoundrel.

Northern Dancer, flying the turquoise-and-gold silks of Edward Plunket Taylor's Windfields Farm, streaked the mile-and-a-quarter in 2 minutes flat as he ended an 89-year losing streak for Canadian-breds in the storied stampede.

The time slashed two-fifths of a second from the former record of 2:00 2/5, established by Decidedly in the 1962 Derby.

Decidedly, incidentally, also benefitted from the riding talent of Hartack, the controversial little guy who does almost nothing but sneer and win Kentucky Derbies.

Hartack has made six appearances in the glamor gallop and four times has wound up buried in roses. In addition to Northern Dancer and Decidedly, Hardtack made it with Iron Liege (1957) and Venitian Way (1960). Hardtack is perfect.

Having Hardtack on his back this bright and beautiful afternoon didn't hurt Northern Dancer a bit — in fact, it may have been the difference. Hardtack rode a perfect race.

Northern Dancer and Hill Rise, ridden by the little millionaire who wound up picking a loser, Willie Shoemaker, were in the middle of the pack and going head-and-head for the first five lengths of a mile. The Dancer was sixth and Hill Rise was seventh. Then approaching the far turn Hardtack made the move which resulted in victory. He clucked to his mount — and the Dancer took off, stealing at least three lengths on Hill Rise in a twinkle.

The Dancer, in high gear, charged for the leaders — Mr. Brick, Royal Shuck, The Scoundrel and Quadrangle. At the quarter-pole — the top of the stretch — the Dancer thrust his head in front of Mr. Brick. Then Hardtack hit him "lightly on the behind" — but the Dancer didn't respond enough to satisfy the rider so Hartack hit him hard and Northern Dancer exploded.

The greatest racehorse ever minted in the Dominion rolled into a two-length lead but now with an eighth mile to go Hill Rise was second and Shoemaker was digging into him — and Hill Rise was coming.

Hill Rise, in a few earth-devouring

strides, slashed the Dancer's lead to a length — and then, with 70 yards to go, he was at the Dancer's throatlatch.

It appeared that Hill Rise would run him down. But Hartack alerted the Dancer with some furious left-handed whipping — and the pride of Canada exposed his big heart by holding his antagonist safe in the final breathtaking strides.

"This is a hard-trying, game-running little horse," the smiling Hartack said after dismounting. "He really did some running from the quarter-pole to the eighth-pole, and was running his gamest at the wire."

Shoemaker, who quit Northern Dancer in favor of Hill Rise after riding the Canadian colt to victory in the Florida Derby at Gulfstream Park, said:

"No, I'm not sorry I chose Hill Rise over Northern Dancer. If I had it to over again, I'd do the same thing.

"The race was a good one for Hill Rise, but not good enough. Northern Dancer got a little far away from us at the head of the stretch and, although we were getting to him, I felt we weren't going to get there when we passed the eighth pole."

The victory was Northern Dancer's fourth in a row and ninth in his last ten starts. The little son of Nearctic and Natalma is 11 for 14 since launching his career at the Ft. Erie Jockey Club on Aug. 2, 1963.

This was Northern Dancer's third triumph in a race worth $100,000 or more. He picked up $114,300 of the gross purse of $156,800 and rocketed his career.

Since most of this has been earned in the United States, the Dancer's owner, the fabulously wealthy Taylor, is eight percent richer than people think.

This was an unforgettable day for the Dancer's trainer — Horatio Luro, the foxy Argentinian.

Luro for weeks and weeks has spent lonely nights.

Thirteen months ago, Californian George A. Pope shipped a 2-year-old to Luro — and the Argentinian turned down the juvenile, claiming the colt was too skinny.

The colt Luro turned down is Hill Rise.

The Scoundrel, the Rex Ellsworth colt, saved third money by a nose over the gallant little gelding Roman Brother, which was a neck in front of the East's big horse, Quadrangle.

Mr. Brick, the pace-setter for almost a mile, was fifth. Then, in order, came Mr. Moonlight, Dandy K., Ishkoodah, Wil Rad, Extra Swell and Royal Shuck.

Ycaza Lauds Mount

Jockey Manuel Ycaza was very impressed with his mount, The Scoundrel. "I tell you this horse very good," Ycaza said. "I think he will improve.

"He ran a marvelous race — and he was right there with the leader at the stretch turn. But he couldn't cope with Northern Dancer and Hill Rise the last quarter."

Maybe Ycaza feels even more kindly toward The Scoundrel now that he knows Northern Dancer ripped that final quarter in 24 seconds flat, equaling the final-quarter record set in 1941 by Whirlaway.

Northern Dancer, second choice in the betting, rewarded backers with across-the-board mutuels of $8.80, $3.60 and $3. Hill Rise, sent away the 7-to-5 favorite, paid $3. and $2.60. The Scoundrel, a 6-to-1 shot, returned $3.20 for show.

A record $2,144,079 was wagered on the Derby.

Next stop for the Dancer — the Preakness, at Pimlico in Baltimore, May 16.

Horse Racing — SECRETARIAT SHATTERS CLASSIC RECORDS

Secretariat shatters classic records in the Kentucky Derby.

Sunday, May 6, 1973

By PHIL RANALLO

LOUISVILLE — Secretariat is everything his trainer, Lucian Laurin, said he was ... and maybe more. He is a super-horse, a 1,100-pound equine thunderbolt, a wondrous and magnificent racehorse who now looms as thoroughbred racing's first Triple Crown winner in 25 years.

Saturday afternoon, at tradition-steeped Churchill Downs, Secretariat, the $6,080,000 colt from the Meadow Stable, smothered the finest 3-year-olds in America with a record-shattering performance in the 99th edition of the Kentucky Derby.

Secretariat, with jockey Ron Turcotte on his copper-coated back, ran the final quarter in an incredible 23 1/5 seconds — fastest last-quarter in the history of the classic — and completed the mile and one-quarter in a breathtaking 1:59 2/5, rubbing out the Derby record of two minutes flat set in 1964 by the brilliant Northern Dancer.

Wins With Authority

Secretariat won with the authority of a champion — by lengths over Sham — as he avenged his stunning defeat of two weeks ago in the Wood Memorial Stakes at Aqueduct, a race in which his credentials came under serious question.

All of the doubters now are firm believers.

Duels With Sham

The final quarter of this richest of all Derbies — the race's value was $198,800 — was a duel between Secretariat and Sham ... with Sham in front as they wheeled into the stretch and Secretariat 1 1/2 lengths behind.

At that point, this pair had already kissed the other 11 horses goodbye.

As they straightened for home, Turcotte buried his head in Secretariat's mane and clucked to the colt, asked him to run — and the bold and swash-buckling son of Bold Ruler responded with an explosive run on the outside.

Secretariat collared Sham at the eighth pole, shoved his clean head in front of the colt from the West, then drove inexorably toward the finish line, widening his advantage with each earth-devouring stride.

Didn't Need Whip

Turcotte never touched Secretariat with the whip during the run through the long stretch. Ron just sat there, calm and relaxed, and hand-rode the spectacularly marked colt whose white stockings on three of his feet make him identifiable to the fans.

Secretariat, with his ears pricking, rushed under the wire 2 1/2 lengths before Sham. The rest of the horses were up the track. Our Native staggered home third, eight lengths back of Sham and a half-length in front of Forego.

Then, in order, came Restless Jet, Shecky Greene, the pace-setter for seven-eighths of a mile, Navajo, Royal and Regal, My Gallant, Angle Light, Gold Bag, Twice A Prince and War-bucks.

Hartack Is Last

The "boy" astride Warbucks, the trailer in the 13-horse field, was the grouchy and abrasive Bill Hartack — a development that gouged a giant hole in that old law, "Nice guys finish last."

The happiest fellow on the premises — and the guys and gals on hand totaled a record 134,476 — was Lucien

Laurin, the 60-year-old trainer who had been criticized since Secretariat's loss in the Wood and badgered for two weeks by Frank (Pancho) Martin, the Cuban-bred who trains Sham.

"I've had more pressure on me than I've had in my life," the jubilant Laurin said. "But this colt turned out to be my redeemer. Ron Turcotte gave him a wonderful ride."

Asked if he had anything to say about his antagonist, Pancho Martin, Laurin said:

"Yes, Mr. Martin is a wonderful trainer."

Was Worried

Laurin admitted he was worried when Secretariat was last as the horses thundered past the stands the first time and headed for the first turn. "I said to myself, 'Please, God, don't tell me it's going to be another one of those!' "

It wasn't.

Secretariat slipped into sixth place after a half-mile, reached a contending position — fifth — at the three-quarters, then uncorked that dazzling move around the last turn and through the stretch.

"I let him run his own race to the quarter-pole," jockey Turcotte said. "Running down the backstretch, he picked up those horses on his own. I didn't ask him to put out until the stretch run. He gave a lot of run right away — and I knew we were going to take Sham."

Trainer Laurin had a few words for Jimmy (The Greek) Snyder, the Las Vegas odds-maker who two days ago circulated a report that Secretariat had a sore knee. "Tell Jimmy the Greek he overplayed his hand. Tell him he should fire the agent who gave him that bad information."

Derby History

Secretariat rewarded backers in the huge crowd with a $5 payoff — a rather generous price for a horse who two weeks ago was rated at 4-to-5 in the Derby winterbook. The colt's slice of the purse was $155,050, lifting his career earnings to a thumping $675,322.

Secretariat enabled Laurin and Turcotte and his owner, Mrs. John Tweedy, to make Derby history. They are the first trainer, jockey and owner to win two successive Derbies in 99 years. They won last year with Riva Ridge.

Laffit Pincay Jr., rider of Sham, said: "He ran his race. I think it might have been better if I had waited a little longer take the lead. The horse on top, Shecky Greene, moved out on us as we were beginning to take the lead. But Sham ran a good race ... and he'll win lots of races."

The races in which Secretariat stays in the barn, that is.

A member of the Churchill Downs publicity staff asked "friendly" Bill Hartack if he had a comment on the race, and Hartack never batted an eye. He just took a big bite of a sandwich and walked away.

Near World Mark

Secretariat's time for the race — 1:59 2/5 — was 1 1/5 seconds over the world record of 1:58 1/5, set in 1950 by Noor at Golden Gate Fields and equalled last July by Quack, in the Hollywood Gold Cup at Hollywood Park.

The colt's final quarter of 23 1/4 seconds erased the Derby's last-quarter record of 24 seconds flat, set by Whirlaway in 1941.

Secretariat, with his marvelous run on this warm and clear afternoon consolidated his position on top of the 3-year-old class and took the first long step toward the Triple Crown, which he can capture with victories in the

Preakness and Belmont Stakes.
Who's going to beat him?

Horse Racing — SECRETARIAT STUNS 'EM AGAIN

Derby champion takes Preakness in classic style.

Sunday, May 20, 1973

By PHIL RANALLO

BALTIMORE — Secretariat, the charismatic colt, is still the "big kid" on the block. The Meadow Stable's "Red Beauty" ran the legs off his rivals Saturday afternoon in the $182,400 Preakness Stakes and took another giant stride toward equine immortality.

Running powerfully and easily and beautifully, Secretariat won as convincingly as a racehorse can win and tipped off the racing world that three weeks hence, in the Belmont Stakes, he will become the sport's first Triple Crown winner since 1948.

Lured by the magnetic Secretariat, an all-time Pimlico Race Course crowd of 61,657 watched Mrs. John Tweedy's marvelous colt snatch the Preakness prize in the same manner that he won the Kentucky Derby two weeks ago — by charging from last place.

Early Pace Is Slow

This time, Secretariat made an early move — thanks to Ron Turcotte, who judged correctly that the pace was unusually slow — and the move was awesome, electrifying. It brought a gasp from the vast army of witnesses. Secretariat had gotten away slowly, leisurely, and when the field had gone a quarter-mile, he was last — despite the fact that the first quarter had been negotiated in the trotting horse time of 25 seconds.

Suddenly, Secretariat turned it on, Turcotte taking him three wide around the clubhouse turn. He looped his five rivals, dramatically — and by the time another quarter-mile had been covered, Secretariat was on top!

Secretariat quickly opened a two-length lead — and that was that. From that point home, he galloped them to death and flashed under the wire 2-1/2 lengths before Sham, the good, good steed who is destined to become a bridesmaid because he was born in Secretariat's year.

Our Native was third, eight lengths back of Sham.

No one will ever be able to say that the 1973 Kentucky Derby and Preakness Stakes were not truly run ... because the two races produced the same 1-2-3 finish — Secretariat, Sham and Our Native — and the identical margins separated the three.

Remarkable!

Too Much for Sham

Sham, in defeat, was rated brilliantly by jockey Lafitt Pincay Jr. But it was simply a case of Sham again running against too much horse.

While Pincay was whipping furiously, even desperately, during the long run down the stretch, Ron Turcotte was just sitting there up front, calmly letting Secretariat breeze home.

"I never hit him, not even once," Turcotte said. "I didn't even show him the whip. I just hand-rode him. I had more horse if a challenge had come. He was very strong at the finish."

Wins In 1:55

Despite the slow early pace, Secretariat ran the third fastest Preakness of all time, covering the mile and three-sixteenths in 1:55. The Preakness record of 1:54 was set by Canonero II in 1971. The second swiftest Preakness was the 1955 edition, when Nashua did 1:54 3/5.

Almost everybody at Old Hilltop bet on Secretariat with both hands, and the colt's win price was $2.60 — smallest Preakness price since Nashua rewarded backers with a similar payoff.

For Ron Turcotte, this Preakness was a redeeming as well as rewarding experience.

Critics Answered

With the memory of last year's Preakness still lingering — that's the test in which Turcotte failed with Riva Ridge — Ron needed a sparkling performance on his part Saturday to stave off the critics.

Turcotte got what he needed. He was letter-perfect and a help to his horse all the way around.

But he refused to take credit, electing to give credit to Secretariat. "My colt let me know the pace was too slow and he just took off. I gave him his head and he did the rest; ordinarily, it's a very bad move when you go three-wide round the clubhouse turn — but not when the other horses aren't running very fast."

Laurin Beats Jinx

Lucien Laurin, the gentle little French-Canadian who trains Secretariat, at long last got his chance to breathe a sigh of relief after a Preakness.

"I was really beginning to believe that I might never win a Preakness — that this race was a jinx for me. I know we have a wonderful horse, a great horse — but I couldn't relax until he was near the finish-line and I knew he couldn't lose."

Mrs. Tweedy, the mistress of Meadow Stable, who accompanied Turcotte and Laurin to the Pimlico press box, said: "I'm still trembling, and I'm hot and thirsty — and I'm very proud."

Triple Crown Team

It is a remarkable team, this Mrs. Tweedy - Laurin - Turcotte threesome. They have won four of the last five Triple Crown races — last year's Kentucky Derby and Belmont Stakes with Riva Ridge, and this year's Derby and Preakness with Secretariat.

Pincay, Sham's rider, said his horse ran a good race and had no excuse. "That other horse is too much. I didn't expect Secretariat to go to the front so soon. At the head of the stretch, I thought I might have a chance because I figured he might give up after that big early move. I kept waiting for Turcotte to hit him, but he never did. Secretariat is a great one."

Has Won $805,122

Secretariat earned a purse of $129,900 for Mrs. Tweedy, who doesn't need it. This boosted the colt's 1973 money figure to $348,719 and his career bankroll to $805,122.

Secretariat is the seventh horse in 24 years with a chance to win the Triple Crown after the running of a Preakness. The others— Tim Tam (1958), Carry Back (1961), Northern Dancer (1964), Kauai King (1966), Majestic Prince (1969) and Canonero II (1971) — all failed in the Belmont.

And in the Belmont, Secretariat will be bidding to become the ninth horse in history to win the Triple Crown. If he does, he'll earn a place among these eight greats — Sir Barton, Gallant Fox, Omaha, War Admiral, Whirlaway, Count Fleet, Assault and Citation.

Secretariat has given every indication he belongs.

Horse Racing — SECRETARIAT RUNS AWAY WITH TRIPLE CROWN

Copper colt adds Belmont "Jewel" in record time.

Sunday, June 10, 1973

By PHIL RANALLO

NEW YORK —Secretariat, that magnificent dude — that unreal, coppery-coated colt who is worth five times his weight in gold — planted an indelible hoof on the world of thoroughbred racing Saturday afternoon as he streaked to an incredible 31-length victory in the Belmont Stakes.

I'll wait right here a second, on this line of type, while you glance up and take another gander at that figure — that victory margin — in the first paragraph.

Okay?

The victory margin, racing fans, is absolutely correct — 31 lengths.

Secretariat, the "Perfect Horse," the equine Adonis, the $6-million chunk of marvelous and matchless horseflesh thus pulled it off — became the thoroughbred racing game's first Triple Crown winner in 25 years.

Sets American Record

That, though, isn't all this charismatic charger accomplished on this sweltering afternoon. The Meadow Stable flyer established an American record for a mile-and-a-half in the bargain, flashing the distance in an electrifying 2 minutes, 24 seconds.

Secretariat's performance was totally devastating. He demolished his four rivals, winning with ridiculous ease. When he rushed under the wire across the finish line, only those with powerful binoculars could locate the second horse.

But believe it or not, it was a simply brilliant horse race for two horses ... for 5 of the 12 furlongs.

Secretariat and Sham went at it, head-to-head for those first five furlongs — Secretariat on the inside.

Second Largest Crowd

Then Ron Turcotte whispered a sweet nothing or two in Secretariat's ear — and the wondrous racehorse exploded. He quickly opened up two lengths at the six-furlong mark, then kept widening and widening — to 7 lengths at the mile, 20 lengths at the mile-and-a-quarter, 28 lengths in midstretch, and finally that eye-popping 31 lengths.

The second largest crowd in Belmont Park history, 69,138, cheered him to the echo as he ran off and hid from his leg weary adversaries ... and most of those 69,138, as they watched in disbelief, had to be asking themselves a question: "Who's Man O War?"

The 31 lengths represented the greatest victory margin for a Belmont Stakes winner. The previous "biggest" Belmont victor was Cont Fleet, who romped by 25 in 1943.

Longshot Second

When the second horse in this Belmont finally arrived at the finish line, it turned out to be a steed named Twice A Prince, the longshot of the race, at 17-to-1. My Gallant was third, a half-length back of Twice A Prince, and 13 lengths in front of the fourth horse, Pvt. Smiles.

The "caboose" horse in the five-horse field was Sham, the plucky colt who had finished second to Secretariat in both the Kentucky Derby and Preakness Stakes.

Saturday, Sham dropped an anchor — his attempt to run with Secretariat early obviously tearing the heart out of him.

Secretariat's feat of snatching racing's three big ones ... the Kentucky

Derby, Preakness and Belmont ...
had not been achieved since Citation
wrapped his hooves around the Triple
Crown in 1948 — when Harry Truman
was in the White House and everybody had short hair but Einstein and
Toscanini.

Spot Besides Greats

Secretariat is the ninth Triple Crown
winner. He has earned his spot beside
these eight greats of the turf — Sir
Barton (1919), Gallant Fox (1930),
Omaha (1935), War Admiral (1937),
Whirlaway (1941), Count Fleet (1942),
Assault (1946) and Citation.

Secretariat's time for the mile-and-
a-half — 2:24 — slashed 2 3/5 seconds
off the former Belmont record of 2:26
3/5 set by Gallant Man in 1937. It also
rubbed out the American record of
2:26 1/5, established by Going Abroad
in 1964 at Aqueduct.

Dirt Track Record

And Secretariat's 2:24 is the best
clocking for the distance on a dirt
track.

And Secretariat's 2:24 is the best
mile-and-a-half ever run on dirt anywhere. The world mark for the distance is 2:23, but it was turned in on
the grass — by Fiddle Isle three years
ago at Santa Anita.

Secretariat's quarter-mile fractions
were dazzling — the quarter in :23 3/5,
the half in :46 1/5, the three-quarters
in 1:09 4/5, the mile in 1:34 1/5 and the
mile-and-a-quarter in 1:59.

The 1:59 is two-fifths of a second
faster than his record run in the Derby
five weeks ago.

The Meadow Stable thunderbolt has
equaled one track record and shattered
two others in six races this year — and
there are those who will always believe
he was robbed of a third due to the
faulty Pimlico teletimer.

Earnings Reach $895,242

Secretariat picked up a purse of
$90,120 for his happy owner, Mrs.
John Tweedy. This boosted his 1973
earnings to $438,562 and his career
bankroll to $895,242.

Secretariat rewarded his legion of
backers in the Belmont crowd with
a $2.20 win price. But he was worth
more to place — $2.40. Twice A
Prince's place price was $4.60. There
was no show wagering. The 2-5 exacta
of Secretariat and Twice A Prince paid
$35.20.

Now the stress and strain of this
nerve-wracking game is over for the
Meadow Stable triumvirate of owner
Mrs. Tweedy, trainer Lucien Laurin
and jockey Ron Turcotte,

They've got their Triple Crown
champ.

Secretariat has stamped himself of
the stuff of racing dreams. He is the
racehorses' racehorse.

He is a legend in his own time.

Horse Racing — SECRETARIAT LOSES TO UNKNOWN HORSE

Unknown horse named "Onion" defeats Secretariat.
Thursday, October 4, 1973
Phil Ranallo: What's New, Harry?

H. ALLEN JERKENS IS A man of magic. Jerkens, in case the name escapes you, is the fellow who trains horses for Hobeau Farm — and who twice in the last two months has saddled Hobeau "unknowns" which have gone out and made a "bum" of Secretariat.

Jerkens first did the "impossible" early last August, at Saratoga, in the Whitney Stakes, when he sent out Onion, a sprinter whose name was not a household word even among chaps who pay close attention to the bangtails — and Onion made an omelet out of Secretariat, whipping "Sexy" by one length.

Onion's victory was one of the all-time upsets of the turf — since Onion was a steed who never before had won a stake race, who never before had gone more than a mile.

But Secretariat had an excuse. The big red colt had left his race on the training track, with that spectacular workout five days earlier, his entourage reasoned — and he had banged his head on the starting gate in the Whitney, remember?

IT JUST WASN'T SECRETARIAT'S day, they said. What happened to the Meadow Stable marvel in the Whitney would never happen again. Well it did happen to him again last Saturday, in the Woodward Stakes at Belmont Park.

And H. Allen Jerkens was the trainer who did it to Secretariat again.

This time, Jerkens dared to challenge Secretariat with another Hobeau Farm horse — Prove Out, another horse who never before had won a stake race — and Prove Out ran the legs off Secretariat, flogging him by 4-1/2 lengths.

This guy, H. Allen Jerkens, is too much!

The startling success he has experienced the last dozen years — while sending his "poor, little steeds" against racehorses with the "super-horse" stamp — can hardly be written off as luck.

Jerkens has done it too often. He is the scourge of champions. He keeps plucking feathers from the wings of Pegasus. He may be a training genius.

A DOZEN YEARS AGO, THE greatest racehorse in the land was the marvelous gelding, Kelso, the "people's choice," but three times "Kelly" was humbled by a horse trained by Jerkens.

That Jerkens horse was Hobeau Farm's Beau Purple.

In 1962, Beau Purple defeated Kelso in the Suburban Handicap and the Man o' War Stakes. Then, in 1963, Beau Purple made it a "hat-trick" by upsetting Kelso again — in the Widener Handicap.

In 1967, the most respected racehorse in the world was the extraordinary Buckpasser.

In the Brooklyn Handicap that year, Jerkens had the temerity to send a nonentity named Handsome Boy against Buckpasser — and Handsome Boy dashed to an electrifying eight-length victory.

So knocking off champions is old hat to Allen Jerkens. He has made a career of proving his point — by knocking them off at the height of their popularity.

MRS. PENNY TWEEDY AND Lucien Laurin will always remember

Jerkens as the trainer who would not keep out of their hair ... as the fellow whose "no-name" horses — Onion and Prove Out — badly tarnished Secretariat's image.

When Secretariat suffered his first loss of the year to Angle Light last April in the Wood Memorial, he had an excuse. The excuse was a bad ride — a misjudgment of pace by Ron Turcotte.

The charge against Turcotte was substantiated, in the eyes of the racing world, by Secretariat's sweep of the Triple Crown, especially by his 31-length victory in the Belmont Stakes.

Secretariat had an excuse in the Whitney — it wasn't his day, he banged his head, the workout took too much out of him, he was developing a fever, etc.

But Secretariat ran out of excuses Saturday.

The brilliant trainer, H. Allen Jerkens, with the likes of Onion and Prove Out, has exposed Secretariat as something less than "The Horse of The Century."

Even as something less than a super-horse.

Super-horses simply do not get beaten by racehorses such as Angle Light and Onion and Prove Out.

I think.

Horse Racing — SECRETARIAT ROMPS IN RACING FAREWELL

Runs the last race of his career at Woodbine Racetrack in Ontario, Canada.

Monday, October 29, 1973

By PHIL RANALLO

TORONTO — "Super Red" went out with a flair.

Secretariat, that matchless, magnificent dude, bade farewell to the racing world with another of his devastating performances Sunday afternoon as he romped to victory in the $142,700 Canadian International Championship Stakes at Woodbine.

In the 21st and final appearance of his spectacular career, the most expensive racehorse ever to step onto a racetrack — and the flashiest, if not the greatest — "blackjacked" his 11 opponents in the grueling mile-and-five-eighths Canadian classic.

The powerful chestnut colt with the white star on his forehead and the three white stockings made it look easy — almost as easy as he did in the Belmont Stakes.

Kennedy Road Leads

Secretariat stalked the pacesetting Kennedy Road for 10 furlongs then put that gallant Canadian-bred away three-eighths a mile from home — when jockey Eddie Maple said, "Go" — and that was the end of the horse race.

As Secretariat went to the front, the crowd of 35,117 let loose a deafening cheer. The Meadow Stable colt, in a twinkling, built his lead to five lengths — and he was boss by 12 lengths as he thundered into the stretch.

He galloped under the wire 6-1/2 lengths before Big Spruce — without Maple, who was pinch-riding for the suspended Ron Turcotte, ever asking him for his best in the stretch.

Touched Him Once

"I touched him with the whip only once," Maple said, and that was around the three-eighths pole when I thought it was time to go after Kennedy Road."

This 36th edition of the Canadian Championship was more an emotional experience than a horse race.

Almost without exception, the 35,117 fans were on their feet as Secretariat turned into the stretch with that huge 12-length lead — some with their fists clenched, others waving in salute ... and all applauding or shouting with vigor.

If there was any disappointment, it was that Secretariat, who this year shattered five track records and two world records, failed to break a record in his grand finale.

Track Is Slick

But there may have been a reason. It rained during the running of the race and, as Maple pointed out, the grass was a bit slick.

Secretariat negotiated the mile and five lengths in 2:41 4/5 – four fifths of a second over the turf course record set by The Axe II in the 1963 Canadian Championship.

Secretariat, in scoring his 16th victory in 21 races, rewarded his army of betting backers with across-the-board mutuels of $2.40, $2.50 and $2.10. The customers bet a total of $181,485 on the race — and $107,337 of it was wagered on Secretariat.

Secretariat picked up a purse of $92,755, raising his 1973 bankroll to $330,404 — an all-time single-season record for a racehorse.

The loot lifted his career figure to

$1,316,308, moving him ahead of Carry Back and Nashua, and into fourth place on the all-time career money list — behind Kelso ($1,997,896), Round Table ($1,749,869) and Buckpasser ($1,462,014).

But money won — and even record times turned in — are poor gauges of this particular race horse. Secretariat has been exciting to watch — and he made fans of people who normally pay little attention to racing — and that is the true measure of "Super Red."

Big Spruce Second

Big Spruce, the place horse in this race, rallied from dead last to earn second money, 1-1/2 lengths before Golden Don. Presidial was fourth, another three-quarters of a length away. Then, in order, came Fabe Count, Triangular, Top of the Day, Twice Lucky, Kennedy Road, Tico's Donna, Roundhouse and Fun Co K.

It no longer is possible to write anything new about Secretariat. All of it has been said. But now that he is through, thoroughbred racing is minus its No. 1 superstar of all-time.

Ron Turcotte put it perfectly the other day.

"We may never see his like again."

Horse Racing — RON TURCOTTE

Jockey who rode Secretariat to the Triple Crown is paralyzed from the waist down in an accident at Belmont.

Sunday, December 10, 1978

Phil Ranallo: What's New, Harry?

FIVE MONTHS HAVE passed since that fateful July afternoon at Belmont Park — the day jockey Ron Turcotte came away from the starting gate astride a filly named Flag of Leyte Gulf.

Flag of Leyte Gulf was the 20,130th mount of Ron Turcotte's outstanding riding career — his 20,130th and last.

A few jumps out of the gate, Turcotte glanced to his left and saw big trouble. Small Raja, a horse with Jeff Fell in the saddle, was rapidly drifting toward Flag of Leyte Gulf.

Turcotte "grabbed" his filly, tugged the reins, in an effort to check her. And, as he tugged, he yelled:

"Hey, Jeff! Watch out! Jeff! Hey!"

But it was too late.

Small Raja bumped Turcotte's mount, and Flag of Leyte Gulf instinctively reached out with her forelegs in an attempt to keep her balance.

But Flag of Leyte Gulf, in reaching out, stepped on the hind quarters of the horse in front of her and fell, head first, catapulting Turcotte from the saddle and sending him somersaulting on the track.

Turcotte remained conscious, and knew almost immediately that he was paralyzed from the waist down.

"I COULDN'T GET my breath," Turcotte said later. "So I pushed my stomach in, and it was like I was pushing in a bag of water. The muscles had all let go.

"Then I reached down and touched my legs, and I knew for sure that my bottom part was gone — because it was like touching the legs of someone else."

That was July 13.

In the weeks immediately following the accident, almost everything went wrong. Turcotte contracted meningitis, which threatened his life. Then he developed an ulcer.

Only fine work by the medical staff at University Hospital in Manhattan — and the support of his wife, Gaetane — brought Turcotte through.

In late August, Turcotte, while experiencing the shattering psychological impact of an uncertain future, was given the worst kind of news.

THE DOCTORS INFORMED him that his chances of ever walking again were extremely slender, then had him transferred to Rusk Institute, the New York University Medical Center's Institute of Rehabilitation Medicine.

Today, at Rusk, the doctors are definite about their prognosis — Turcotte's chances of walking again are zero.

But Ron Turcotte refuses to believe them.

"I really believe that I will walk again," Turcotte said the other day. "Doctors are human. They make mistakes. They can't see what's inside the spinal cord.

"They don't know the extent of the damage and a lot of things can happen."

TURCOTTE, THE TOAST of the thoroughbred racing world in 1973 — when he rode Secretariat to a sweep of the Triple Crown — is a tough fellow to keep down.

During the last three weeks, he has made a half-dozen visits to the jockeys' quarters at Aqueduct — since he has learned to get in and out of his wheelchair, and in and out of a car.

"I still don't have any feeling in my

lower part," he said, but I manage to transfer in and out of cars to get around."

In the hospital, Turcotte spends considerable time lifting weights.

"I can lift all the weights they have here. As far as strength in the upper arms and upper torso, I have gained it back."

TURCOTTE SAID HE and his wife now go out to dinner on occasion, usually with the Jean Cruguets and the Eddie Maples.

"Whenever I get the longing for steamed clams and lobster, we go out."

Although he realizes that his riding days are definitely over, he believes that he one day will be back at the track and working in some capacity.

"I'd like to train horses. I've always loved horses and have been around some very fine trainers. I used to hang around the barn a lot in the mornings. I wasn't anxious to work a horse and then leave.

"I think I've picked up quite a bit about training but of course I'd want to know more.

"I don't think I'd want to be an official or an administrator. I couldn't stand to be cooped up in an office all day. I want to be out in the fresh air."

TURCOTTE SAID THAT everything depends on how well he recovers. "I'll walk out of this place, even if it means wearing braces. But I'll walk again. I really believe that I will walk again."

Personally, I'd never bet against Ron Turcotte.

He's nine feet tall — when it comes to determination.

Olympics — EDWIN MOSES

Edwin Moses wins a gold medal and Mike Shine wins a silver medal, and they embrace and unite as Americans.

Thursday, July 27, 1972

Phil Ranallo: What's New, Harry?

A PICTURE, THEY say, is worth a thousand words. Some pictures, though, are worth more. Take, for example, the picture of those two young Americans — Edwin Moses and Mike Shine — that appeared on a couple of hundred million television sets around the world Sunday afternoon.

Edwin Moses, a lean and lithe Ohioan with a stride as smooth as silk, has just earned his chunk of Olympic gold by obliterating his seven rivals with a super performance in the 400-meter hurdles.

Mike Shine, a kid from Pennsylvania, had just won himself a silver medallion with a second-place finish in the event.

A couple of dozen strides past the finish line, Shine caught up to the world's new 400 hurdles champion, Moses, and the picture of their spontaneous reaction was worth tens of thousands of words.

Shine, a white young man, and Moses, a black young man, embraced, wrapped their arms around one another. Shine planted a kiss on Moses' cheek. They jogged a turn of the track, side by side — each with an arm around the other's waist.

Then, every few steps, they hugged.

It was an unforgettable picture.

It was beautiful.

THE PICTURE MADE by Edwin Moses, the black man, and Mike Shine, the white man, symbolized what America is supposed to be all about, what the Olympic Games are supposed to be all about.

Brotherhood and peace.

The picture is worth a limitless number of words.

Beautiful words.

Words such as:

"Love thy neighbor as thyself."

"All men are created equal."

"One nation, indivisible, with liberty and justice for all."

BIGOTRY AND RACIAL prejudice and stupidity are still with us, yes, but the picture Moses and Shine made Sunday symbolized how far the world — how far America — has progressed to overcoming them.

The picture gave heart to those who dream the American dream and struggle for its realization.

The picture gave credence to the cry, "We shall overcome!"

That picture, of Moses and Shine, told it all. It defined for Americans, and all peoples of the world, certain words — "brotherhood" ... "love" ... "equality."

THE BEAUTIFUL PICTURE from my vantage point told it better than any scene I have witnessed — or anything that has transpired in this year of the American Bicentennial.

Because America is not in the flag, and not in The White House, and not in the speeches that are made — and not even in prayers we recite.

The real America, what it's meant to be, is in the hearts of Americans like Edwin Moses and Mike Shine.

Moses and Shine are two Americans who practice what some Americans preach, but fail to practice.

THESE RECENT OLYMPICS are remembered as much for their chaos and tragic incidents as for the achievements of the athletes. Montreal, perhaps, will be remembered for the "dirty tricks" Canada played on

Taiwan.

But Montreal will also be remembered for that picture the world saw Sunday.

That picture of Edwin Moses, the black kid from Ohio, and Mike Shine, the white kid from Pennsylvania — hugging and embracing, planting kisses on one another's cheeks, jogging side by side.

It was a beautiful picture, an unforgettable picture, a picture in which a black kid and the white kid showed hundreds of millions what the colors red, white and blue are meant to be all about.

Olympics — BORIS ONISCHENKO

Russians caught cheating in numerous Summer Olympics events.
Monday, July 26, 1976
Phil Ranallo: What's New, Harry

IF MEDALS WERE AWARDED for cheating in the Olympic Games, the winner of the "gold" would be Maj. Boris Onischenko, the Russian who rigged his epee with an electronic device in the fencing portion of the modern pentathlon competition.

The Russians, in these Olympic Games, have been guilty — or have been charged with being guilty — of just about everything but snatching Queen Elizabeth's purse, or doping Princess Ann's horse.

The Russians are a determined bunch.

And the most determined Russian of them all has to the major — Boris Onischenko — the swordsman who came into the Games heralded as the world champion in the modern pentathlon.

Onischenko, whose propensity for cheating indicates he could make it big in harness racing as a driver, rigged his epee with an ingenious device that enabled him — via the pressing of a button hidden in the handle of his epee — to register a "touch" on the electronic scoreboard, at will.

WELL, IN A MATCH against a British chap named Jeremy Fox, the anxious Onischenko got very careless. He pressed the button — and a "touch" was registered on the scoreboard — at a moment when the tip of Onischenko's epee was not in the vicinity of Fox's torso.

Fox lodged a claim of foul and demanded that Onischenko's weapon be examined. Officials then discovered the device, disqualified Onischenko and booted him out of the Games.

The Soviet Union's Modern Pentathlon Federation, on learning of Onischenko's "dirty tricks," condemned the major and expelled him from the organization.

WHY DID MAJ. ONISCHENKO do such a thing? Well, the poor guy is 38 years old and probably figured he was running out of chances in the Olympics. So, when he gets back to Russia, he'll surely face the music and get shipped to Siberia — for getting caught cheating.

The following day, in Montreal, the Russians were in the news again when the manager of the U.S. Olympic diving team, Tom Gompf, accused Soviet officials of attempting to fix the judging in the springboard diving events.

A Russian who had been a diving judge at the Games in Munich four years ago, believing that Gompf would get a judging assignment in the current competition, made an offer to trade points that would favor two divers — Russia's Irma Kalinina and the U.S.'s Phil Boggs.

Gompf's revelations reddened the faces of the Reds back in Moscow.

THEN THE RUSSIANS suffered another embarrassment when it was discovered that the Soviet's declaration that their water polo team's withdrawal from the competition—because of "sickness and injuries" to five of the team's 11 members — was a bald lie.

It was learned that all members of the team were in the pink, physically, and that the team had been withdrawn because it had no chance of successfully defending its Olympic title — and chose to avoid the humiliation of elimination.

An International Olympic Committee official has stated that disciplinary action will be taken against the Russians.

AFTER MAJ. ONISCHENKO rigged his epee, the feigning of illness by the Russian water poloists and the Soviet attempt to get a diving judge or two to take a dive, a Russian gymnastic coach wondered aloud about the high scores awarded the doll of the Olympics, Nadia Comaneci.

The Russian coach, Larissa Latynina tried to downgrade Nadia's extraordinary gymnastics performance by hint that something is rotten not only in Denmark, as the saying goes, but also in Montreal.

Larissa Latynina scoffed at those perfect 10s Nadia racked up in the competition.

What Latynina was saying, in essence, is that if nobody's perfect, as is generally accepted, why is Nadia Comaneci?

ANYWAY, THE RUSSIANS' past-performance lines in these 1976 Olympics make one wince when one looks ahead and realizes that the 1980 Olympic Games will be staged in Moscow.

After seeing what the Russians were brazen enough to do last week in Montreal, where they are guests, you've got to concede they could have some beauties in store for the world — in the "dirty tricks department" — when those 1980 Olympics are held in Moscow, with the Russians as hosts.

Olympics — JESSE OWENS

Olympian passes away; he won four gold medals in the 1936 Olympics, prompting Adolf Hitler to walk out.
Wednesday, April 2, 1980
Phil Ranallo: What's New, Harry?

WELL, WE'VE LOST another of the special people.

Jesse Owens was the greatest Olympian of them all. But, more importantly, Jesse was a man who for 44 years provided inspiration for young dreamers, black and white.

From those days in August of 1936 — when he infuriated Adolf Hitler by winning four Olympic gold medals — to the day he died, Jesse Owens made many marks — and all were indelible.

Jesse made his mark on the cinder path.

His remarkable accomplishments in Berlin — especially his achievement on Aug. 2, 1936, when he won the 100 meters and became the "World's Fastest Human" — are etched on the minds of sports fans whose heads have turned gray.

Jesse made his mark as a trailblazer for blacks in America along with Joe Louis and Jackie Robinson. What Owens did for blacks was project an image — the image of what a black boy could be like, what he could become.

And Jesse Owens made his mark as an American. He was a life-long ambassador for this country — despite the bias and indignity and the discrimination he encountered along the way.

BITTERNESS COULD have come easily to Owens. But it never did. "Hey, I live here," he often said. "It's all I know and I have. My job is not to complain about it, but to make it better."

And Owens tried to make it better by dedicating himself to young, black and white.

For the last 16 years, for example, Owens conducted the nation's biggest track meet for children.

Playground kids of both sexes, ranging in age from 10 to 15, competed in the annual Jesse Owens Track Classic — with qualifiers held in 14 cities, Buffalo to Fairbanks, and finals staged at UCLA.

A couple of years ago, at the local qualifier at Buffalo State, we were privileged to spend a few moments in conversation with Owens.

"If you don't believe in kids," Jesse said, grinning, as he watched a half dozen youngsters straining for the tape, "you got to hate Santa Claus."

THE SIGHT OF THE kids striding out and giving it their all brought back memories, to Jesse Owens, of when he was a boy in Cleveland, at Fairmount Junior High — when he first began to dream his dream,

"I was 13 at the time," Owens said. "And there was this remarkable man, my gym teacher. His name was Charles Riley. He and I used to sit on the grass and watch the swans swim in the lake.

" 'See how gracefully the swans swim, Jesse?' " Charles Riley used to say to me. " 'See how perfectly stationary they keep their heads as they move?'

"My gym teacher taught me to run with my head stationary, perfectly straight — as if I was running with a glass of water on my head and trying not to spill a drop.

"My gym teacher, Charles Riley, is the man who started me dreaming.

"HE CONVINCED ME that every child and every person should have his own private dream. He made me believe that dreams, although they come hard, can be realized — and that you can get there if you pay the price.

"The sacrifices Charles Riley made for me, as my coach, gave me the determination that got me to Ohio State — and to the Olympics."

Charles Riley, Jesse Owens said, was white.

Then Owens spoke of that unforgettable day in his life — Aug. 2, 1936, the day he became the "World's Fastest Human."

"Before the running of the 100 meters," he said "I stood there — at the starting line — and looked down the track, to the tape that was 109 yards and two feet away.

"And a number of thoughts flashed through my mind.

"I remembered Charles Riley as I looked down that lonely straightaway — all the coaching he gave me, all the counseling.

"I THOUGHT OF THE other people who helped get me there, in Berlin — all my other coaches and the sacrifices they made for me. Then I thought of my hometown, Cleveland.

"Then I looked down at the uniform I was wearing and saw those letters on it, 'U.S.A.' Then I looked around the stadium and found my flag — our flag.

"As I stood there, I felt as if my legs wouldn't be able to carry the weight of my body. My stomach ached. My mouth was dry as cotton. The palms of my hands broke out with perspiration.

"I realized that nine years of hard work and sacrifice had boiled down to this moment, and that it would all be over in 10 seconds. I had given nine years for these 10 seconds."

Owens, with a magnificent run in the 100 meters, made the nine years extremely worthwhile.

Jesse Owens then went on to make the next 44 years of his life extremely worthwhile.

Jesse Owens was a winner — all the way.

Our Country — NAT KING COLE

Legendary vocalist passes away.
Wednesday, February 17, 1965
Phil Ranallo: What's New, Harry?

"I NEVER met him, Sam," Honest Harry remarked, "but I felt I knew him intimately – and I regarded him as a warm friend.

"He always did something for me, particularly when I was 'down.'

"I'd just sit there all alone — and listen.

" 'Unforgettable' ... 'Tenderly' ... 'For Sentimental Reasons' ... 'Portrait of Jennie' ... 'The Very Thought of You.'

"HIS VOICE was soothing. It lived the lyrics. It reminded me of all the beautiful things in this life.

"And right away I'd start looking forward to tomorrow.

"He had talent, and he had humility and modesty.

"And this set him apart, at least for me, because humility and modesty so often are lacking in the gifted.

"HE WAS ONE of the miracles of this day and age, Sam. He made half-a-million dollars a year just singing naturally!

"He did it without a guitar, without a ton of hair, without twisting his hips, without a crazy tune, and without inane lyrics.

"He did it the hard way – with a beautiful voice and with beautiful lyrics.

"HE WAS a whole man, Sam, a man who loved the basic things — his work, his wife, his children, his home, his fellow man.

"The fine reporters who wrote his obituary all pointed out he was not active in the battle for civil rights. They reported he confined his activity to financial contribution — but I disagree.

"I HAVE THE feeling that every time he'd sing one of those tender tones in his wonderful style, that for three minutes even the most bigoted bigot would forget prejudice.

"He was my kind of guy, Sam.

"I would have regarded it an honor to have lived on Nat King Cole's block."

Our Country — ROBERT KENNEDY (Part I)

Robert Kennedy is assassinated.
Thursday, June 6, 1968
Phil Ranallo: What's New, Harry?

ANOTHER AMERICAN tragedy!
Another diabolical act!

Another horror that reflects and magnifies the gruesome and appalling image we are creating — the image of a monster — a monster that maims and slays and devours its own.

The image is terrifying.

It is difficult — in fact, almost impossible — to argue that the image is not real ... or almost real.

WE FIGHT AND BLOODY and kill one another on our streets — black against white ... white against white ... black against black.

We set fire to our homes and our buildings — and then we stone our firefighters.

We defy and battle and spit at our policemen.

We fight on our college campuses — student against student ... student against college official.

We defy our government.

We burn our draft cards.

FOR MORE THAN 250 YEARS the United States of America has been described as the "Great Melting Pot."

One doesn't hear that description too often these days because the phrase has a ludicrous ring.

The fire under "The Great Melting Pot" seems to be dying out.

The contents of "The Great Melting Pot" are solidifying ... hardening ... getting stone cold.

TOO MANY OF US, BOTH the educated and the uneducated, are "majors" of hypocrisy.

In the baseball and football parks, at the first strains of the National Anthem, we stand at attention and sing about "The land of the free."

The words mean nothing to many of us.

The words are sung by too many hypocrites who, just the day before, resented and despised the black man who moved into a home on the previous all-white block.

SOMETHING TERRIBLE HAS happened to our moral values. They have deteriorated and cheapened to a frightening degree.

With too many of us, in this day and age, absolutely everything goes.

Everything goes in most of our movie houses.

Everything goes between the covers of most of our best-sellers.

Everything goes in our garb.

And, when everything goes, a price — a very expensive price — must be paid.

PART OF THE PRICE WAS paid 4-1/2 years ago, in Dallas, when the life of a young and vibrant President of the United States was snuffed out.

Part of the price was paid two months ago, in Memphis, when the life of the great black man — "The drum major for peace" — was snuffed out.

Part of the price was paid Tuesday night, in Los Angeles, when a candidate for the Presidency of the United States was struck down by gunfire.

THE CANDIDATE LAY THERE, supine, on the cold floor of the hotel kitchen — a bullet in his brain ... a rosary in his hands.

The picture of the candidate, lying there, was a picture of the hate and hypocrisy and violence that prevail in our sick society.

God help us!

Our Country — ROBERT KENNEDY
(Part II)

After RFK is assassinated, Phil looks back several years earlier when his son John attended John F. Kennedy's funeral in Washington.

Friday, June 7, 1968

Phil Ranallo: What's New, Harry?

THE YOUNG MAN'S ROOM IS A rather spacious one on the third floor of our home. The young man, John, hasn't slept in his bed since Labor Day of 1966 — the day his 72-hour pass ended and a week before he was shipped to West Germany for duty in the United States Army.

The walls of the young man's room are adorned by five pictures. Only one of the pictures is housed in a frame. It is framed because it is so extra-special to the young man — a beautiful 8-by-10 color photograph of President John F. Kennedy.

The other four pictures are held in place by thumbtacks. One is a large team photo of the 1965 champion Buffalo Bills. Two are Life magazine covers — of Mickey Mantle (July 30, 1965) and of Frank Sinatra (April 23, 1965).

THE FIFTH PICTURE IS OF Robert F. Kennedy, seated at a desk and coatless and with the sleeves of his white shirt rolled up. It is actually a campaign slinger, whose caption reads: "Let's Put Robert Kennedy to Work for New York."

Once, perhaps 2-1/2 years ago, the young man's father walked into this particular room, noticed the five pictures, turned to his son, then 19, and remarked maybe he didn't think Sinatra's belonged.

The young man, who has had a mind of his own since he first toddled, looked his father straight in the eyes and said: "Is it my room, Dad — or isn't it?"

The Sinatra picture stayed put.

LONG, LONG AGO, the young man with the mind of his own became enchanted by the Kennedys ... as did millions of Americans.

He was especially fascinated by the Kennedy who won his way into the White House.

That dreadful day in Dallas, when the life of the President was taken away, the young man, then 19, went to pieces.

He begged his parents to permit him to go to Washington for the funeral — in the company of four of his friends, one of whom was 18 and owned a 1958 Ford.

The parents said no ... definitely no.

THE YOUNG MAN, THOUGH, has a mind of his own. The next day — it was the evening of Nov. 23, 1963 — his parents, on arriving home from grocery-shopping, found a note on the dining room table.

The note read:

"Dear Mom and Dad:
"I have left for Washington. Please forgive me for disobeying. I can't help it. My heart tells me I must go. I will take good care of myself. So don't worry about me.
"Love,
"John"

One of the young man's brothers — a little pepperpot with a marvelous sense of humor — on reading the note, said: "We had better hope and pray that nothing ever happens to the Pope."

The young man, on his return home, was reprimanded — but rather mildly — since it was obvious the trip had been punishment enough. He had spent three nights trying to sleep, sitting up, in the back seat of that 1958 Ford.

IN MID-MAY OF 1966, the young man with the mind of his own enlisted in the United States Army — for four years. He has been stationed in Fulda, West Germany, since September of 1966.

Exactly a week ago — May 31 — the young man became 22. Part of his birthday present, from his family, was a telephone call to his base in Fulda.

The young man told his mother how much he loved her and how much he missed her and everyone else, and how much he missed her cooking — especially her spaghetti.

Then the young man said something his parents will never forget.

"I'M 22 AND I REALLY FEEL I'M a man — because this year, for the first time in my life, I will vote for a President.

"Bobby lost in Oregon — but Oregon doesn't mean anything.

"Bobby'll win in California and he'll get the nomination and I'll vote for him — and he'll be the next President of the United States.

"Bobby Kennedy's an amazing man, Ma.

"He's a phenomenon.

"He's the black man's white hope."

THE YOUNG MAN'S MOTHER and father can picture the young man — this very minute, sitting on the edge of his Army cot in Fulda, West Germany — sobbing and weeping.

Our Country — ROBERT KENNEDY
(Part III)

Robert Kennedy's funeral.
Saturday, June 8, 1968
Phil Ranallo: What's New, Harry?

IT WAS AN UNFORGETTABLE morning and afternoon and evening and night — this particular day, June 7, 1968 — this day for remorse and for mourning and for soul-searching.

In two endless lines, they walked — people of every race and every creed and every color — down the long and marble center aisle of the magnificent cathedral.

The men and the women and the children in the two endless lines represented the highest and the lowest stations in America — and all the stations in-between.

In the two endless lines, the most affluent and the most indigent walked side-by-side.

The two endless lines were America.

SOME OF THE MEN AND WOMEN were garbed in suits and dresses cut from the finest cloths. Others wore their very best — their Sunday suits and dresses.

Some wore their work clothes. Others wore the only clothes they possess.

The men and the women and the children reacted in different ways when they reached the head of the aisle, where this special man's body lay in the mahogany coffin that rested on the two-foot-high catafalque — the catafalque draped in maroon velvet.

There are many, many ways to say goodbye — and the people in the two endless lines said goodbye in every possible way.

THERE WERE THOSE WHO paused at the head of the aisle and gently placed their right hands, just for an instant, on the coffin of the special man — the man the nation lost on his night of victory.

There were those who, without breaking stride, simply took fleeting glimpses at the coffin — perhaps in deference to the thousands and thousands of people in the endless lines that stretched dozens of blocks beyond the massive portals of the cathedral.

There were those whose lips moved in prayer as they passed the coffin.

There were those who stopped and genuflected.

THERE WERE THOSE WHO made signs of the cross.

There were those who stopped and leaned over and kissed the mahogany coffin.

There were those who sobbed and who wept and who cried out and who broke down, physically, and had to be assisted from the cathedral.

There were those who moved their heads, slowly, from side-to-side — in disbelief.

And, always, as the people in the two endless lines passed and said goodbye, there were the special man's intimate friends — usually six — standing vigil facing the coffin, three to the side.

And, at times, those standing vigil included the special man's teen-aged sons.

THEN THERE WAS THE appearance of the special man's widow — the beautiful and courageous lady in whose womb God is forming an 11th baby — a baby that will never lay eyes on its father.

The widow, accompanied by part of her family, took her place in a pew, removed her black, elbow-length gloves, knelt, folded her hands and bowed her head, and prayed — dry-eyed.

Five minutes later, the widow got up, left the pew and walked slowly out of the cathedral — still dry-eyed.

Then there was the appearance of another widow — another remarkable woman who 4-1/2 years ago went through a similar ordeal and now was experiencing another one.

IT WAS AN UNFORGETTABLY tragic day, this particular day, June 7, 1968. It was the special man's final full day on this earth. Today, before sundown, he will be placed under the earth.

It was a day for remorse and for mourning and for soul-searching.

Mostly ... for soul-searching.

Our Country — MARTIN LUTHER KING

The peaceful warrior's funeral.
Wednesday, April 10, 1968
Phil Ranallo: What's New, Harry?

"IT WAS A DAY PACKED WITH such emotion, Sam," Honest Harry said, "that it was utterly impossible to give thought to horse racing ... or to baseball ... or to hockey ... or to any sport.

"Truly, it was "Brotherhood Day."

"First, there was the sight of this Baptist church in Atlanta, a church in which blacks and whites shared common pews and prayed for, and paid tribute to, the peaceful warrior — the 'Atlanta Brave.'

"Then, Sam, there was the sight of this black and beautiful extraordinary lady who reminded so many so much of the white and beautiful extraordinary lady of 4-1/2 years ago.

"THIS EXTRAORDINARY LADY, too, had her heart cut out and her world shattered — but she, too — just like that extraordinary lady of 4-1/2 years ago — somehow managed to remain dry eyed.

"There was the sight of this pretty little black girl, seated beside the extraordinary lady, who is her mother — and the pretty little girl was sleeping the sleep of the young and the innocent.

"Later, there was the sight of this casket — the casket which bore the body of the peaceful warrior — and the casket resting on a bare wood farm wagon that was being drawn by a pair of mules.

"THEN THERE WAS the awesome sight of this mass of humanity that followed in the wake of the farm wagon — a mass of humanity that extended blocks and blocks farther than the eye could see.

"Perhaps a hundred thousand Americans, black and white, marched silently down the street of Atlanta, under a hot Georgia sun, toward the final resting place of the peaceful warrior.

"Then during the long march, there was the sight and the voice — via a super-imposition on the television screen and a tape recording — of the man lying in the casket on the farm wagon.

"THE PEACEFUL WARRIOR, in the little picture in the upper left-hand corner of the television screen, was standing on the steps of the Lincoln Memorial in Washington, and he was saying, 'I have a dream today.'

"And as he uttered the words of that memorable address, chills ran up and down the spines of millions and millions of people, black and white, in millions and millions of living rooms.

" 'I have a dream,' the peaceful warrior was saying, 'that one day sons of former slaves and sons of former slave owners will sit down at the table of brotherhood.'

"THEN, SOMEWHAT LATER, when the burial site was reached, the peaceful warrior was seen again and heard again — in that little picture in the upper left-hand corner of the television screen.

"This time he was uttering the final public words of his life, the moving and prophetic words he uttered the night before he was gunned down in Memphis.

" 'I may not get there with you ... but I want you to know that we, as a people, will get to the promised land.'

"Yesterday, Sam, never will be forgotten.

"Truly, it was Brotherhood Day."

Our Country — MAN ON THE MOON

The historic lunar landing, and what it means to mankind.
Tuesday, July 22, 1969
Phil Ranallo: What's New, Harry?

SUNDAY NIGHT, AT 10:56 P.M., a half-billion men and women and children in this world of ours sat there — entranced — in living rooms and in barrooms and in all places on this planet where television sets could be plugged in.

More than a billion eyes, zeroed in on those millions of television screens, saw a mere mortal — Neil A. Armstrong — place his left foot on the surface of the moon and mark for eternity, with his foot's imprint, the beauty and the pride of human triumph.

Then another mere mortal — Edwin E. Aldrin Jr.—crawled through the hatch of the landing craft, Eagle, and gingerly made his way down the nine-rung ladder and joined his "brother" in that place, out of this world that is almost a quarter of a million miles away.

THEN THE TWO COURAGEOUS MEN — Armstrong and Aldrin — walked, in a floating and gliding manner, on the moon — in another world — and there seemed to be about them, as they walked, a great physical and mental pureness.

There they were, those two mere mortals from Earth, those two "brothers" — standing on the moon, bound together on the surface of this satellite which Aldrin described as "magnificent desolation."

No hatred in their hearts. No jealousy. No avarice. No prejudice. No bigotry. No urge to destroy one another.

There they were, those two men — all alone, out of this world — each dependent on the other.

THERE THEY WERE THOSE TWO mortals — all alone — experiencing a feeling for one another, a need for one another, a love for one another that no other two humans ever experienced.

A half-billion Earth people watched the two men on the moon and what they witnessed had to bring to mind a wonderful and a daring and a hopeful thought:

The thought that the ugly incidents of those recent ugly years may one day soon be no more — ugly incidents such as the slaughter of our leaders — President John F. Kennedy and his brother, Robert, and the drum major for peace, Martin Luther King.

Perhaps this magnificent human triumph — man setting foot on the moon — will be "one giant leap for mankind" toward the end of the assassinations, the racial upheavals, the wars, the starvation, the burning and looting of our cities.

PERHAPS THIS ACHIEVEMENT OF the ages will serve as an example of what this country, this world, is capable of doing if the money and the attention and the efforts truly are placed against physical problems.

"Perhaps one day, poor, pitiful people no longer will have to stuff rags into broken windows to keep out the cold in the pitiful dwellings that make up the slum arenas in all of our major cities.

"Perhaps one day a mother will lay her baby in a crib and not have to spend the night lying nearby, with one eye open, ready to fight off big rats — rats that, because of their large number, get bold and sometimes slither into cribs and gnaw at the flesh of screaming babies.

PERHAPS ONE DAY THERE WILL be wholesome food on every table in every home — and all the fathers and mothers and the children will be happy — and none of them will have this feeling that the people next door, people whose skin is another color, are their enemies.

Perhaps one day all whites will regard all blacks as brothers — and all blacks will regard all whites as brothers.

Perhaps one day soon the killing and the maiming will end in Vietnam — and the people of Israel and Egypt will embrace — and the Russians will move their tanks out of Czechoslovakia.

All this is possible.

Because nothing is impossible.

This was proven Sunday, at 10:56 p.m., when Neil A. Armstrong made his way down that nine-rung ladder and set his left foot on the moon.

THE "GIANT LEAP FOR MANKIND" has been taken. Now, it is our responsibility to do the possible — to do everything. If we don't, we might have to answer to a place that is a lot further away than the moon.

Pool — MINNESOTA FATS

Phil interviews Rudolph Walter Wanderone, aka "Minnesota Fats" and "The Hustler."

Sunday, April 8, 1973

Phil Ranallo: What's New, Harry?

HIS NAME IS Rudolph Wanderone, but in pool halls around the world he is known as Minnesota Fats — for obvious reasons. The renowned hustler has considerably more than his share of avoirdupois.

Saturday, at the new Sheraton Inn Buffalo East, Minnesota gave an exhibition of his skill with a cue. His "opponent" was Donna Abbatessa, one of the establishment's cocktail waitresses.

Donna took the first shot and missed, and Fats cleaned the table, talking non-stop as he toiled.

While the balls were being re-racked, Fats consoled Donna, eying the well-constructed lady as he spoke.

"Don't feel bad honey, because you got a lot of things going for you. You are a lovely tomato."

Fats got on the subject of champions.

"There are all kinds of pool champions. There are city, state, regional, national and world champions. Then there's me, who beats everybody for cash. Nobody living challenges me any more for cash."

FATS SAID IT'S A different game when a fellow is playing for his own money. "Evel Knievel was right when he said golfers don't know what pressure is, because they don't play with their own money.

"When you're playing with your own money, instead of for a jackpot — money somebody else puts up — it's as different as night and day."

The cue master confessed he does not know what sets him apart from other pool stars and what gives him an edge when he's playing with his own money.

"All I know is that nothing can make me flinch. The other players fall apart when they're playing with their own money. When I'm playing you could take a machine gun and shoot it-off behind me and it wouldn't bother me.

"It's mind over matter.

"You gotta have eyes like an eagle, a heart like a lion, and iron nerves — all of which I've got."

"NOW, WHEN THE OTHER guys are playing Willie Mosconi and the rest of them — even when they're playing for money other people put up — you aren't allowed to breathe. It's like playing in a cemetary.

"If somebody takes a cigarette out of his mouth while they're playing, they notice it — and they consider it a personal affront.

"EVERY champ who ever lived is a nervous wreck — every one of them but me.

"Masconi is a tremendous player, but he couldn't make a living playing pool if he had to put up his own money. He'd starve to death. He couldn't beat Mickey Mouse or Whistler's mother."

Fats cited the Depression years — the '30s — as an example. He said the other fellows couldn't make a living playing pool and had to go to work to exist, dig ditches and things.

NOT MINNESOTA FATS, though. "I made a bundle playing pool for cold cash, and I lived in $100-a-day ocean-front hotel suites and drove Dusenbergs while they were on foot, putting air in their sneakers."

Does Fats mind being called a hustler?

"Why should I? You're a hustler. Everybody's a hustler. We're all trying to get a hold of something ... and we hustle for it.

"Why even the President of the United States — the most important man in the world — is a hustler. He goes around shaking hands 24 hours a day, and that's hustling."

Fats, who is 60 years old, claims he has been playing pool for 58 years- since he was two.

"My father and uncles spent a lot of time in saloons, drinking nickel-beers — and they'd set me on the bar, near the free lunch where I learned to eat with both hands.

"THIS WOULD GET THE guy who owned the joint hot — so he'd pick me up and set me in the middle of the pool table, which was nearby. So I'd sit there and roll the balls into the pockets with my hands.

"When I was about four I was grabbing a cue. When I was five or six, I was running a couple of racks. At eight, I could run 50-60 balls, and at 10 I could run them in the 100s."

Minnesota Fats' upbringing paid off.

He has parlayed pool and a gift of gab into a fortune. There is Minnesota Fats Enterprises, which manufactures billiard equipment; there were six-figure receipts from the movie, "The Hustler."

There was his best-selling book, "The Bank Shot." There was his three-year television series, "Celebrity Billiards," in which Fats was challenged by the Hollywood stars.

Minnesota can afford to play for cold cash.

The Rockpile — WAR MEMORIAL STADIUM

Phil pays tribute to all of the fans and sports legends that passed through the gates of this great arena.

Sunday, December 10, 1972

Phil Ranallo: What's New, Harry?

SHE'S IN HER DEATH THROES, THAT wonderful old "gal" — War Memorial Stadium. She is expected to take her last breath this afternoon, a couple of hours before dusk ... and when she dies, the old lady should be mourned by every lover of sports in this community.

Born during the Great Depression, a daughter of a federal WPA project of the '30s, the old gal is proof that something good can come from anything — even from a depression.

She's gnarled and she's creaking and she's cracking — and she's a terminal case, this plucky old gal — War Memorial Stadium, nee Civic Stadium — but she has lived a most worthwhile life.

For 35 years the old gal has stood in the Masten District — at first, majestically; later, not so majestically — and has served as an inspiration for thousands of little white boys and little black boys who dreamed of one day running with a football, like the wind, on her worn and scuffed green apron.

No ordinary lady, this old gal.

She is the mother of major league sports in Buffalo.

THE OLD GAL WAS THERE, IN THE MID '40s, ready and waiting — when Jim Breuil decided to invest in a football team, in the All-America Conference — and she pressed the old AAC Bills to her bosom.

Had she not been around, there would not have been any old Bills.

In 1960, when Ralph Wilson was shopping around for a site for his team in the new American Football League, Ralph was able to settle in Buffalo — because the old gal was there to em-brace the new Bills.

Had she not been around, there would not have been any new Bills.

And without the Bills — whose financial success spotlighted Buffalo as a major-league team — it is conceivable that we would not have the Sabres or the Braves.

The old gal — War Memorial Stadium — made it all possible.

The old gal — the beautiful old rockpile — was the catalyst.

She gave Buffalo the chance to be major league.

THE OLD GAL IN HER LIFE-TIME, HAS had wondrous talent, marvelous football players dig their cleats into her green apron — players whose deeds generated eardrum-taxing cheers from millions — cheers that reverberated off her tired concrete walls.

The football marvels are unforgettable ... and some of them come back to me now.

Marion Motley of the old Cleveland Browns, the most thunderous, destructive runner these eyes ever witnessed — Motley ramming the line in a resounding explosion of leather and plastic and muscle, and leaving bruised and battered bodies strewn in his wake.

George Ratterman — the thinking man's quarterback of the old Bills — Ratterman faking a handoff or two and fading back, nonchalantly, the ball hidden on his hip, then suddenly wheeling and rifling a long strike to a streaking receiver.

Tommy Colella, the "Albion Antelope" of Canisius College — and later of the champion Los Angeles Rams of the NFL and the champion Cleveland Browns of the AAC — Colella, the most gifted kicker ever to appear regularly in the stadium, booming those prodigious punts and, as a Griffin tailback, running swiftly and smoothly, with the grace of a Nijinsky.

FRANKIE ALBERT, THE BRILLIANT southpaw quarterback of the old San Francisco 49ers — Albert, rolling out and faking a pass, then running for a long-gainer.

Flashy Howie Willis, the tiny Canisius tailback — Willis, running with the ball, threading his way for yardage among players twice his size — and somehow surviving.

And the exploits of Dan DeSantis and Toni Cahill and Roman Piskor, all of Niagara ... and Bona's Frank LuVuolo and the 180-pound Canisius center, Bill Piccollo, both of whom made it with the New York Giants.

The magical Otto Graham of the Cleveland Browns — and Rocco Pirro, Harold Lahar, Jonn Kissel, Vince Mazza and Chet Mutryn of the old Bills — and Chet Kwasek of Canisius and Eric (The Red) Tipton, the fabulous Duke punter.

All the fellows who made Lou Saban's old AFL champions tick — Billy Shaw and Tom Sestak, Jack Kemp and Wray Carlton, Stew Barber and Al Bemiller, Jim Dunaway and Ron McDole, Mike Stratton and Harry Jacobs, George Saimes and Ernie Warlick, Cookie Gilchrist and Elbert Dubenion, Booker Edgerson and Tom Day, John Tracey and Paul Maguire — and the gallant warrior, Ed Rutkowski.

SOME OF THE INDIVIDUAL EFFORTS will be forever etched on my mind:

— Marion Motley, a two-way player, recovering from his middle-linebacker position and chasing the fleeing Al Coppage and somehow catching

up with him and, with the overhand smash of one of his massive arms, almost obliterating Coppage, swatting poor Al to the turf as one swats a fly.

— Mike Stratton putting that spine-chilling block-tackle on San Diego's Keith Lincoln in a championship game, as Keith was leaping and reaching for a pass — and all but breaking Lincoln in two.

— Cookie Gilchrist, the closest thing to Motley as a power-runner, destroying the New York Titans with a 243-yard rushing performance.

— Jack Kemp, entering an exhibition game in relief and, with a merciless volley of boos ringing in his ears, firing a pass on his first play, to Elbert Dubenion, for 64 yards and a touchdown.

—Edward (Buckets) Hirsch of the old Bills, cutting across from his linebacker spot and broadsiding and crunching the sweeping blur of a runner, Buddy Young — and almost putting Young into the seats.

It all happened on the green apron of the old gal — War Memorial Stadium. The beautiful old rockpile.

This afternoon, when the Bills and Lions have had it out and I am walking down one of the old gal's crumbling concrete ramps for the last time, I'll pay her my final respects.

I'll walk with my hat placed over my heart.

THERE IS A BARBER FRIEND OF mine who feels the same way about the old gal. He's the Yankee clipper, Joe Frisa, who shears hair in a Hertel Ave. shop.

Frisa, incidentally, is incensed at the recent declaration of another barber — an unidentified barber who had the audacity to state that he planned to tear his seat out of the old gal today and bring it home as a souvenir.

"I'm going to find out who that

barber is," Frisa said Saturday, "and I'm going to make a citizen's arrest of him and have him thrown out of the barbers' union.

"The nerve of that guy! He's got no respect. The old gal has been the greatest stadium in the world. I will forever grieve her death."

Small wonder.

For years, Joe Frisa has operated the large parking lot at Best and Jefferson — and, for every Bills' game, he parks almost a thousand cars — at a buck-seventy-five a pop.

Tennis — BILLIE JEAN KING VS. BOBBY RIGGS

Billie Jean King beats Bobby Riggs in the "Battle of the Sexes."
Sunday, September 23, 1973
Phil Ranallo: What's New, Harry?

"IT WAS HUMILATING, SAM," Honest Harry said. "The other night, Bobby Riggs carries the banner for American manhood and Billie Jean King tears the banner to shreds and stuffs the shreds in Bobby's ear and the ears of all the guys who roam this land.

"Billie Jean has given the gals a new lease on life."

"You're right," Sam the Immigrant said. "Since Billie Jean humbled Riggs, all the women I've seen have been walking with their heads held high and their chests out, and to be perfectly honest with you, Harry, they look fantastic that way."

"They tell me, Sam," Harry said, "that the pharmaceutical company people are panicking because the unfrocking of Bobby Riggs has set vitamin pills back at least 50 years.

"Friday morning I flushed all my vitamin pills down the drain.

"THINGS HAVE REALLY changed around my house since the big match. For the last three mornings, I have served Ruby breakfast in bed — and I'm not doing it because I lost a bet to her, or something. I'm doing it because she has threatened to strike me if I don't — and because I now am afraid of her.

"Ruby has got me feeling a lot like Riggs. I began to get this feeling Friday morning — when Ruby went downtown and bought a big rolling-pin.

"What Billie Jean did to Riggs is also going to cost me my car.

"Ruby, who has always been afraid to drive a car — she's been riding a bike for 20 years — isn't afraid any more.

"Right after Billie Jean polished off Riggs, Ruby said to me:

" 'Monday, I am going to start taking driver lessons — and you, big shot, are going to start taking it easier — by taking a bus.'

"WHAT KILLED ME THURSDAY night, Sam, was to have to sit there and watch a 55-year-old geezer with skinny legs and skinny arms and deep wrinkles in his face and thick glasses and disheveled hair represent me in the 'Battle of the Sexes.'

"Ruby doubled up and laughed every time Riggs patty-caked a ball into the net or made a fruitless move toward one of Billie Jean's cross-court zingers.

"Poor Bobby, when he was on the move, sort of looked like Sam Ervin running for a bus.

"Between laughs, Ruby kept saying:

" 'This fellow, Bobby Riggs — this withered up wretch — is your perfect representative, big shot.'

"It hurt me deep inside to hear Ruby keep saying that, because just a couple of mornings before, right after showering, I'd glanced in this big mirror we've got on the inside of our bathroom door — and what I saw reminded me of Riggs.

"THURSDAY NIGHT, WHEN Billie Jean's victory was sealed, Ruby turned to me — with this big grin creasing her face — and told me there was a moral to the story we'd just seen unfold in the Houston Astrodome.

" 'Any 55-year-old geezer,' Ruby said, 'who thinks he can play with a 29-year-old girl is doing nothing but kidding himself.' "

"It appeared to me, as I watched the

match, Harry," Sam said, "that the most stunned fellow in the Astrodome — next to Riggs — was the commentator, Howard Cosell.

"Poor Howard had trouble getting in a word or two edge-wise, in his give-and-take with Rosemary Casals, an incredibly bitter babe whose enemy list is headed by every man who breathes.

"Cosell was so startled by a couple of Rosemary's feminist remarks that I thought his toupee was going to fall off.

"THERE'S A RUMOR MAKING the rounds now that Rosemary has applied for Cosell's job with ABC, and has offered to hand-wrestle Howard for it.

"Cosell had better not accept the challenge because he's in the neighborhood of 55."

"What happened Thursday night, Sam," Harry said, "has changed the world a little — maybe more than a little.

"Never again will it be said in my house, for example, that this or that is a woman's job.

"Billie Jean King has moved up the girls many, many lengths — as the guys were saying at Batavia last night.

"A pretty girl now is more than like a melody.

"She's a worthy opponent, too."

Wrestling — TEDDY THOMAS

The inner secrets of professional wrestling in Buffalo, N.Y.
Wednesday, February 19, 1969
Phil Ranallo: What's New, Harry?

TEDDY THOMAS SAT THERE, IN A CORNER of the restaurant. His meaty right hand wrapped around a luscious beef-on-weck. The colorful referee of Buffalo's golden era of professional wrestling — when grapple "addicts" filled Memorial Stadium almost every Friday night — was reminiscing.

As Thomas reeled off yarn after yarn, his luncheon guest pictured Teddy in his heyday — leaping up and down in the Aud ring, with his stubby legs spread far apart and with the ring shaking and reverberating due to the "punishment" inflicted upon it by the bounding 300-pounder.

"Nowadays," Teddy Thomas said, "everybody knows wrestling is a fake. Not so, though, in the good old days. In the late forties and in the fifties, most of the fans didn't realize wrestling was just a show — just a form of good entertainment.

"PRO WRESTLING WAS SORT OF LIKE a game of Cowboys and Indians. It was the good guys against the bad guys ... the heroes against the villains. And the reason it was a box-office smash was that the 'good guys' or the 'heroes' seldom won.

"The fans came — and paid their money — to see the 'bad guys' and the 'villains' get what they deserved — a real pasting — but went home disappointed 90 percent of the time. When a 'good guy' or a 'hero' did win, it was usually via a disqualification — after he had taken a 'merciless' beating from the 'bad guy' or villian.

"This kind of victory for the 'good guy' or 'hero' certainly didn't satisfy the fans. What it did was infuriate the fans — to the point where they'd come back the following Friday, hoping to see the 'bad guy' or 'villain' get left for dead.

"Wrestling, you might say, was sort of a 'Continued Next Week' thing.

"IN THE ROLE OF REFEREE, I WAS AN extremely important part of the plot. A referee could make or break a wrestling show.

"I'd look away at the wrong time, for example — just when the 'villain' was doing something terribly unfair to the 'good guy.' This would rile the customers — really get them upset, I mean, where they wanted to get their hands on me and do me physical harm — like break one of my legs or something."

The 5-foot 5-inch Teddy Thomas, currently down to a 'svelte' 240 pounds, took a bite of his beef sandwich and laughed, heartily.

"These days," Thomas said, "whenever I pick up a paper and read where one of the pro football teams has just signed a guy who can run the hundred in, say, :09.6 — I'm really not impressed.

"I'LL TELL YOU WHY. WHEN I WAS a ref and had to make it from the ring to the dressing room — after I'd rubbed the fans the wrong way — I was running for my life, literally. While I was making my mad dash, the customers would flail away with fists and umbrellas and things — so I'm sure I was at least a :09.4 man.

"Since I was taking such risks, the promoters used to give me 'hazard' pay — sometimes as much as three times a ref's normal wage. Which reminds me of a pretty good story about this promoter who told me I was going to have to settle for normal pay on this particular night, because it was going to be a calm show and wouldn't involve any risks on my part.

"Well, this boiled me. I thought I was entitled to the hazard pay, regardless, because the previous show had been a gasser and the fans had almost got me. The promoter, though, made it clear that I had to agree to his terms ... or else. So I agreed. But I fixed him.

"ON THIS NIGHT — I THINK IT was in 1951 — The Great Togo, the Japanese wrestler, was making his first or second start in Buffalo. Togo, a villain who was being built into a headliner by the promoter, was in against Fred Blassie — and the script called for Togo to win.

"But Togo didn't win — because I disqualified him for judo-chopping Blassie. The stunned promoter, his face chalk white, screamed at me: 'What are you looking for, Teddy, your pension?' The promoter, with that remark, meant he was going to cross me off his list.

"Then the promoter leaned over and whispered something to Dick Trout, who had wrestled earlier on the card. And, a few seconds later, Trout leaped into the ring, rushed over and hit me with three tremendous Sundays that loosened all of my front teeth.

"WELL, I HAD TROUT ARREST-ED ON a third-degree assault charge. Trout, believe it or not, claimed he had struck me because he was Blassie's friend and because I had waited too long before disqualifying Togo.

"This, of course, was a lot of hogwash — which was proved a year or so later, when Togo sued Trout for $16,000. Trout, you see, really was Togo's manager, off the record, and had struck me because the disqualification had put the brakes to Togo's buildup.

"Anyway, a couple of days after I had Trout arrested, I dropped things for steady work as a ref, hazard pay every time, and full payment of my dental bill."